T5-ASR-892

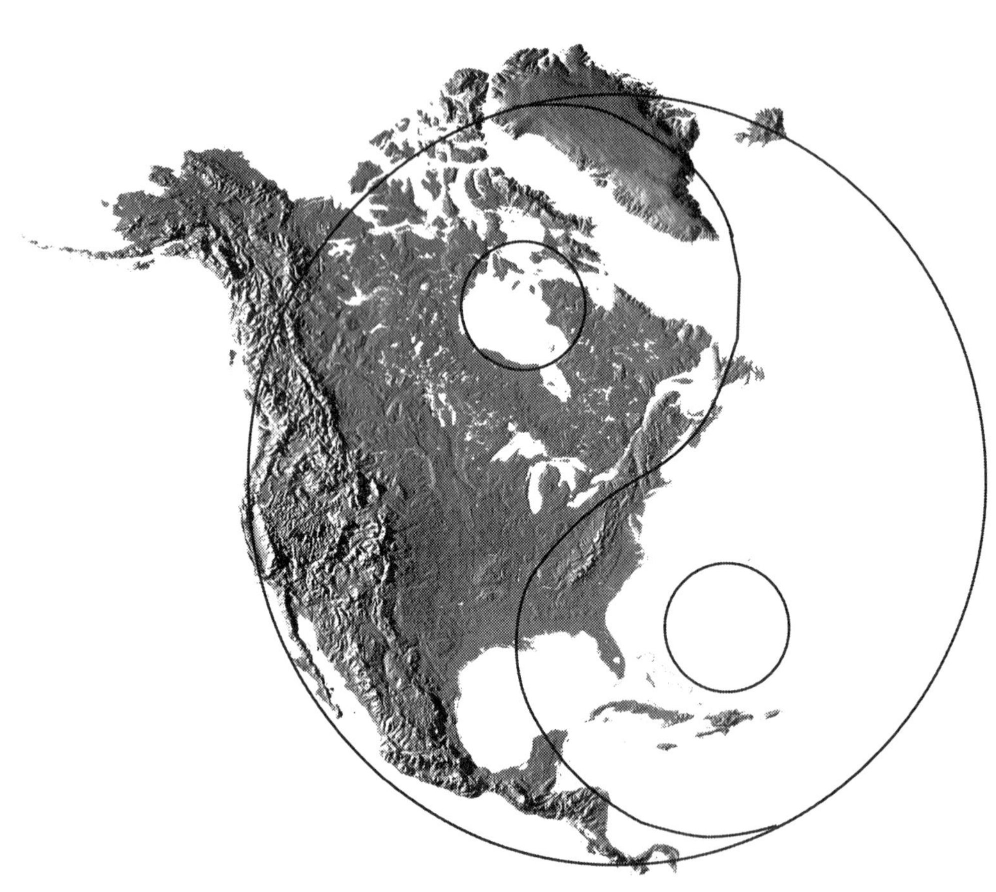

Gaia Matrix

The **Celestial Basket** was first presented in the summer of 1999 in Tenerife, Canary Islands at the Oxford VI International Archaeoastronomy Conference. It will be published in forthcoming Conference Proceedings and is published herein with the permision of the author (c. Bethe Hagens).

"The Paradise" paper was given as an invited keynote lecture in 1992 to the 24th Annual "Meeting in Finland", an international congress sponsored by the Assoiation of Finnish Adult Education Organizations. It was first published in the Conference Proceedings and presented again at the 1994 to the Annual Meeting of the American Anthropological Association. It is reprinted here with the permission of the author (c. Bethe Hagens).

First edition.
Library of Congress Catalogue Number- 99-72805
ISBN 0-9672328-0-5

Book Categories:
Spirituality/ Natural Science/ New Age /Travel

Printed in the

United States of America

Gaia Matrix

Arkhom and the Geometries of Destiny in the North American Landscape

Peter William Champoux
author / illustrator

friends / contributors
William Stuart Buehler
Susan Franklin Wilson
Bethe Hagens, Ph.D.
August T. Jaccaci
Henry Phelps MacLean

First Edition

Washington, The Commonwealth of Massachusetts

9/99

Disclaimer

This book is intended to provide information as a guide and is not intended to be the ultimate interpretation. The purpose of this book is to educate and entertain.

Every effort has been made to make this book as accurate as possible. The text and graphics should be used only as a general guide and not as the ultimate, definitive information. There are mistakes both typographical and computer generated. As to content, every effort has been made to verify geological, social, historical, and other information and facts.

We have tried to respect the privacy -of the personal- when making mentions in the book. Although the work is original, there is no doubt that people, places, and things have influenced the author. The opinions expressed are often humorously overstated by the main author, and in cases are those of the author, and not that of Arkhom, Inc. (non profit organization) or Franklin Media (publisher).

This book is a visionary piece, much of the information it contains, therefore, amounts to early deductions about a field much unexplored in the current venue. It is not the purpose of this book to render advice or direction for individuals or groups.

It is sold with the understanding that neither the publisher nor its authors advocate or endorse any particular religion, spiritual or earth mystery practice or political belief.

In the spirit of the book each individual or group should take responsibility for their own interpretation. You are urged to use this book to open yourself up to this beautiful planet we are all a part of.

Please be respectful of others, their property and their spirit.

We extend this book to the public in hopes that it will encourage an intimate, responsible relationship with the Mother of us all -- Gaia.

Dedication

This book is dedicated first and foremost to you the reader and all your relations. It is also dedicated to everyone who participates in the construction of this millennial Ark. The book acknowledges with appreciation the accumulative knowledge, direction, support, and insight received from friends, family, teachers, authors, colleagues, and the Great Mother Mystery God.

Next, grateful for the curve balls of life, this book is dedicated to the hands of the Fates, who grace this road less traveled. Dedicated further to Love and the lessons of the broken heart, this book is in gratitude to the matriarchy!

A deep gratitude to all my editors who literally translated this book. Bonnie B. Schwab the mother of my son and a most patience ex-wife. Matthew U. Champoux, my son the Biosphereologist. August Jaccaci, a most ardent visionary supporter and mentor. Special thanks to the meticulous questioning, gentle considerate nature, and sense-of-place attunement of Susan Franklin Wilson and her old soul.

Especially to Sig Lonegren, Keith Critchlow and John Michell for their open minds and support. Dan Winter for his verbosity, and networking. All the folks who adamantly insisted that this book be written and promptly.

The synthesis provided by the World Institute of Social Architecture, LightGate, The American Society of Dowsers, NorthEast Sustainable Energy Association, New England Artist Congress, Massachusetts Museum of Contemporary Art, the City of Providence RI, Boston MA, 'Maple Dragon', and 'Dragon Fly', for giving Arkhom venue and opportunity to evolve and discover.

A special appreciation to the support by the many individuals in corporate America and in the mainstream of influence that grasped the idea. My compassion goes out to the frustration inherently a part of communicating such a context. My hats are off to you for your enthusiasm and working insight. I sincerely hope this helps you to find a way to present this further so it can happen and we can assist in it. To all those people along the way —this speaks to you and our appreciation for financial, task, and valuable support. Particularly a note of gratitude to the diverse and individual youths who expressed their understanding and enthusiasm. To those that requested presentation of the material, sponsored return speaking engagements, and made me realize that this had so grown to be best absorbed on one's own time in book form. And most of all thank you for understanding!

I am Grateful to the diverse people who participated in and supported this process of discovery. Specifically the contributing team: Susan Franklin-Wilson, Bethe Hagens, William Buelher, and Henry MacLean. Thanks to Christopher, Rachel, Sibila, Reava, J. Martin, Noor, Jill, W.G. Lombard, D. Yarrow, J.S.R, Berrieres, the Anandas of Starseed, and those that know who you are. Appreciation to all those who have been actively engaged in this in their own way, doing by example, throughout even the infancy of my understanding.

This book is dedicated to Our Mother

Foreword

Arkhom is a celestial trumpet call. It trumpets in the emerging whole-
Earth renaissance that is opening a long foretold golden age of humanity.

Arkhom is also a signature art work of our renaissance. Like Leonardo Da Vinci's painting of the visitation of the angle to Mary announcing the birth of Jesus the Christ-- wherein elegantly realistic humans are placed in a scene of vanishing point perspective, Arkhom calls to the divinity within us all and places us in planetary-- point perspective.

The signature image of our space age is the blue marble, the image of Earth from space. It is that image which all the astronauts tell us-- when they see it on their travels-- that transforms them into seers and sages for the sanctity of the borderless life on Earth. And now Arkhom is showing us that same holiness of the whole Earth itself, rebirthing her into human consciousness in planetary-point perspective.

Arkhom is the first 'social architectural' groundplan of our planetary cathedral. There are / will be others. But Arkhom is 'first'.

Whereas the ground plans of the medieval cathedrals were crucifixes celebrating Christ's sacrifice and ascension.

Arkhom is a flower of life, a rose of the world celebrating our planetary-point perspective and our conscious rebirthing of the sanctity of all life.

When James Lovelock and Lynne Margolis introduced the concept of GAIA, the awareness that planet Earth is a living being, they rejoined our scientific industrial era to the fact all former ages and peoples have always known-- the Earth lives and breathes, and she is our mother. All indigenous people know this and all farming cultures. They all know that their economy is their environment. Their environment is their economy. How we utterly lost that simple-- obvious-- truth in our rational parade of toxic arrogance is a mystery. The greater and more glorious mystery is, however, how we are getting it reborn among us. Talk about angelic visitation of the universal christic spirit, and you are holding it in your hands.

One of the wonderful things about a renaissance is that the distinctions between different domains of human endeavor dissolve as the new higher order of unity of being: emerges. Religion, science, politics, art, and all else become one, at the new higher level of being.

Is Arkhom religion? Yes, it rebonds us together and to the Earth in the experience of the holiness of all being.

Is Arkhom politics? Yes, it guides our steps together in collaborative self-governance creating a sacred planetary one-world culture.

Is Arkhom science? Yes, it forms a working testable hypothesis about the energy fields within and on the Earth and how we live amists and have our being amid and in honor of these energies.

Is Arkhom art? Yes! It is an inspired and inspiring message to you saying: Congratulations, you are alive at a second great awakening of humanity, our human species mid-life passage to mature service to life in the cosmos. Arkhom is an ever-so elegant invitation, high renaissance artistry.

You are holding the announcement to the wedding of heaven and earth in your hands. Congratulations! You are invited.

August T. Jaccaci
Social Architect
Cape Elizabeth, Maine

7/28/99

Preface

The continuing discovery and evolution represented by the Gaia Matrix is essentially a synthesis study and a visionary experience, drawn from spiritual training, education, travel, and a passion for geography. The six year study, emerging in 1993, represents this book and work, it was an incremental process of discovery that spans twenty five years.

My reasons for writing this book are many. Struck early in life with the disunity of the worlds peoples it is hoped that Gaia Matrix will promote a peaceful interaction within humanity's family. This book was written to enlighten as it informs, to give historic preservation and environmental conservation a social frame work, and to objectify humanities relationship with the sentient Earth, thus enabling us to see the effect of our actions or inactions on the greater pulse of life.

The methodology herein is admittedly lacking scholarly validation and protocol. For this I apologize. It is in the first degree a visionary work. Determining these models is reliant upon the accuracy of any flat representative of a curved surface. Working with maps of a variety of scale and projections, tracing a straight line over a projected flat surfaced of a not quite spherical very large object is tricky at best. Inaccuracies do exists but the overall geometries presented, as with all naturally occurring forms the geometries are implicit. If these landscape geometry were perfectly drawn one would greatly question its natural origin. Spherical trigonometry has yet to be applied on these models, however; I am confident that once applied to a Government level global digital model the proof of these geometries will be evident.

Throughout this book the reader will be introduced to viewpoints and language which some may consider indecipherable. To interpret this information a synthesis mind and the whole of one's brain must be put to the task. As the Gaia Matrix is an ideal/ idea germane to millennialism the authors and editors have opted to print the document in its present unfinished form, as a gift of hope for the dawning twenty first century.

As unpopular as common sense, synthesis thinking, is nonetheless the cognitive capacity most needed in a world without borders. Examined in total the synthesis of this information results in a model of a bioelectric lifeform that coalesces into a organic self-organizing mechanism connecting cultures and universe.

In 1997, Dragon Fly, a Northeast synthesis group, co-validated the Arkhom Geometry and contributed greatly to its evolution. Convened to address what appeared to be a terrestial vestige of the celestial constellation Orion, the co developers were Dr. Wayne London, and Henry MacLean who scaled Orion to key the stars Aldebaran and Sirius to Montreal and Boston. The point of synthesis for this group was the Arkhom geometry.

This group presented grid models, supported by myth and cultural, that mapped both terrestial and celestial web structures. Within these grids, an overlighting matrix- geometry (Arkhom) is anchored like a ship to the center of the continental plate. Like a pilot of this vessel, Orion, a world-wide icon of wisdom, is positioned as pilot of this ship matrix. His hat (wisdom) geopositioned on Hatley, Quebec, is the crown point of the Gaia Matrix, corresponding to both the "Reshel" and "Arcturus" templates. The knee of this terrestial Orion is common to the center points of Eng, a zodiacal landscape pattern developed by Steve Nelson, and described in the Inner Life of this Gaia Matrix (the center of North American Tectonic Plate). Following this synthesis- thinking to its logical conclusion, illustrated through the eyes of many, revealed an entwined human/ landscape biology. The common factor was the Arkhom pattern and geography of which you will soon learn. Dragon Fly's fellows are some of the contributors to this book.

Generally speaking, generalized thinking, a real open mind, the sixth, seventh and eighth senses (the senses of intuition, humor, and commonsense) are the only prequisites needed to comprehend this evolutionary view of the North America.

Throughout this book are some value judgements that meant to illucidate the point rather than to offend. There are descriptions and personalities that some may find disagreeable. Throughout the book the term God is used as my preferred name for the Creator, Allah, Great Spirit, Goddess, all that is, Ahura Mazda, the I AM, etc. ... please substitute the 'term' with your deity of choice. I ask that you take my digressions with a grain of salt and appreciate the truth and beauty of this sublime vision of a loving landscape-- A landscape alive with evolution-- Humanity included.

Long live the evolution!

Peter Champoux

Note from the Publisher

As publisher of this book, I am using this one space to communicate to you the reader. I use this old fashioned book part, as my place to comment on the book and bring to the fore a tradition going back to early printing.

The contained information is new and follows few conventions, allowing for creative liberties with the book's provocative content. This work consequently reflects the original process of creative discovery. In presenting this original version we are attempting to maintain the process the author took... the motivations are often expressed in hyperbole and with a whimsical tone. Done to show the motivations and glimpse the dynamics, the comments here-in are the authors frank, extrapolated remarks, somewhat like asides -you can make informally- in a live presentation.

Use of words - There were, in ancient times, specific languages and vocabularies to allow for understanding subjects and relationships to time and space, weight, velocity, resonance, etc. to sing a few your way. Same words often have other meanings.The meaning of some of the words are out of their popular-culture contexts. If it seems unfamiliar! Look it up! There will probably be some mysteries solved. There are concepts and words that are little used in American, and without that meaning-- other descriptions would be redundant and over-simplified to others. Being as the book is represented as avant-garde, we opted to stay with the word! rather than ignore the use of the word because of misinterpretation. We have therefore had several independent editors go over the book to allow for this more in-depth meaning.

Additionally, some styles are used beyond the common conventions. For example, to separate a string of place names: consistently -we will use the: / thus handled in the same way to indicate a connected ley line. We used state zips rather than the conventional state designations because of the repetition of state names necessary in this book, and everyone knows zips-- it was better. Much of the style used, allows for clarity of rather complex information; use was logical. We have stayed diligently with our styles throughout the book. In a single sentences it is often necessary to discuss multiple relationships. There is very little common ground and no expected level of understanding. This just may not make sense to some people, and others will be excited that it is finally something that does make sense. The book was authored, not by a professional writer but an original creative thinker. To get this material out to the public we did not have the time to ensure everyone would understand. This was not written as a traditional mainstream edition.

Some material in the book intimately takes you on journeys through relationships in place. We hope you appreciate this style and use your discernment as with all things! We caution you to error on the side of the highest good in mind and heart.

We look forward to future color editions and indexing. We are honored to present this to the general public and look forward —making this information available to the widest audience. There is much more to discover and record! and it is here that we hope to focus in the future. In presenting it here and now, the book offers the opportunity to, as a people, assess our relationship with the environment at the turning of the millennium.

Consider - always - the effect of your actions on the next seven generations !

Susan Franklin Wilson
Franklin Media
publisher, Gaia Matrix

Table of Contents

1: Beginnings

Understanding the nature of Nature has been a point to ponder since humanity awoke to knowledge in our mythical past. We have developed many sciences and pseudo-sciences in our attempts to describe the complexity and simplicity of the natural world. Throughout the ages humanity has created tools to understand and affect nature for the benefit of the individual and group. Examples of these proactive endeavors include the stone "henges" of England, and the Great Pyramids of Egypt, and ceremonial sites worldwide. Researchers have documented sacred sites associated with the ancient cultures of China, Japan, Africa, India, Western Europe, and the Americas. These sacred sites were designed to communicate with gods and goddesses, and the deities worshiped at them were personas of nature. Placating the god of rain, for example, helped produce abundant harvests. This principle extended to a pantheon of all the attributes of nature's cycles. In fact most pre-Christian cultures related proactively with the Earth through such earth-based technologies as site alignments. They used them to collectivize ceremonies, channel the earth currents during eclipses and solar flares, focus these currents to enhance the season's crops and organize the populations. For all of human history the question of the nature of Nature has remained paramount in our minds.

In 1993 a new perspective was gained into this question. That year marked the discovery of a pre-existent, coherent sacred geometry encompassing most of the New England landscape. This core geometry expands harmonically into multiple geometries across the entire continent of North America. Taken together, these embody the Gaia Matrix. Possessing the attributes of ancient systems, the Gaia Matrix is a living Ark, an unconscious cocreation of humanity, Gaia, and the Creator. Coalescing over millennia, this Ark, a home to millions, evolved to a point where it is now visible and accessible to all-- we are now able to see the face of Gaia and interact consciously with this Great Mother.

The language of this interaction is geometry, the common language of nature. This same geometric language speaks to us through the worldwide crop circles phenomenon found imprinted in cereal crops with elegance and beauty. Consider for a moment the possibility that Gaia creates these crop circles to communicate with another sentient life form, humanity. What then?

Plato once described the world as a dodecahedron.

1.1 dodecahedron

Recent years have seen a resurgence of interest in earth-based spiritual technologies. The work of John Michell, Byron Dix, Sig Lonegren, Christopher Bird, Buckminster Fuller, Becker & Hagens, Dorothy Leon, and many others, have returned this study and practice to a place of prominence in an emergent creative culture. Common to these rediscoveries is the language of geometry. It is to this field of study that I contribute in this exploration of landscape geometries.

The name we have given to the core of the North American landscape geometries is "Arkhom". This first book on the subject introduces those tools necessary for determining landscape geometries. This common-sense inquiry links human settlement, culture, history, and spirituality to the surrounding landscape in a nested fractal form. The information gained from such investigation is particularly expansive.

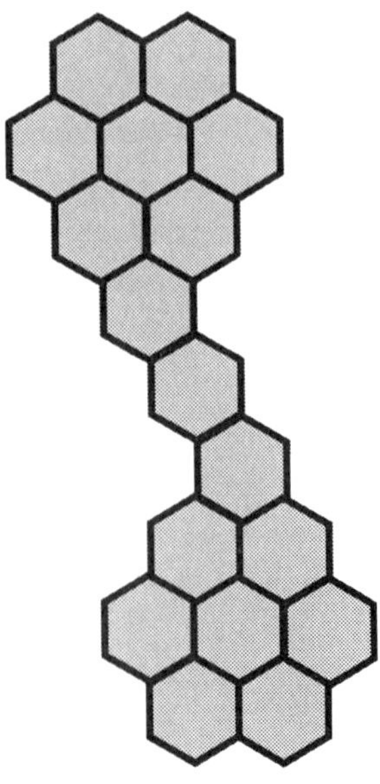

1.2 The Hive
The hexagon is the building block of both bee hives and human community.

It is a body of knowledge useful to regional planners, ecologists, architects, spiritual seekers, and anyone concerned with creating a sustainable future in harmony with the sentient Earth. Such knowledge carries with it a responsibility to act conscientiously and appropriately.

The premise of the Gaia Matrix -- that unseen natural influences affect our lives -- flies in the face of the notion of free will. Yet our actions as agents of free will seem to conform to the Earth's biology, lending more evidence to the idea of a sentient Earth. As a species, we organize ourselves in a hive-like, or natural manner. Are bees taught how to construct honeycombs, or beavers how to build dams? No, these are species traits. Peer into antiquity and you will see as the marks of humanity: the Great Pyramids, Stonehenge, Machu Picchu, Solomon's Temple, St. Peters, the Kaba. All were built for eternity, all are signs of our species. We are a spiritual species, mobile megaliths whose very biology links Earth and Sky. After 100,000 years of creating sacred space, this behavior has become second nature; a species trait, the automatic bioelectric signature of an instinctive relationship between humanity and creation. Our knack for building sacred structures marks time and civilization.

What remains veiled to the general public is that we create sacred space on a much larger scale. We do so without knowledge or compunction. Accomplished through acts of human free will, the cumulative effects result in an ordering of chaos, along the same lines as the geometric canon found in classical and ancient architecture. Applied in any scale, these naturally occurring forms enmesh to create whole systems models. As possible models of social architecture, these naturally generated landscape forms offer a renewed sense of place and community through relationship to one another, and connection to the Earth itself.

From the simple placements of three mountains to the complexities of the full Gaia Matrix, these geometries appear to underlie and shape specific cycles of North American history and cultural development. From the creation of the League of the Iroquois, to the births of the United States and Canada, to a future of spiritual maturity, the geometries key human evolution. Seeming to have a mind of its own, the Gaia Matrix requires human cooperation to fulfill the sequential cycles of destiny.

The discovery of the core of the North American landscape geometries in 1993 was the result of twenty years of labor, research, travel, and study, involving world mythologies and religions, the sacred architectures of land and structures, physics, economics, and the environment. I call this geometric work of cocreation "Arkhom"

By coincidence, I was born on the day Pacal's vault was opened, June 15, 1952. Pacal of Palenque graces a stone sarcophagus lid on which he rides what appears to be a carved seat. Some say this Maya of the Yucatan is piloting an unknown flying vessel. Others speculate that he is travelling between worlds along earth energy lines. He might also be seen as a man in the jaws of death with the "Tree of Life" growing from his belly. The exact meaning of the scene portrayed on that stone sarcophagus lid remains one of many enigmas associated with this Palenque ruler and the Temple of Inscriptions under which he lay buried. Pacal's four decade reign of peace based on wise leadership and community building, during which his culture flourished. is an inspiration for all. The spirit of Pacal is very much a part of the American spirit, along with all the peoples, places, and events woven into the tapestry of this book.

Being born on this auspicious day afforded me the opportunities available to the son of a union rubber worker's family, including Catholic education, and the benefits allowed the lower middle class in fifties America. I endured throughout my years, what creatives so proudly point to as their license to create, dyslexia. Raised on a rockpile of a hilltop, I floated above the world. This aviary looked out on Westover Air Force Base, then the base of the United States Strategic Air Command. From my bed I envisioned the Nuclear Bomb ready to explode there any minute like the rising sun.

My parents named me Peter after the rock that came out of the Champoux house foundation hole. Beginning at age 12, when collecting dinosaur footprints with my family amongst the shale of the Connecticut River Valley, blasted for the construction of Interstate Route 91, stone became one of my greatest teachers: when I lost a fingernail to a rock and a hard place. Alone, hurting, and on the sidelines as George, my Father, kept digging. We amassed one of the largest known private collections of dinosaur footprints.

All through art school and in my studies as a photographer, I did my best work with rock. And when I learned to split boulders with hand tools, the energy released from the rock was a religious experience for me-- I awoke to the memory held in stone.

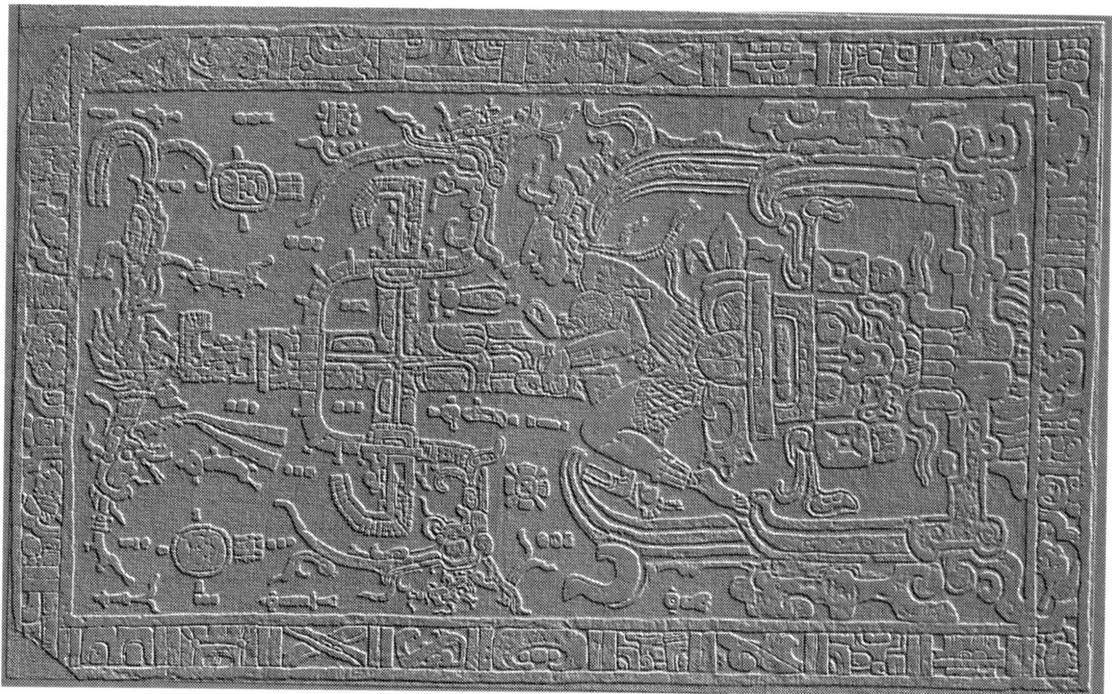

1.3Pacal's Sarcophagus Lid

Unearthed on 6/15/52 from the Temple of the Inscriptions in Palenque, Yucatan, Mexico, this enigmatic carving has been an object of debate as to its meaning since its discovery. From a rubbing by Merle Greene Robertson

During a crises as a young adult, searching for meaning and purpose to my life, I found it in my name: Peter Champoux, "rock of the field". Perusing the encyclopedias I came across some rather large stones here and there; stone piles such as Stonehenge, Chartres Cathedral, and the monuments of Easter Island. These icons inspired me to pursue a twenty-year study on the cultural use of stone. For me, stone had become the unifying matrix of humanity.

Professionally this coincided with two decades of "hard labor" as a stone mason. With rock as a symbol of the universal and enduring nature of creation, I aspired to build cathedrals. Studying and practicing stone masonry design techniques from all over the world ultimately led me to a deeper understanding of our relationship to sacred space and the crust of the earth as a matrixed landscape.

We introduced the initial Arkhom geometry and concept in a variety of venues. First exhibited at the 1994 First New England Artists Congress at the Massachusetts Museum of Contemporary Art (Mass-MoCA) in North Adams Massachusetts, Arkhom was displayed again as part of the 1996 Convergence

1.4 Ark in the Park
A conceptual sculpture designed by the author as an interactive model of the New England Landscape. Stones were brought from Staten Island and Portland Maine to symbolically link the seaports of the Yankee coast in this sense of place installation.

IX sculpture series in Providence Rhode Island (International Sculpture Conference).

Arkhom was clearly currently relevant and held power as a millenium project. Early on, the-journey-of-discovery pointed towards enchancing various expressions of community. Included in this proposed sense of place celebration-- was the installation of twelve Noah's Ark proportioned pillars in a circle around the center of the Arkhom landscape geometry. By popular demand speaking engagements, work-shops, and presentations followed and inspired others to see Arkhom's value as a community- building tool. A non-profit formed in its name laid the groundwork for its use as a teaching aid and data base for cultural inventorying, thus positively impacting historic preservation and regional resource planning efforts. Regular presentations at the New England Sustainable Energy Association's (NESEA) yearly conference, explored the application of the matrix to sustainable planning.

The name "Arkhom" perplexes many. Where is the "e" for home, if pronounced ark-home? Does it have anything to do with "Arkham", the notorious prison of Batman fame where the Joker domiciles? Was it taken from the place name in the novel by H.P. Lovecraft, that New England town where the clinically insane reign supreme? In truth, it arose spontaneously at the eureka moment of the discovery of the Arkhom Gaia Matrix. Surprising confirmation came by way of the preponderant use of "ark" at many of the sites, such as Arkville, Arkwright, Barkhamstead, and Newark. Odd to call it a discovery, when Arkhom identifies a structure we have been part of for millennia. My best guess as to its meaning is: "Arkhom delineates a geosacral (ark) community structure (home)".

The "e" of home was dropped to encourage the use of the sacred sound OM. The C# tone OM is the sound of the Earth -- the tone of sonic cacophony, and the note to which traditional musicians both East and West tune their instruments.

A universal sound, A-R-K translates from the Runic Alphabet (Northern European) as "the transmission of knowledge through light". The Ark of Noah preserved life in cataclysmic biblical times not too unlike our own. The concept of Noah's Ark is a universal archetype which is analogous to the sustaining Earth. Many world myths refers to a great flood and a lifeboat that survived to seed the cleansed world. An apt analogy for a world and its creatures that are three-quarters water. The nomadic Jews believed that the Ark of the Covenant contained the Spirit of God, affirming their pact of peace and stewardship with the I AM.

Thus the core Arkhom geometry of the Gaia Matrix, whose study prompted the writing of this book, describes a specific geographical area that transcends time and space to become an Ark, a Home, a kind of New Jerusalem within which we can experience a sublime relationship with the divine will in us all.

Though conceptionally new to modern thinking, the component parts of this terra-- form remain commonplace and accessible. The modern evolving myth for which this book makes a case is populated by heroes like you, the reader. Entering into this world can be disconcerting and may shake your very sense of reality. It will place your feet firmly in two worlds that diverge in acts and deeds, yet remain in the same place. This multi-dimensional nature of Arkhom, and the Gaia Matrix as a whole, unites the sacred and profane, making for a shift in the sense of reality. This single tent, this Temple of the Ark, covers all and includes all. Accepting this world-view places slums, estates, corporate towers, Lenny's Garage, paste-faced and mahogany people, pristine wetlands and congested highways into a sacred relationship.

Applying this new sense of place to your personal life makes for greater health and holistic living. Experience your own body as a model or microcosm of the whole: a holographic map of landscape consciousness, global biology, and, most seductively, power.

Throughout the book you will encounter concepts and disciplines which assist in understanding the nature of this collective terra form and its natural landscape pattern Sacred geometry, Platonic science, fractals, history, physics, and geography inform and build the book. Within its pages you will experience for yourself the adventure of discovering Arkhom and the Gaia Matrix. We hope that your personal discovery of this space, place, and grace may lead you to reassess the nature of free will, divine will, Gaian will, and personal will, as their edges appear to blur in light of your discoveries.

The goal of this book is to afford the reader a substantive sense of place one which includes a sense of God's grace. Divided into chapters addressing each consecutive geometric generation of the Gaia Matrix, the reader goes on a journey from the mountains of northern Vermont out across the North American continent in a seamless interrelated exploration of place. We will explore the Gaia Matrix from its seed form in the mountains of New England to the western arc that delineates the sweep of the West Coast from Panama to Seattle. The findings include newly revealed geometries of the Maritimes, the Great Lakes, the South, and the western United States.

In this treatise on American geomancy, the reader will also learn of the geomantic practices of the Masons who designed the Constitution of the United States and related governmental structures. The chapter on Masons in America describes the geometry that was used to focus the inherent power of America's landscape to create and preserve the United States of America. This mechanistic model, when combined with historical and cultural patterns, lends proof to the existence of an accessible etheric biology.

We will examine the works of such Geomancers as Washington, Jefferson, Franklin, John Brown, Brigham Young, Maasaw, and the Peacemaker. These historic characters illustrate cultural cycles of destiny between Natives, non-Natives, and the environment in the context of the Gaia Matrix.

Offering practices appropriate for personal and community growth, the book helps the reader through this complex and enlightening subject matter with original graphics, and also cites ideas about the nature of the Gaia Matrix from a variety of authors who offer individual responses to this multi-disciplinary model.

Of these contributors, anthropologist Dr. Bethe Hagens explores the relationship of our setting in the cosmos-- as a tool and language for growth and culture. Her work describes a geo-matrix she developed with William Becker (Unified Vector Geometry, UVG) that is a three-dimensional model of the world derived from the works of Plato and Buckminster Fuller.

Reverend William Stuart Buehler introduces a "metatronic" geometry called a Reshel and a planetary grid design that is related to the Arkhom model. In order to maintain the relationships of his thought development his esoteric dialect has not been translated into conventional idiom. Adding depth and further description of the core Arkhom geometry, Reverend Buehler synthesizes timelines, earth grids, architecture, and landscape geometries into scenarios that premiere the emergence of a "metatronic" group mind -- an assumed next step in the evolution of consciousness.

Henry P. MacLean, a Boston architect, professor, and futurist-- shares his ideas on Boston as a national model and showcase of environmentally sustainable practices. His writing focuses on City Hall Plaza, a formative site of the Gaia Matrix. The actions in and around the City Hall site are shown in the body of this book to positively affect North American cycles of destiny. Many seeds of inspiration for America's future have found fertile ground at this auspicious location. MacLean confirms that a cutting-edge ecological retrofit of Boston City Hall can be done, as well with the appropriateness for the creation of a regional environmental center. Such focus, leadership, and innovation emerging from this auspicious location could inspire the sustainable transformation of cities across the continent and throughout the planet.

The contributors, as well as other visionaries provided valuable depth of insight meeting in a salon environment over the last five years. We hope that you too can express your ideas and expertise to evolve this synthesis that is the Gaia Matrix. Its nature will be fully understood only through the talents, gifts, and eyes of many people.

Published on the eve of a new millennium, this book is offered as a message of hope and continuity. A time of uncertainty or transition, it could also be a time of taking inventory of our past and seeing a new future --taking a positive spin for the benefit of all.

The center of the Gaia Matrix, Arkhom, marks the geologic center of the North American tectonic plate and radiates harmonically to encompass its expanses. It offers keys to eco-creative, proactive, sustainable relationships between human and Gaian biology. As a sacred enclosure, this trans-national Gaia Matrix can also facilitate global cooperation through example, interconnections, and spiritual power.

The pioneers of this evolving art/science have walked on the thin ice of what is considered reality; an odd thing to say when talking about the rock, water, and biology of a planet. Our evolving human drama, of which we are each a part, is as much due to the Earth itself as to any social, economic or political agenda. We are part of its biology, its evolution, its future. We bring spirit to its matter as the willful, geometric, mobile megalithic star debris we are.

Apologies are extended for my dense style of writing. Like the earth energy lines, grid patterns, and matrices, life expresses itself between the lines.

So with that said, welcome to the Gaia Matrix. We are grateful for this opportunity to share with you this new perspective on the sacred, ancient, sublime, sentient landscape of North America.

1.5 Gaia Matrix
A preview of coming attractions.

2: ARKHOM - The Core Geometry

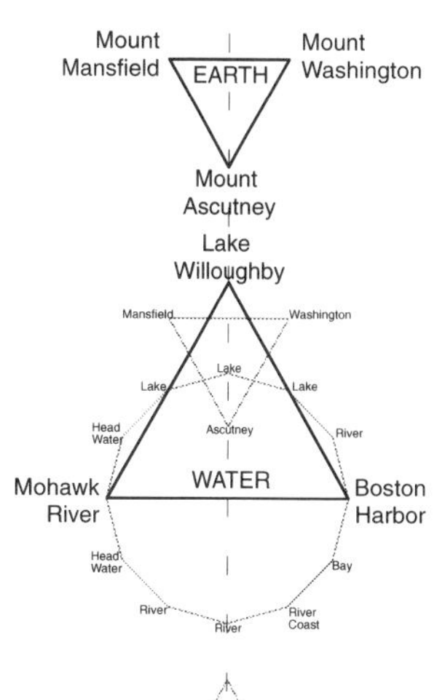

The Arkhom Geometry comprises a number of elements which together make up a biology as complex and interdependent as any life form. This biology embraces human culture and geographic parameters to create a complex system that is best understood via the sum of its parts. Throughout the following chapters the elements of Earth, Water, Fire, Air, and Ether act as building blocks of this biological geometry.

The Arkhom is a *Mother Geometry*; that is, many geometries can be drawn from it. It builds from simple geometric forms, generated in a precise progressions to include both natural and cultural features. The compo-

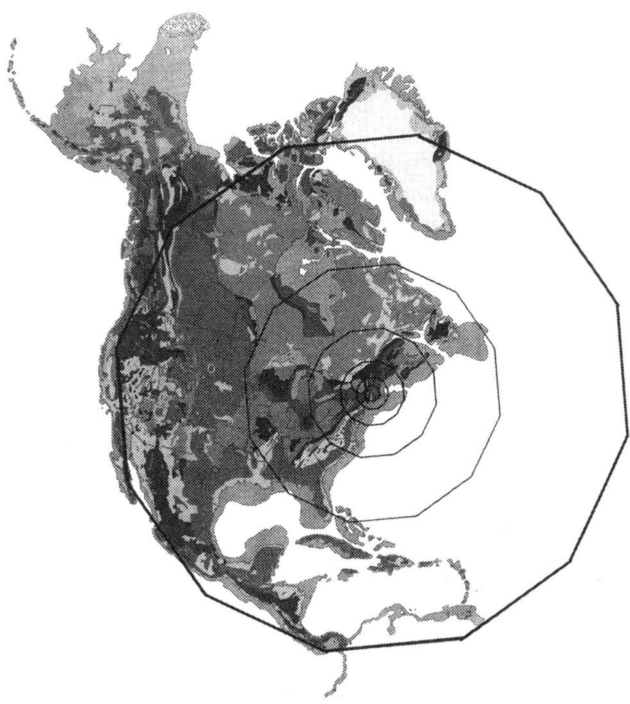

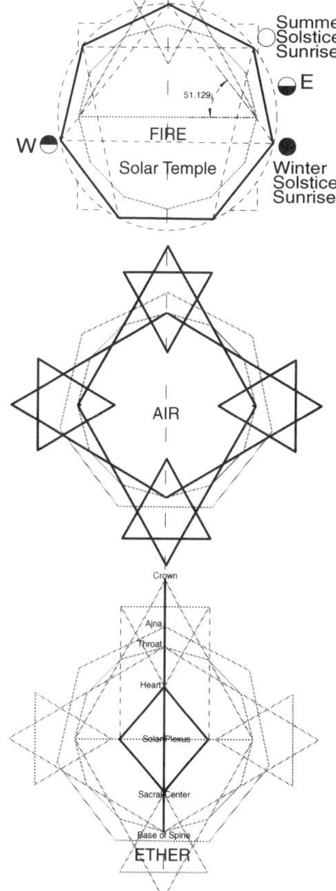

2.1 Development
The geometric growth of the Arkhom core of the Gaia Matrix from triangle to continent.
2.2 North American Geology and Gaia Matrix Harmonics
This geologic map of North America shows harmonic rings of earth energy radiating from the center of the tectonic plate in Shelburne Falls Massachusetts.

2.3 Ferns
The smallest leaf structure of the fern plant is a fractal shape of its largest branch.

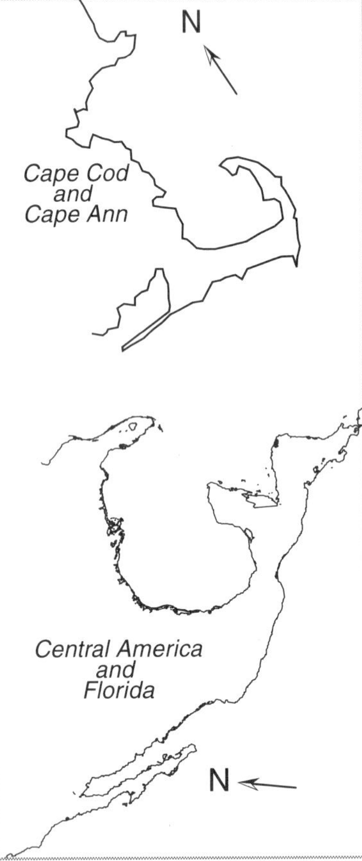

2.4 Fractals of North America

Cape Cod and Central America indicate a fractal relationship and a clockwise directional turn.

nent parts of this unified field system are: line, triangle (3 points), hexagram (6 points), heptagram (7 points), dodecagon (12 points), diamond rhomboid, and circle (infinite points). Each of these geometric shapes offers description of the genesis and qualities of place. These are often expressed as distinctive parts, or organs, of this core biology.

Harmonic growth is yet another building block of the geometry, a doubling of size, number, and diameter. Accordingly, the doubling of the central temple area of 110,000 square miles ought to reference other important geographic features, and indeed it does, illustrating dynamic functions of Nature rather than the author's imagination.

Continued harmonic doubling of the original centric structure reveals striking correlations to the geologic forces that shape the Earth. The outer ring embraces the North American tectonic plate with surprising regularity. It traces the western arc of the plate from Panama through California, Oregon, and Washington, circles through Magnetic North, and then scribes the eastern extent of the tectonic plate, the Mid-Atlantic Ridge. This brings one to an important feature of the Arkhom mother geometry: it lies at the very center of the North American tectonic plate and generates landscape geometries and harmonic interrelationships outward across the continent.

Fractility also plays a very significant part in this. Fractals are forms which replicate in scale. The fern, whose smallest leaf repeats the shape of its largest fern frond, portrays this principle. The sweeping shapes of Cape Cod and Central America are fractal. The shapes of India and Africa are fractals on a planetary scale.

A seed form not only for the generation of landscape geometries, Arkhom also generates the seed form for an economic and governmental system. In turn, the growth of this seed--form through interactions of governmental, political, social, and economic agendas originating at Arkhom's center, mirrors the control and domination of North and Central America historically in the expanding harmonic rings.

The conclusions presented here are the result of over twenty years of research, travel and exploration. Arising first out of physical ramblings to map "Early Sites" in New England, the study has evolved into a geomancy, or feng shui, uniquely American in origin. The Early Sites of New England have been attributed to Native, Templar, Phoenician, Celtic, and Red Paint Peoples. To some degree all of this appears to be true. The Red Paint culture which flourished during a warm period BCE most certainly had trade contacts in North America; signs of this culture are evident all along the North Atlantic shores. This culture naturally shared earth wisdom practices native to societies on both sides of the Atlantic. Where Red Paint cultures existed, standing stones, straight tracks, stone chambers, and odd megalithic stone constructions bear witness to their presence. A seafaring people, they probably formed a cultural bridge between New England and megalithic cultures in Europe. The pre-colonial sites served both utilitarian and ceremonial purposes. They beg to be included in present - day community and regional planning and historic preservation. Many such treasures are being lost as our own suburban expression builds on the sites of this ancient culture.

In the 1970s mapping the Early Sites of the Pioneer Valley of Massachusetts revealed linear patterns suggesting a planned development of sites. Some of these sites displayed solar orientation. Having no readily accessible mechanical time and calendars, indigenous culture depended on Calendar Sites to determine the cycles of the seasons. Calendar sites required a panoramic view of the east, south, and west. An ideal locale looked upon distinctly visible mountain tops or notches on the horizon for tracking the progress of the sun's cycles. In fact, by using such alignments and geographic features, many new

2.5 Whangton Chamber

Putnam County NY. example of typical stone chamber of unknown use that dots the NE landscape. By Lisa Grashow

2.6 North Salem NY-- Dolmen

This megalithic construct is central to the highest concentration of early sites in the Northeast. By Sue Carlson

2.7 Stone Shrine

Located in Shutesbury MA this example of megalithic design is typical for this ancient cultures. By Sue Carlson

2.8 Burnt Hill
An 'Early Site' in western Massachusetts purported to be a calendar site an ancient clock.
Courtesy of New England Antiquities Research Association, NEARA. By Colgate Gilbert.

calendar sites, standing stones, and stone chambers were discovered. Plotting the sites on a 7.5 minute USGS topographical map, it became evident that a conscious culture created a network of these sites in the Yankee hills.

Moving to the Front Range of the Rocky Mountains in Colorado, the founding premise of this study was applied to the foothills west of Boulder. Classical geographic siting factors identified a spot on a topographical map of the region. To no surprise this led to a calendar site made of a circle of moss-blanketed stones some thirty feet in diameter. What a site it was! Located near Ward CO it had a magnificent 360-degree view of the mountains, plains, and foothills, making it very well suited for ceremony, calendar use, and communication with the unseen ones.

Another example of a geomantically based identification of ancient sites came at Point Reyes, in Marin County CA. Right where the San Andreas Fault cuts northwest, a straight-track alignment of stones and cairns crosses the bluff. A hawk accentuated this viewpoint by landing on consecutive points along the alignment. Moss-and-lichen encrusted, these stones are of great age and their placement dates to a pre-colonial era. This coastal site must have performed well in tracking seasonal, celestial, ceremonial, and agricultural cycles. Its alignment no doubt focused the earth energy generated by the piezoelectric current of the San Andreas Fault parallel to the alignment. The State of California, thirteen years later, acknowledged the site's archaic origin and designated the area as a historic site.

These observations eventually led to the conclusion that if divergent peoples from unassociated locations were able to come up with the same underlying model, then an etheric structure must exist which governs their common techniques across time and space. A species' behavioral pattern perhaps? In fact, what existed then must also exist now, so then the question arose of: How modern humanity expresses this relationship with the land? It seemed that there was an underlying geometry to which our ancestors responded intuitively across cultural lines. And if sunflowers, galaxies, humans, and bees all expressed themselves geometrically, then the landscape must as well, and it was these geometric patterns that the ancient earth grid engineers were responding to.

Given this premise, how was this geometry being expressed right now, in the present day?

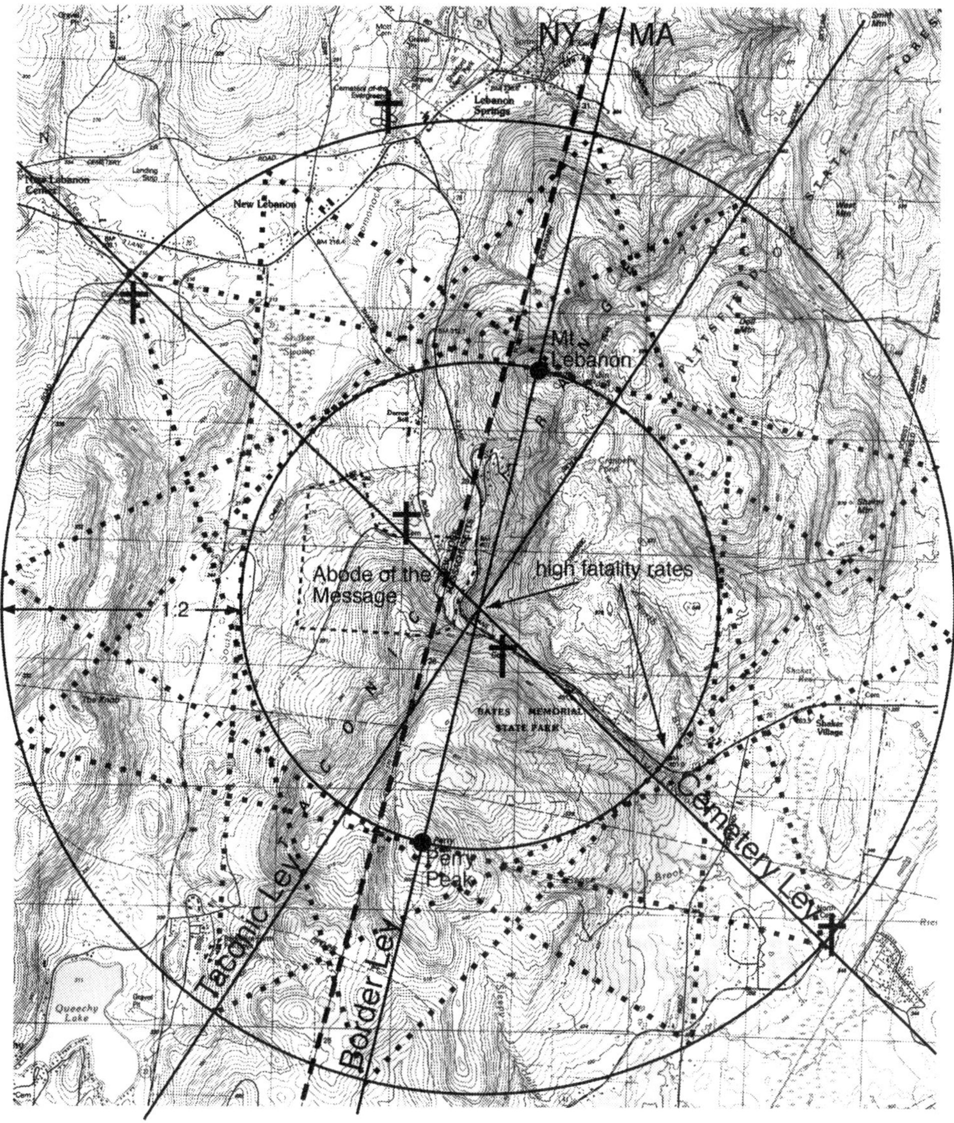

2.8 My First Landscape Geometry
The convergence of three earth energy lines at a point adjacent the Abode spiritual community in New Lebanon NY generates a hexagonal pattern. Crosses indicated cemetery sites

As a model for a master plan I applied these naturally generated cocreative design principles at the Abode of the Message in New Lebanon NY. This 360 acre intentional spiritual community is the present home of the Sufi Order of the West. Located within the New Lebanon Shaker village complex, it was once home to the South Family of the original Shaker community. Mother Ann Lee (founder of the Shakers) held her first revival meetings in what is now an organic vegetable farm at the Abode Community. I found that the property had eight zones arrayed in a radial pattern, suggesting an octagonal master plan. One point of this eight-sided form was marked by a boundary stone of Massachusetts and New York State, and the others by earth energy sites and existing use patterns at the community, such as: a retreat camp, a private residence, wild land, community facilities, and agricultural zones. The plan was never formally adopted, but still stands as a model for their naturally evolving development, which appears to be in step with the land. It is a testament to the many sensitive individuals who have lived and worked the land, both present day Sufis and their Shaker predecessors.

Bisecting the Abode farm is what is referred to in the graphic as the "Cemetery Ley". This alignment, once a native pathway then a Pony Express route, later became Route 20, the Boston to Albany road. It passes through four graveyards in the space of four miles. Alighting through a mountain pass, the MA/NY boundary stone, farm, Shaker graveyard, and stream bed; the Cemetery Ley pointed to a geometry adjacent to the Abode. Notoriously deadly, the mountain pass site hangs over the community like a dark cloud. Its modern history is a counterpoint to the ideals of both the Shaker and Sufi communities in its shadow, a sort of attraction of opposites. The mountain pass has been the site of rapes, killings, and accidental deaths at a rate of two per year, as well as of a bootleg still, and a hot spot for lusting lovers. Needless to say, it is a place of power, but one that has become dysfunctional.

This mountain pass point has three ley lines generating a vortex. These are the Taconic Ley, running along the Champlain escarpment to New York City, the Border Ley, identified by mountains that are equidistant to the killer point at the pass, and the Cemetery Ley. The angle at which these three leys intersect generates a 20-degree arc of separation. This degree of arc divides a circle into 18 equal points generating three hexagrams. By laying this pattern over the landscape at the diameter of the equidistant Perry and Lebanon mountains, it touches on many local geologic and man-made features, including springs, communities, roads, mountains, and another killer turn along the Cemetery Ley. This geometry was the onetime flower of Shaker culture and nature. A doubling or harmonic of this first diameter brings the geometry into context with features of land and culture on both sides of these borderlands of Massachusetts and New York.

This site was not always so manifestly sick. With the advent of modern travel the mountain pass was blasted and rerouted to accommodate car and truck travel. Not long after the construction of this modern roadway the Shaker Community closed its doors. When the pass was cut, so were the telluric currents. Energy and people no longer traveled the old straight track that led to the healing waters of Lebanon Springs Valley. This placed the Shaker Village outside the loop of its earth energy resource, cutting it off from positive expression. This severing of the earth energy meridian in turn served to reinforce the Border Ley, which further isolates and divides the lands.

The site has changed drastically since the Lebanon Shakers hosted an international conference on world peace years in advance of the creation of the League of Nations at the Paris Peace Conference in 1919. As a result of the road construction, a negative vortex was created and reinforced by the negative activities of the location. These conditions can be rectified by applying geomantic techniques appropriate to the spot, the road, the Abode Community, and the surrounding harmonic zone.

Recognizing the significance of this discovery, I pressed on to find more such alignments to verify the premise and identify other geometries. These landscapes were found to have a biological organization based on the canons of sacred geometry, canons which mark and evidence the passage of the Creator. One might call these geometries a universal language of Grace.

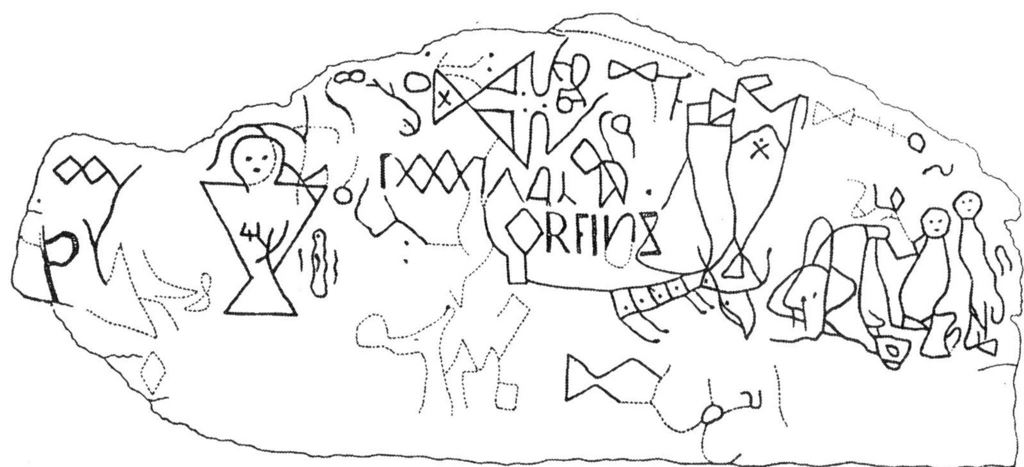

2.10 Dinghton Rock
Located in Fall River MA this native petroglyph shows the cross cultural influence within the area. Note the geometric forms that reflect the Arkhom geometric pattern.

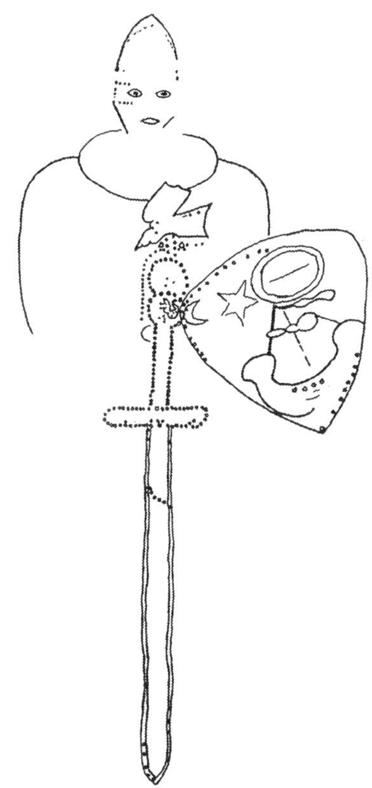

2.11 Westford Knight
This Westford MA petroglyph has elements and proportions that illustrate components of the Arkhom geometry.

There are many gestures in the landscape which suggest geometric shapes, including mountains whose footprints mimic swirling swastikas, phi proportions (1:1.618...), ridge lines with near perfect arcs, and dead straight alignments. One can discern geomorphic structures which suggest dragon heads, lens shapes, and humans. Cities, towns, tribal centers, concentrations of Early Sites, and river systems all self-organize to form a cohesive geometric whole. All of these patternings combine, patterns upon patterns, to generate regionwide matrices. This eventually led to a discovery of etheric landscape structures. Arkhom, the first of these large-scale structures, was uncovered in March 1993.

Noting a rough equilateral triangle cut by the placements of three dominant mountains in Vermont and New Hampshire, I recognized an original measure or unity for a much larger unfolding template. Mount Washington, whose winds and temperature changes are legendary; Mount Mansfield, the "sleeping giant" where the "Sound of Music" plays at the Trapp Family Lodge; and Mount Ascutney to the south form the triangle from which the entire Arkhom geometry is drawn. Mount Ascutney is purported to mean "where the forks end", referring to river and mountain forks. The Mansfield Green Mountains and the Washington White Mountains come together at Ascutney, the heart of northern New England. The southernmost outcrop of White Mountain granite, Ascutney is adjacent to an ancient river plain, which gives the mountain its presence unusual for its relatively small size. Additionally, the forks of the northern rivers come together just north of the mountain, looking like a veined heart, a heart which beats the pulse of river and mountain flow. It may be seen as the Great Mother Mountain, a sacred mountain, an icon of the sacred.

Applying the mathematical laws of fractal geometric generation, a triangle was drawn equal and opposite to the original, creating a hexagram. In sacred space design, this reflects the concept of "as above so below", the interpenetration of Earth and Sky, humanity and Creator, man and woman. The building block of the beehive, the hexagram's role is to create community.

2.12 Orientation
The initializing hexagram of Arkhom is oriented 14.5 degrees east of true north.

The orientation of the mountain triangle points 14.5 degrees west of due south. Laying out the opposite triangle 14.5 degrees east of north the points identify three water features: Lake Champlain, Lake Winnipesaukee, and Lake Willoughby. From this simple hexagonal harmonic the elaborate Arkhom mother geometry is brought to light.

This geometric model of the Northeast can be applied as a tool for demographic understanding, and interdisciplinary applied education. We call it a "mother" geometry or matrix because it has given birth to much of what is known today as North American culture, history, invention, and continental form. The simplest form of this geometry delineates eight geometrically equal regions. The most complex rendition identifies the central point of the geometry integrated with a multi regional structure that encompasses the North American continent. A work in progress, the discovery of the bones of this Gaian (earth) biology, will be fleshed out for years to come. The following chapters serve as your introduction.

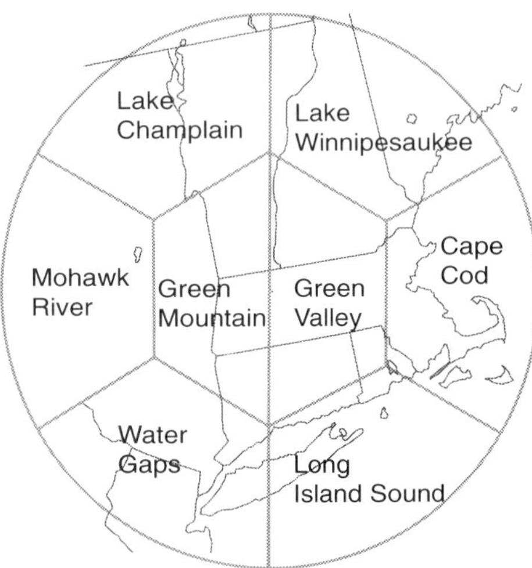

2.13 The Bioregional Hexagram
Eight hexagonal segments define geographic patterns in the greater New England area.

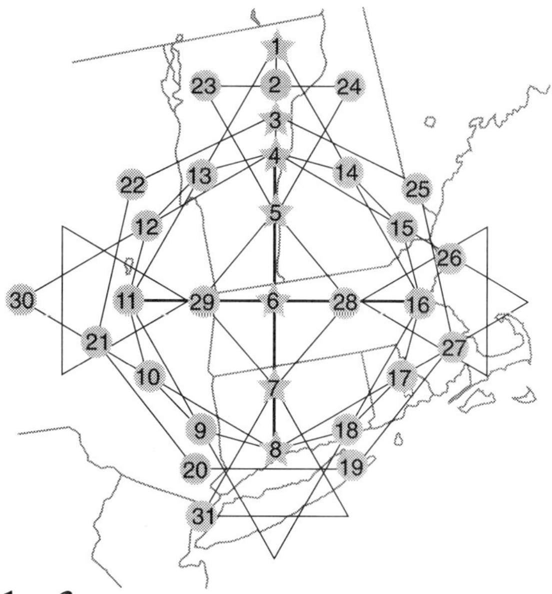

Legend of Sites

1) Newark VT
   Lake Willoughby
2) Danville VT
3) Topsham VT
4) West Fairlee VT
5) Mt.Ascutney
6) Shelburne Falls MA
7) Barkhampstead CT
8) Derby CT
   (Confluence of Rivers)
9) Poughkeepsie NY
10) Arkville NY
    Catskills
11) Canajoharie NY
12) Oregon NY--
    Adriondacks
13) Middlebury VT
14) Meredith NH
    Winnipesaukee
15) Epping NH
16) Boston MA
    City Hall Plaza
17) Arkwright RI
    Narragansett Bay
18) New London CT
19) Shelter Island NY
    Long Island
20) West Point NY
21) Cooperstown NY
22) Vanderwacker Mt.
23) Mt Mansfield VT
24) Mt Washington NH
25) Berwick ME
26) Cape Ann MA
27) Middleboro MA
28) Mt Washusetts MA
29) Troy NY
    (Confluence of Rivers)
30) Oneida Lake NY
31) Manhattan NY
    (Newark NJ)

3: Geomantic Corridors

Throughout the next chapters we will refer to geomantic corridors, or leys. It is best to familiarize yourself with these identifying landscape features. They are the bones that give form to the landscape, the building blocks upon which the more complex geometries and social dynamics rest.

There are no straight lines in nature, as you know. The landscape lines we will be discussing actually describe a wave form much like the DNA spiral. Trans-regional and global, they are similar to the "olde" straight tracks of England, they mark the passage of earth energy where landscape features, healing springs, megalithic constructs, and churches all align. We have found that lines in the New England landscape also mark historical events which have shaped the cultural character of the continent.

The name "ley" was first given to these cultural alignments by an English traveling salesman named Alfred Watkins, because he noted that a preponderance of people whose traditional family homes were located along these alignments had surnames with the suffix of "ley", such as: Conley, Finley, Worley, Barkley, Markley, and Gridley. It was postulated that these alignments were called ley in olden times, and that these families were actually ley keepers, maintaining the pathways and sacred sites.

There has been a great deal of controversy about the meaning and function of leys. Many divergent attributes have been ascribed to them. Generally speaking, a ley current is expressed as signal or wave forms. It is an energetic that can be dowsed, that is, read with a divining rod. It can even be seen, as one might see a human aura. However, leys are also punctuated by culture and historic artifacts.

These old straight tracks, or leys, are regarded as models for similar alignments in the Americas. Prompted by the work of Reshad Field and John Michell, I first identified Early Sites in New England due to their natural and cultural relationship with geographic features.

Sig Lonegren, a noted authority on the subject of dowsing, labyrinths, and geomancy in general, notes that these linear structures refer to wide corridors of activity, and he coined the term "Geomantic Corridor". For literary ease, this book will often use "ley" with the broader meaning of "geomantic corridor".

3.1 Stonehenge
Ceremonial use of the sites energizes the Gaia Matrix.

The terms geomantic and geomancy have many interpretations and connotations. I think they refer to humanity's dynamic, evolving spiritual relationship and co-stewardship with the Earth. Webster defines geomancy as,"divination by random figures formed when a handful of earth is thrown on the ground, or as by lines drawn at random". Geomancy in fact has a much broader definition and richer history worldwide. This first natural science, geomancy, can be seen in the placement of pre-reformation churches, not to mention capitals, cities, farms, and battlefields. The honoring of places of "Manitou", or The Great Spirit, by Native American peoples is a geomantic practice.

Geomancy is much more than simple patterns of dirt thrown on the ground. It is a discipline which includes all the "Geo" sciences and then some. As a "i-mancy" it is associated with magic since it addresses the unseen forces of creation. The Chinese version of geomancy is called "feng shui", literally "wind and water", both transparent elements one cannot hold on to, but which are nonetheless real. Similarly the "Chi" or earth energy with which the geomancer works cannot be held in the hand, but truly exists. In geomantic circles it is acknowledged to be the hand of God (or whatever version of divinity one ascribes) which casts the mud upon the ground to create the patterns which geomancers attempt to divine. Whether by conscious volition or from sublime causation, the family of geomancers includes water witches, bishops, city planners, generals, geographers, gardeners, and your John Q. Average planetarian.

The technology of geomancy is nothing new; it can be traced back many thousands of years. Stonehenge is an example of megalithic geomantic technology. The Great Wall, with its snaking course to the Imperial City of Beijing, is evidence of a highly developed geomantic tradition in China. Geomantic technologies gathered, stored, and dispersed earth energy to assure the vitality of the land, the crops, and the human population. The power being harnessed is attributed to Life Force, Chi, Prana, and the Great or Holy Spirit. It is like the wind and water; transparent and fluid.

Geomantic ley corridors have influenced group mind and community direction. By reading these ley corridors, the social karma, dysfunctions, health, progress, and spirit of the land become clear. Without further ado, let's begin our travels on the geomantic corridors which traverse the body of the Gaia Matrix.

The Empire Ley

A ley of note is the transglobal line that follows the 42nd parallel of North Latitude. This temperate zone alignment delineates the cultural centers of civilizations and empires, and the location of such notable features as the Great Wall of China. The Empire Ley was called the Milky Way by early Romans and Christians because of light centers found there. On or near this ley are Rome / Kosovo / Istanbul / Beijing / Chicago / Boston. The Empire Ley scribes the Massachusetts - Connecticut border/ the Pyrenees Mountains between France and Spain / the Caucasus Mountains / South Pass Wyoming where the Oregon Trail crosses the Great Divide of the Rocky Mountains / and Mount Shasta in California. The power of this geomantic ley corridor carries the emotion of megalomania and the self-righteousness of Empire. Countries along this ley that are not necessarily empires nonetheless act as such. Here we find Serbia acting out this dream of empire, a dream more appropriate to another era.

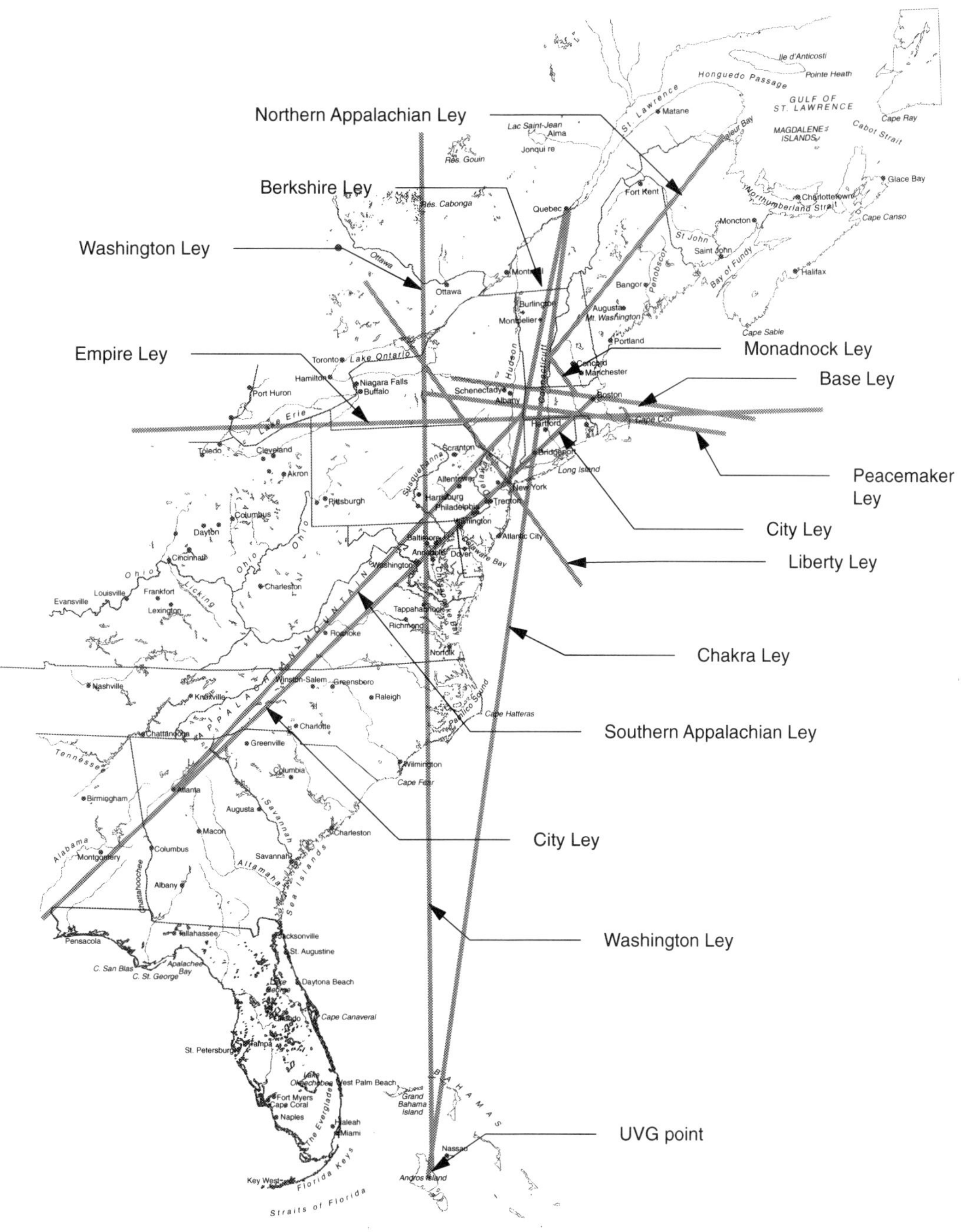

3.2 Eastern Leys
The Geomantic Ley Corridors of the eastern United States affect cultural expansion, governance, power, and peacemaking.

The City Ley

One striking example of a geomantic corridor that has seen extensive contemporary development is the alignment of the cities along the East coast of North America, first noted by Steve Nelson of North Carolina. These include Boston / New York City / Philadelphia / Baltimore / Washington DC / Atlanta / the bonus metropolis of Mexico City. Was this alignment placed there by design, Grace, or by the nature of the geographic landscape? Perhaps it was the work of the founding fathers -- primarily Masons versed in geomancy -- who saw the need to formulate a structure for community continuity. We will explore this more in the chapter on the Masonic Age. A masculine line, this ley is dominated by symbols and centers of male power, including such phallic symbols as obelisks, skyscrapers, and monuments to war.

Stretching out this alignment to the east, the line arcs over the North Atlantic to connect with the Ley of Conflict. This proverbial line in the sand courses through the capitals of Ireland and England / the Franco - German border / the Balkans / Cyprus / and Israel. Through this alignment control, power, and spiritual lineage is conveyed to North America. Conversely, this ley also draws the United States into the conflicts of those regions.

The two zones crossed by the City and Empire Leys are Kosovo and New England.

The Appalachian Leys are divided in two by the whirl and activity associated with our central mother matrix Arkhom. These leys can be seen on the geologic map (Illustration 3.3) as two propeller -- like forms attached to this matrix.

Upper Appalachian Ley

This mountain ley is marked of course by mountain points. These include Mount Ascutney VT / Mount Washington NH / Mount Katahdin ME / Mount Carleton, New Brunswick, Canada. The distance between Mt. Washington NH and Mt. Ascutney VT, marks the unit of measure from which the Arkhom geometry is drawn. In the chapter "Three Mountains" the significance of these peaks will be described in greater depth.

Lower Appalachian Ley

Coursing south, this alignment includes many significant historic sites and mountains along its wave form into the heart of Dixie. A list of the sites is as follows from north to south: Mount Everett MA / High Point NJ (Port Jervis) / Harpers Ferry WVA / Mount Rogers VA / Grandfather Mountain NC / Mount Mitchell NC. The unique feature of this ley is that all these mentioned points are in multistate areas. It follows a river of granite and marble the length of the mountains, ending at the quarries of Marietta GA. Backbone of the southern states, the history of this Lower Appalachian wave form chronicles some of the greatest victories of the Confederacy and, passing close to Gettysburg, speaks of its demise.

The Peacemaker Ley

This cultural corridor was named after the native prophet Deganawidah, who introduced a code of life to the tribes of the Iroquois Nation with the help of his spokesman Hiawatha. This code of unity and peace was the inspiration behind the Constitution of the United States.

One of many social customs instituted by the Peacemaker was the communal longhouse. By analogy on a regional scale, the Peacemaker Ley is the central corridor of a longhouse to the sea. Tribal lands, life, and family spaces were placed on either side of the ley stretching from Seneca Falls in the Finger Lakes Region of New York to the elbow of Cape Cod, Massachusetts.

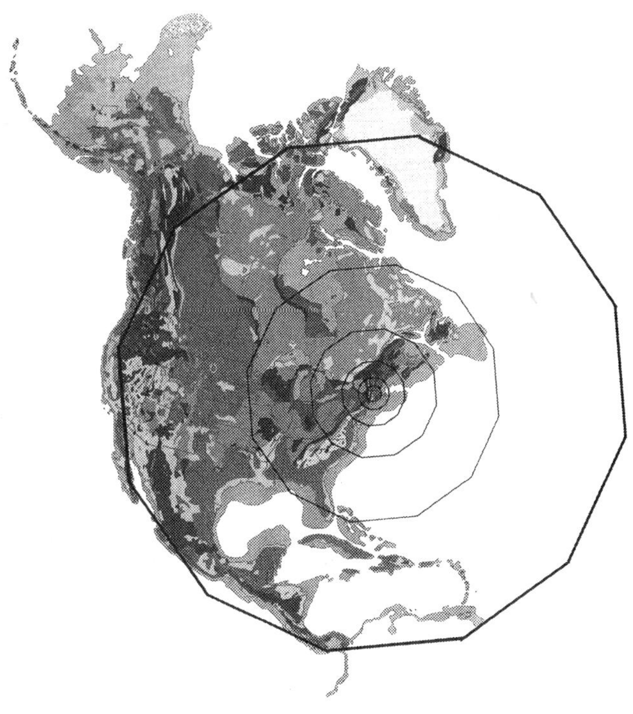

3.3 North American Geology and Gaia Matrix Harmonics

This geologic map of North America shows harmonic rings radiating from the center of the tectonic plate in Shelburne Falls Massachusetts. The Appalachian Leys are seen as a propeller-like geologic structure spinning from the center.

Where leys associated with colonial settlement have qualities of place to do with power, war, science, and education, the Peacemaker Ley sets a tone of cooperation, play, spirituality, and equality. Two salient points on this alignment are Cooperstown NY (Baseball Hall of Fame) and First Encounter Beach on Cape Cod where the Pilgrims met the Native Americans (the Thanksgiving archetype). The Peacemaker Ley also correlates to a line that is part of the Unified Vector Geometry (UVG; see the chapter by Bethe Hagens), a model which keys into many important points of the Arkhom geometry.

Washington Ley

Another alignment of the Universal Vector Geometry (UVG) is a north / south ley which passes between Washington DC and Baltimore MD. Earlier we identified the Empire Ley along the 42nd parallel. The Washington Ley follows a meridian of 76 degrees 50 minutes longitude. Tracing this meridian is a real surprise. It lays bare a dark reality of the American psyche.

Towns such as Williamsburg VA and Hershey PA are on this line, places known for tobacco and chocolate. By themselves of little consequence, add to them other sites found on the Washington Ley and a story unfolds: all around the globe this line highlights places which one would consider drug-related The short list of sites on this global alignment is as follows: Kingston, Jamaica (marijuana, rum) / Cali, Colombia (cocaine) / Lima, Peru (coffee) / Golden Triangle (heroin). All have risen to prominence as suppliers to America. This is oddly appropriate, considering that our own economy got its start dealing drugs such as rum and tobacco. In fact to this day our economy is known for such drug-related products as Coca-Cola, Pepsi, and burgers made from drugged beef. It doesn't stop there, however; America's chemical and pharmaceutical industry, and the export of consumerism globally, have hooked the world

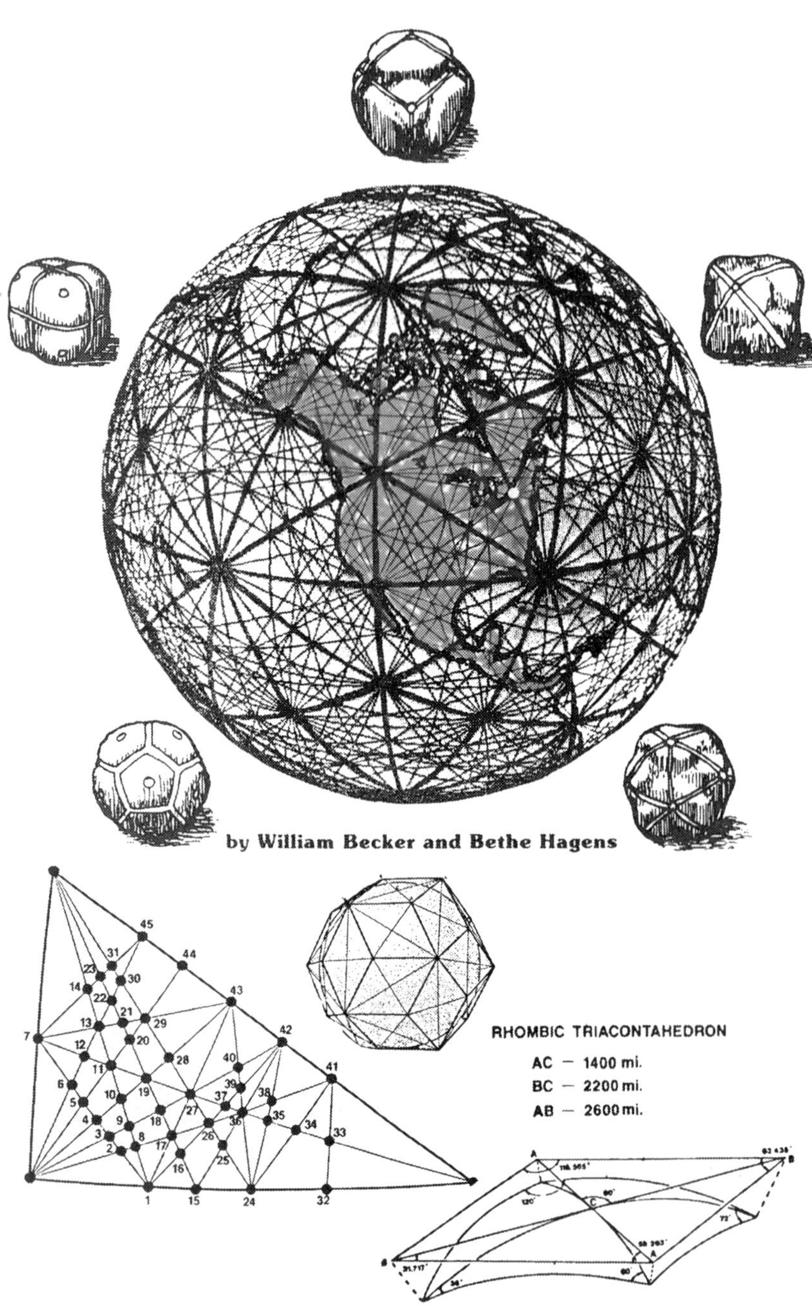

3.4 Universal Vector Geometry (UVG)

This evolutionary geometry, the work of the designers Becker, Hagens, Plato, and Fuller, is a spherical projection of the five geometric solids, seen here as a grid pattern of 120-3/4/5 triangles or 15 equal interlaced "Rings of Gaia". The UVG represents the crystalline earth as tectonic, and biospheric patterns mimic this Earth Grid pattern.

Three of the ley alignments noted as part of the Gaia Matrix are associated with this hexakisicosahedron.

Geopositioned to snap into the North and South Poles, and the Great Pyramids this planetary model has been used in geographic education.

Know generally as the Earth Grid, the UVG is a framework for the Gaia Matrix biology.

Compiled from graphics by Becker and Hagens.

on their drugs. Small wonder that when our children eat and drink foods made of sugar, caffeine, growth hormones, and steroids, they need to be fed Ritalin to counteract their overdosed nervous systems. Prozac is prescribed for cultural malaise. Vitamins to supplement lifeless food.

This is a prime example of how a ley can speak volumes about and affect a cultural reality. It is safe to say that Americans are unrivaled in their use of drugs. What does this say about Washington DC specifically and the United States in general? They dutifully consume vitamins, growth hormones, painkillers, laxatives, caffeine, nicotine, alcohol, skin cream, gasoline, TV, sex, video games, endorphins, and most of all power. Confronted with the dominance of pestilence, and the numbness of suburbia, it is not a big leap to turn to marijuana, cocaine, heroin, LSD, and sundry other escapes to supplement this diet of drugs. How does a government fight a war on drugs on one hand, while on the other encouraging their wholesale distribution through medicine, commerce, and agriculture?

Located at the crossing of the Empire Ley and the Washington Ley, one can see the results of a culture based on these contradictory economic practices. At this auspicious locale is one of the toughest prisons in New York State, Elmira. Populated by drug dealers and users, this national disgrace is a potent symbol for our civilization and power elite to contemplate. Located in the shadow of the Elmira Prison is Woodlawn, a National Cemetery for the honored war dead of the United States armed forces. The population

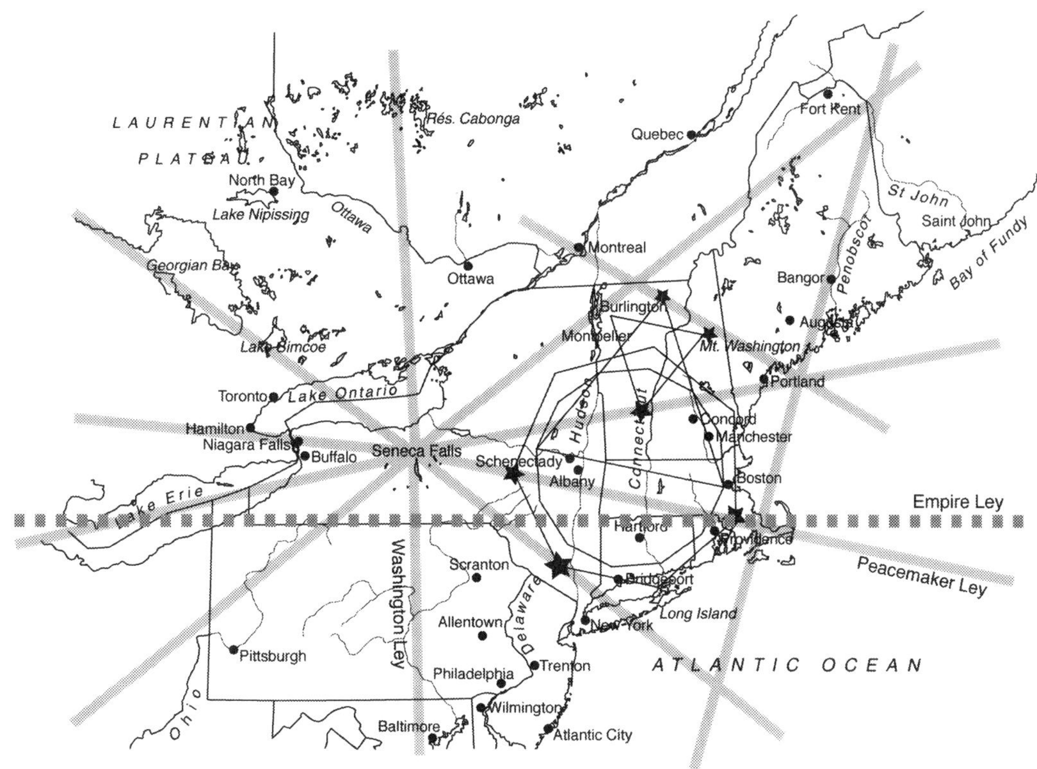

3.5 Seneca Falls UVG
Planetary grid lines of the UVG frame Arkhom and generate some of the ley corridors that energize the Gaia Matrix. Several UVG lines converge on Seneca Falls.

of this prison is there as a result of the "War on Drugs". The living dead without freedom across the street from the honored dead who died for freedom.

3.6 Elmira, New York Ley Intersection

The Washington Ley and the Empire Ley (42nd parallel) cross in Elmira NY. The energy of this site is affected by the placement of a prison and National Cemetery.
It is the resting place of Mark Twain.

Liberty Ley

Named after the Statue of Liberty through which it passes, this line crosses and connects multiple leys. Starting at the estuary of the Oswego River in Oswego, NY, it matches the river's course south. Expressed in the Pennsylvania / New York border passage of the Delaware River, it crosses Port Jervis at the north end of the Delaware Water Gap. The line continues southeast through New Jersey / then to the Statue of Liberty / and out to sea via the Hudson Trench. This ley in its passage southeast hits on Syracuse / Onondaga Castle / and an area of land where the Peacemaker accomplished his forty-day vision quest. The Liberty Ley, a feminine line, shines its light from the Statue of Liberty to the matriarchy of the Iroquois Confederacy.

Berkshire Ley

Crossing the Peacemaker Ley, another alignment of cultural importance must be included. The Berkshire Ley transects the Peacemaker Ley in the Stockbridge Bowl. This scene of the *Tanglewood Tales* was also where Nathaniel Hawthorne wrote *The House of the Seven Gables*. It is the contemporary site of the Tanglewood Music Center, summer home of the Boston Symphony Orchestra. The Kripalu Yoga Center is also located there.

This line runs from New York City to Quebec City. In its passage through Berkshire County MA, it crosses at least thirteen schools, hence the name Berkshire Ley. The county has three primary mountain features: Mount Greylock, Monument Mountain, and Mount Everett. All are connected by this ley and share the distinction of being sacred mountains of the Mahican Indians.

Any visitor or resident will attest to the enchantment of the county. This is no doubt due in part to the many choral groups, monasteries, and music schools that call this line home. Close to both the Berkshire and Peacemaker leys is the town of Stockbridge. Here, illustrator Norman Rockwell painted an ideal of home, family, and country that became America's self-image. Saint Norman, as he is affectionately called in the county, documented and propagated this accepted vision of the American spirit more than anyone else.

Monadnock Ley

Simply three mountains in a row, this corridor connects the two following leys in our review. It is unusual because it links the three Monadnocks of the region: Mt. Ascutney, Mt. Monadnock, and Mt. Wachusett. A monadnock is a mountain that stands alone on a plain. These three mountains named by Native peoples are proportionally placed on a line whose three points generate a phi ratio (1:1.618).

Chakra Ley

This ley is a geologic structure that stretches from Quebec City to the Connecticut Coast. It is marked by a high concentration of minerals, especially garnet, and has many distinctive granite dome intrusions, markers for the Gaia Matrix geometries. Garnet found in high concentrations along this ley has a high level of geometry in its crystalline form and is the most prevalent mineral in the New England region. This ley is best seen in a ridge line which runs 14.5 degrees southwest from Mount Ascutney to Putney Mountain in Vermont.

Along its course one finds retreat centers, artist colonies, treaty sites, Peoples State Forest, environmental education centers, international youth prep schools, the home of the American Society of Dowsers, copper deposits, and some of the most beautiful land around. An eclectic blend, this ley has some of the most diverse qualities of place found thus far. In total this line could be described as the spine of New England. The centerline of Arkhom, its place qualities are similar to qualities ascribed to the human chakra system. It was also a dividing line between two local tongues of the Algonquin language, and forms a powerful, stable, metamorphic landmass that births river systems that course in and around it like the neural and vascular systems of our own bodies. This will be described in much greater detail in the chapter, Chakra System.

The Chakra Ley bisects the Base Ley at the Shelburne Granite Dome, which you will come to know as the center of the North American tectonic plate. Shelburne Falls is also known as a treaty site between Native groups. Following the course of this Geomantic Ley Corridor southward it aligns with a major vector point of the UVG in the Bahamas.

Base Ley

This Geomantic Corridor is the most important of the series. As you will see, it is the base line of our developing geometry, so more detail will be given here as a classic example of cultural site sequencing for the identification of leys.

A colleague, David Yarrow independently discovered and identified a part of this ley, describing it energetically as a green dragon. Its tail curves around Cape Cod and coils in the bay, giving force to its body, which courses past Old Boston's Green Dragon Tavern (established in 1697) and the adjacent "Boston Stone" along the Mohawk Trail and the Mohawk River (NY) corridor. The dragon's mouth is at Syracuse NY's Onondaga Lake, home of the Firekeeper for the Iroquois Nation. According to the Arkhom geometry, this ley starts north of the tip of Cape Cod in waters where whale pods gather to feed on zooplankton (as well as small fish such as Herrings), and completes its course at the eastern head of whale-shaped Oneida Lake of central New York state. This wave form was a primary line used by European colonists to project their spirit and worldview deep into the body of the continent. These independent discoveries, using different methodologies, confirm the existence of this geomantic corridor.

The Base Ley courses westward out of Cape Cod Bay, and comes ashore near and in line with the Boston Stone, Green Dragon Tavern, and Boston City Hall Plaza. This auspicious site, the neck of land where the Charles and Mystic Rivers meet Boston Harbor, was once the home of the Shawmut tribe.

The Boston Stone is the zero mark from which all distances were measured for the Massachusetts Bay Colony. The Green Dragon was where the boys got ready for the historic Boston Tea Party. (Curious that they dressed as Mohawk Indians.) Old Scolley Square was the site of the first livery (taxi). A fellow named Revere quite likely got his information and a horse here for his famous ride. This was also the site of the Grand Hall of American Masons where the activities of the 18th-century Sons of Liberty prepared the American Revolution, fueled by the nearby Boston Massacre. Millerites built a temple here to greet the end of the world in 1848, it turned into an opera house and then a burlesque house. Even Alexander Graham Bell used this place of beginnings to demonstrate the telephone for the first time. On this sacred ground all expressed the exuberance of life in communicating this distinctive sense of place.

Harvard University and the Massachusetts Institute of Technology are both on the base ley, as is the Walden Pond area, where Thoreau wrote his famous treatise which inspired the American ecology movement. From there King Philip, the mighty Metacom, bent his bow to drive the English to the sea. The King Philip War of the 1600's was what defined the mutual sentiment of Colonial and Native relations, perhaps even to the present. Philip's war castle was at Mt. Wachusett. A Wampanoag, he united the tribes of New England for their first collective endeavor. Mt. Wachusett's old growth forest, now a new ski run, sheltered both brave King Philip in his battle to preserve and protect his homeland, and Henry D. Thoreau as he contemplated the nature of the world under the shade of its trees. Mt. Wachusett to this day is held as sacred by Native peoples.

3.7 The Hub of the Boston Hex

This war memorial marks the center point of the hexagonal Boston Hub.

Wachusett is followed to the west by "Bears Den", a natural fortification, and falls where Metacom met with his war chief prior to the attack on Deerfield. Proceeding westward one comes to the Canada Hill site. Canada Hill was a seasonal camp for the annual spring salmon run, used cooperatively for millennia, until one cold spring morning when 300 Native Americans of all ages and sexes were cut down there in retaliation for an attack on Deerfield. This site is also where Professor Hitchcock undertook the modern study of paleontology, researching dinosaur footprints. It is a river confluence, a major falls, and the industrial town of Turners Falls, a typical northeast rustbelt city which is returning to its roots by retrofitting its old mills to an aquaculture industry. Turners was also hometown to the Brotherhood of Spirit Community, one of the largest 'hippie' communes in America.

The Greenfield / Deerfield area next in line is included in many early American histories. Greenfield is home of North East Sustainable Energy Association (NESEA) a leader in solar and alternative energy education. Crossing the Connecticut River at Greenfield our Base Ley matches the famous Mohawk Trail.

3.8 Cabin
A replica of Henry D. Thoreau cabin, where he wrote the book Walden Pond.

Shelburne Falls, the center point of this ley, as well as of Arkhom and the Gaia Matrix, and is underlaid by a basaltic dome of granite, a potato-shaped rock feature sited at the main confluence of the Deerfield River system. The location of another falls, it is considered locally to be the site of a treaty agreement between the Mahican and Pocumtuck Indians which later included the colonial powers. The long-supported treaty allowed for free travel, trade, hunting and fishing within a day's journey of the falls. This center has always been a place of peace and cooperation. It is kind of like the eye of the storm.

3.9 Walden Pond

Nearby is the town where Leonard Bernstein wrote the musical *Westside Story.* Shelburne Falls

3.10 Straight Track
Looking westward along the Base Ley of Arkhom as it passes through Shelburne Falls MA, the center of the North American tectonic plate and of the Gaia Matrix.

was also first during the early days of the industrial revolution with a cooperative community and industry hydro-electrification of the river. In the early 1990's, a watershed study was part of the relicensing of all of this rivers hydropower operations to issue new federal permits, created a nationally recognized approach. Residents evaluated the qualities of the river-watershed. For the study, the entire community was encouraged, supported, and invited to participate and inventory the resources. Specialists were available throughout the study to further the evaluation. The impact was addressed in the resulting regulatory aspects of river's future.

Shelburne Falls is a beautiful town of glacial potholes (world's largest), a flowered bridge started by the community when the trolley stopped running, fine examples of Victorian country-style architecture, and a stone tower with a great view of this center point of the North American tectonic plate. Shelburne has long been home to artists and craftspeople. Nearby is where Mary Lyons started her first school before going on to start Mount Holyoke College. A contemporary locale of meditation retreats, Shelburne Falls has always been a good place to get to the core of things. This rings true for the Buddhist Rinpoche who has identified the Shelburne area as the site of a Dakini treasury.

Coursing westward our ley passes through another old growth forest and past the Zoar Gap, the deepest river canyon in Massachusetts and where Olympic White Water trials are often held. At this gap is the entrance of the Hoosic Tunnel. This railroad passage through the Yankee granite was where nitroglycerin was first used as an explosive. The tunnel was a portal for the first rail trade route to the west. The rail lines exit the mountain at North Adams, entering into northern Berkshire County.

3.11 Shelburne Falls MA-- Glacial Potholes
The 'world's largest' Glacial potholes show the intensity and whirling vortex of the water at the center of the tectonic plate. It was also a Native treaty site.

In North Adams, the former buildings of the Sprague Electric Company, whose electrical capacitors helped propel humans to the moon, are presently the location of the Massachusetts Museum of Contemporary Art (MassMoCA). MassMoCA in its formative years has been heralded as a cutting edge synthesis model for modern museums. Combining arts, industry, and education, its huge floor space will provide a dynamic arts venue for the next century. It is a model that brings dance repertories, Hollywood special effects firms, computer educa-

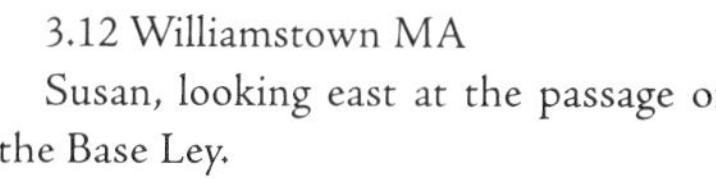

3.12 Williamstown MA
Susan, looking east at the passage of the Base Ley.

tion, music, and traditional museum exhibitions under one roof.

Heading west from this town of rainbows (due to the humidity and geographical conditions) past the foot of Mount Greylock and the crossing of the Berkshire Ley, one enters Williamstown, home of Williams College and the Clark Art Institute. Heading up the escarpment of the Taconic Range, the ley crosses Petersburg Pass into New York State.

The Taconics, a deflection resulting from the clash of the African and American tectonic plates, mark the dividing line of bioregions. The view west from the pass reveals the passage of the ley over the Peace Pagoda in the Grafton Hills. These hills hold many pre-colonial stone structures, and places of Manitou (spirit) to the Native peoples. Many of these sites are threatened by quarry operations mining some of the oldest and hardest rock on the planet.

Carrying on westward along Route 2 into the city of Troy we come to another important site, the confluence of the Mohawk and Hudson Rivers. Here we find Uncle Sam City, Rensselaer Polytechnic Institute, Russell Sage College / the clothiers of Cohoes / and the New York State Department of Historic and Urban Parks / through GE Schenectady /The Shrine of American Martyrs / the traditional home of the Akwesasne (Mohawk) Indians / and the Erie Canal, this ley courses out to its completion at the mouth of Oneida Lake.

As is made clear by this passage across this historic landscape, the Base Ley affords a perspective and window into the American experience, karma and future, a sine wave of culture that is still in the process of becoming. From the "Mohawk" Tea Party in Boston to the struggle of modern Mohawks to re-enliven their traditional heritage, the Base Ley "is" the story of 'America'.

3.13 Peace Pagoda
Positioned by Grace on the Base Ley, the Grafton NY Peace Pagoda sends a pulse of peace westward into the continental body.

It is important to familiarize oneself with these leys or Geomantic Corridors. To recap, these lines or bones inscribe pulses or wave forms which carry a signal of world civilization, mountain orogeny, western control and power, native spirituality, and crystalline structure. When combined they make a compelling case for the convergence of forces on the center of the North American tectonic plate. As good a place as any to be the omphalos of American myth and spirituality. The lines described, when combined, lead to more sophisticated triangular dynamics which give form and focus to the Gaia Matrix and geometries of destiny in the North American landscape.

4: Sacred Geometry 101

Sacred Geometry is a language whose origin predates the time of Cheops, the Pharaoh of ancient Egypt who built the Great Pyramid. At that time it had already developed into a high science.

The simplest form of sacred geometry is a circle. Marking a circle in the dirt is an act which in its simplicity describes the Earth, cosmos, and cycles of life. In reflecting upon this geometry of the circle, the movements of the planets and the sun's cycles are marked according to the season. So inscribed, a seven-pointed matrix is brought into form. It includes the four cardinal directions of North, South, East, and West, as well as the Zenith, the point directly above, the Nadir directly below, and the center point of the circle. Within the context of this sacred space all that is within and without the circle is part of the circle.

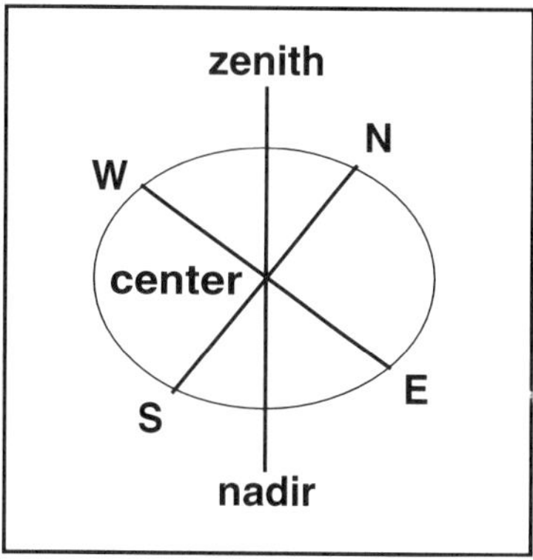

4.1 Sacred Circle

Standing at the center of this sphere with seven points, one is symbolically united with all that is above, below, around and within. Below the surface of the circle is an underground river, faultline, or subway, the effects on the nature and resonance of this sacred form are directly impacted. Our circle of activity, circle of friends, and cycles of life all refer to the great circle symbolized by this original sacred geometry. Whatever one finds in any of these seven directions affects and is affected by the sacred circle and its environs.

To establish one's geometric relationship with the land, one needs to take into account the geographic qualities which are included by the placement of the circle. For instance, the Great Pyramid is placed so that its four cardinal alignments cross the most dry land on Earth, a characteristic unique to this spot near Cairo, Egypt. A good exercise with this is to discover what geographic features are in the six directions set by your personal location in space, because these qualities of place all contribute to your personal and community sense of place.

As we all know, it takes two to tango. The circle typically represents both Sky and Earth as the horizons are clearly circular. The circles of Earth and Sky represent matter and spirit. A simple geometry using these two circles of equal dimension is to combine them as two intersecting circles with a common radius. If you make a circle with a compass, and then place your point anywhere on its circumference and scribe another circle the same radius as the first, the resulting shape scribed by the bisection of the two is what is called a Vesica Piscis, or "Vessel of the Fish". Classically this is seen as the unity of spirit and matter. It is the shape of the mouth, the eye, and the vulva, and is the

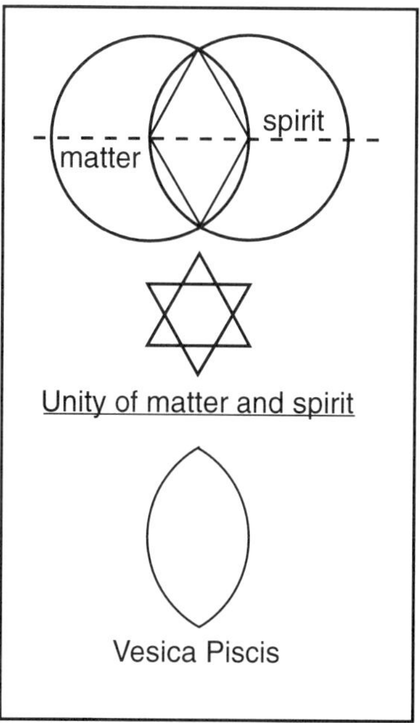

4.2 Vesica Piscis

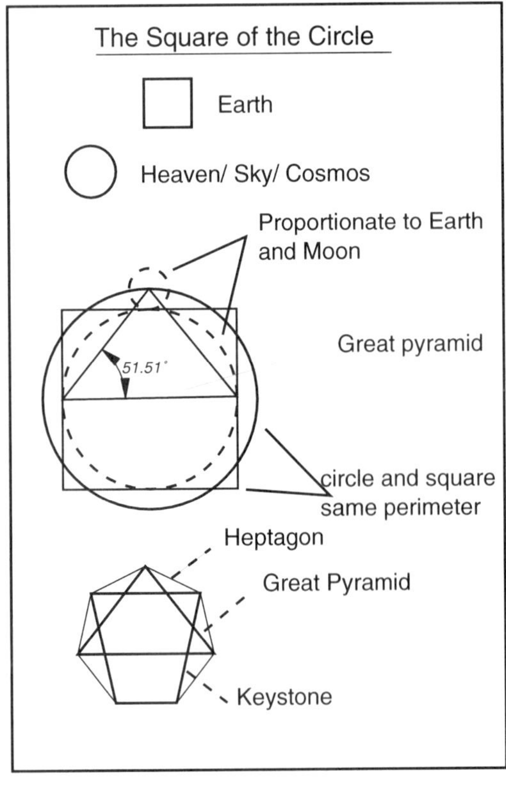

4.3 Squared Circle

base form of all sacred geometry. It is called a *mother geometry* because multiple geometries can be drawn from it by expanding on its intersecting points. This subject is nicely covered in Robert Lawlor's book *Sacred Geometry*. This vesica is found in religious art framing the images of Jesus or Mary, again representing the unity of matter and spirit. It is the basis of Gothic architecture, and the Christian symbol of the fish.

A further evolution of this form is described with lines connecting the two radius points and the points of the football. This draws two equilateral triangles pointing in opposite directions. Combine these, and you have the Star of David, the symbol of the Jewish faith.

Another more complex rendition of this unity is the Squared Circle. The square represents earth or matter and the circle sky or spirit. In Islamic architecture three geometric elements are generally utilized. The basic form of a Mosque is a cube, symbol of earth, capped by a dome, symbolic of the one truth that covers all. The combination of the two represents the unity of spirit and matter. The octagon or eight-sided form is the transition between the cube and dome. Symbolic of the Koran, the octagon links matter to spirit. Venturing farther back into antiquity, one finds the Squared Circle as a sacred geometry and the inner message of the Great Pyramid. This geometry creates two forms, a square and a circle; these have different shapes but are the same length. That is, the square's perimeter is equal to the circle's circumference. As seen in the accompanying diagram, the great pyramid is drawn to connect these two simple forms, generating this epitome of sacred geometry.

This same pyramid marks three points of a heptagon, or seven-sided geometry, whose other four points scribe a keystone. They are all symbols of the unity of spirit and matter. To express this is the essential purpose and function of sacred geometry.

Perhaps the most known sacred geometry is the pentagon or pentagram. It is, of course, the shape of the United States military headquarters in Arlington, Virginia known as the Pentagon. Another is the Chrysler automobile manufacturer's symbol. The pentagram, the five-pointed star within the pentagon, is considered a symbol and tool of Paganism. It is in these contexts that this five-pointed form is usually seen contemporarily.

The human body is also a pent or five-pointed form. The pentagram and pentagon are thus symbols of humanity as well. A common ratio is found both in the human form and the pentagram, 1:1.618, or phi. This phi ratio is the ratio of life, found in many natural geometries, such as the nautilus shell, the pine cone and pineapple, and sunflowers. The phi ratio is also embedded within the source of physical life, water, as the angle of separation between the two hydrogen molecules attached to the one oxygen molecule. It is common sense that water beings like humans would have this ratio as the basis of their form. Other expressions of phi are seen in the cross of Jesus and the Fibonacci number series, 1-2-3-5-8-13-21-34-55-88-... Proportions of this ratio can be found in the Great Pyramid, the Greek Parthenon, and Thomas Jefferson's building design. Phi proportion gives life. It is no small wonder that modern building, ignoring this proportion, creates disease. Most indigenous structures worldwide have this proportion in their geometries. This is a logical result of using the body as a measuring device in their construction and layout.

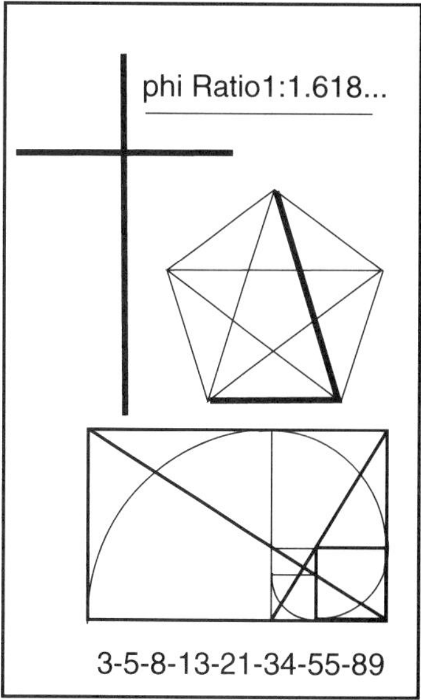

4.4 Phi

Noah's Ark was also a phi structure. The Ark's dimensions were 30x50x300. 3-5 is a phi proportion, while 30x50=1500/300=5. The Ark was a multiplication of the power of phi, a perfect vehicle to preserve life, expand it, and return it to five, the geometry of humanity. Phi is a proportion from antiquity with a timely message.

Similarly, the geometries of Arkhom and the overall Gaia Matrix are expressly sacred with many expressions of the phi ratio of life. The Arkhom geometry is a mother geometry in the sense that from its original form can be drawn the triangle (3), pentagon (5), hexagon (6), heptagon (7), nonagon (9), and dodecagon (12). The Arkhom combines these with the Vesica, the squared circle, and the land features, into a unity matrix that both literally and symbolically represents of the union of spirit and matter.

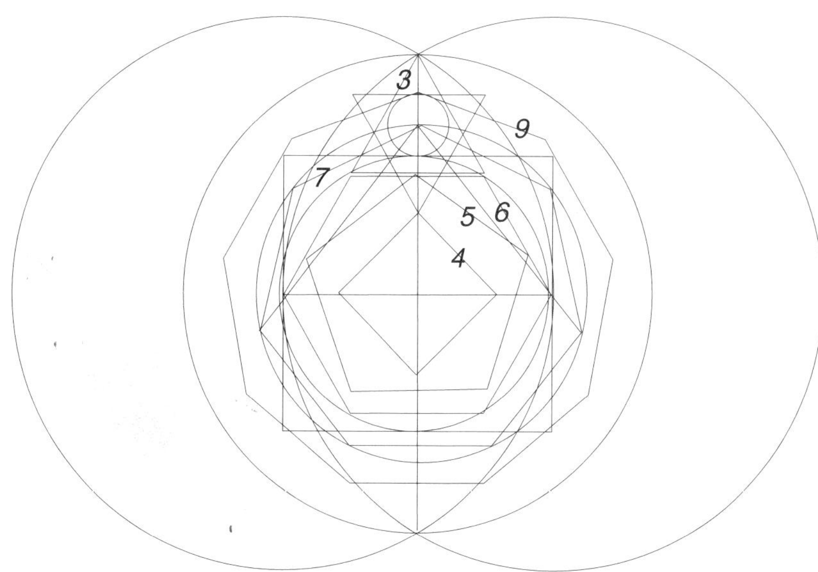

4.5 Mother Geometry -- see description of numbers in text.

5: Three Mountains

Testing our theory that geometries exist within the scale of mountains, we return to the individual and grouped footprints of Mounts Ascutney, Mansfield, and Washington.

5.1 Mount Ascutney
Known as "the place where the forks meet", Mount Ascutney is the southernmost point of the White Mountains. This spiralling peak is the Heart of the Gaia Matrix. This view is looking northeast.

5.2 Bretton Woods
Mount Washington's western face shadows the historic Bretton Woods, the site of treaty summits.

5.3 Mount Mansfield
The east slope of Mansfield shows the profile of Gaia's Face.

Mount Ascutney, a mountain of no great size, is nonetheless majestically luminous and is shown as such in many of Maxfield Parrish's landscape paintings. Its footprint creates a rough square with four arms that spiral towards the peak, a whirling swastika-like vortex of White Mountain granite. It stands as sentinel at the "place were the forks end", so named by the Native peoples. These forks refer to the upper tributaries of the Connecticut River and to the Green and White mountains which all meet here. Ascutney is the southern entrance to the mountainous northern kingdoms of Vermont and New Hampshire. This distinct bioregion, a world unto itself, is within a dish of land bounded by these same White and Green Mountains.

5.4 Ascutney to Washington Ley Passage

The distance from Mount Ascutney to Mount Washington marks the unit of measure which builds the entire geometry.

Mt. Washington, highest peak of the Presidential Range, it is the central apex of the spiral of the White Mountains. It is legendary for having the most changeable and severe weather in the world for a mountain under 10,000 feet. The third of this trio, Mt. Mansfield, is called the sleeping giant because its profile resembles the face of a green giant. The footprint of this mountain generates a shape that measures a golden rectangle (1:1.618). The three mountains create a nearly perfect equilateral triangle, whose size and orientation is the basis from which all the geometries were spun.

This simple triangle of three mountains would not be of note if it weren't for other landscape markers. The triangulation is further verified by alignments of valleys, towns, and watersheds. Astrologically speaking, the trine is the most harmonious relationship between planets, and speaks to the manifestation of unity.

The triangle is the first true shape. Its three-dimensional cousin, the tetrahedron, is the first true solid. To create a star tetrahedron one combines two tetrahedrons as one would two triangles to create a hexagram. The star tetrahedron is theorized by Richard Hoagland to be the energetic structure of the Earth and many planetary orbs of our solar system. This mountain trio powers the entire region with the piezoelectric, or electromagnetic charge, generated by their orogeny, or mountain building. Thus this force produces an engine of spirit for the genesis of culture. Symbolically these three mountains are representative of the element of earth.

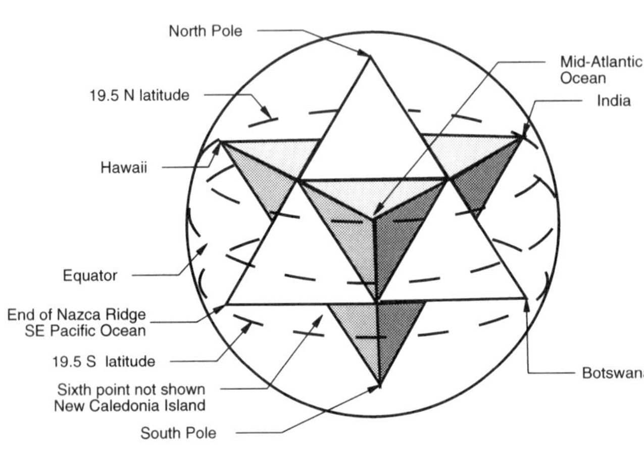

5.5 Hoagland's Tetrahedron -- see accompanying text.

In the world of threes, even going back to ancient times, there always exists a balancing second three. Since the first trio is mountainous, or Earth (matter), the second would logically be Water (spirit), to balance and feed the soil with its waters of life. The balancing water triangle of the same size has a reversed orientation, creating a hexagram (six points). The mountain trio is complemented by the lake regions of Willoughby to the north, Winnipesaukee in the east, and Champlain to the west. A positive (mountain) and negative (water) triangulation combines to generate a hexagram, the symbol of the unity of spirit and matter, the Star of David, the building block of our species-level hive.

When this water trine is doubled in scale as a geometric harmonic, another equilateral triangle is inscribed on the land. The base of this triangle matches the course of the Base Ley alignment (which was described in the preceding chapter). The generation of this Grand Trine brings our study to a new level of interconnection. Like the first, this trine is water based and shares the northern point of Lake Willoughby, known as America's Lake Lucerne (one of the most picturesque and restorative lakes in Switzerland). Boston Seaport and Canajoharie NY (on the Mohawk River) anchor the base of this triangle. Referenced historically to Native culture, this Grand Trine identifies the regions of the Haudenosaunee (Iroquois) to the West, the Wampanoags and Massachusett to the East, and the Abeneki to the North. It triangulates the colonial powers of the Dutch, English, and French respectively.

Water is the moniker of this Grand Trine. You have seen how the Base Ley crosses river systems, falls, lakes, and bays. The other two sides of the Grand Trine also have a preponderance of water features along their linear wave form. From Boston Harbor to Lake Willoughby, the eastern side of the triangle follows the course of the Merrimack River to the Lake district of New Hampshire, and on through the river valleys of the White Mountains. Where the eastern side has water in motion, the western side has water contained along its alignment. Here you will find lakes George, Champlain, and Great Sacandaga.

As the Grand Trine is a harmonic expansion of the water trine in the original hexagram, it geometrically indicates the generation of a star with twelve points, doubling the original six-pointed star; and so the geometry unfolds to our next section.

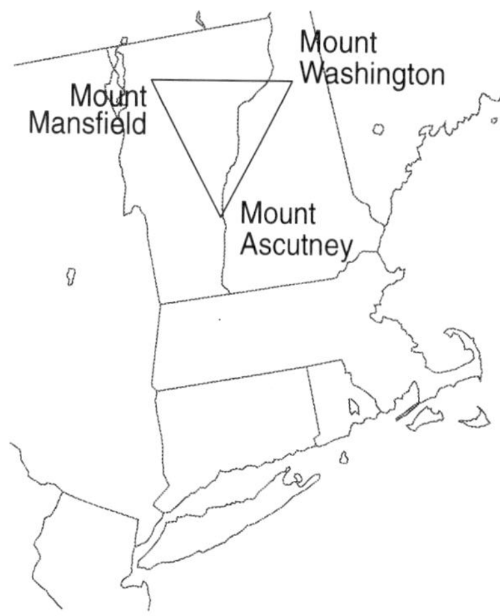

5.6 Three Mountains Triangle
The three mountains in situ on a map of the region, shown linking left and right brain functions manifest in the sense of place of Vermont and New Hampshire.

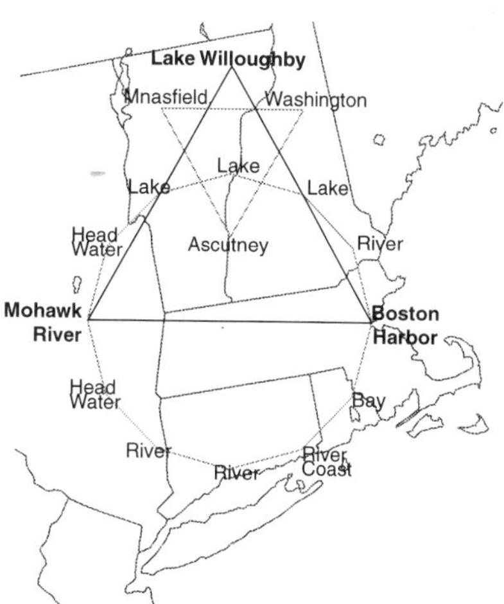

5.7 Element of Water
Balancing the earth element of the mountains, water features are positioned to expand mountain energies into the next fractal form.

6: The Circle of Twelve

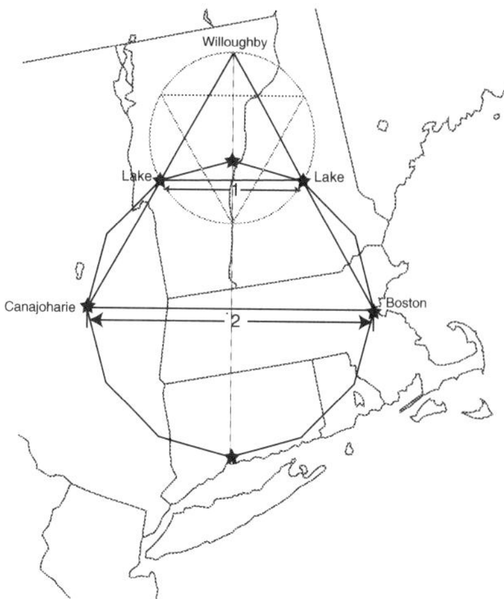

6.1 The Circle of Twelve
This figure illustrates how the Arkhom geometry evolved from a three- to six- to twelve-pointed form.

We have seen how the original hexagram and the Grand Trine are written into the landscape, and that the Base Ley is a major cultural corridor. These forms are further confirmed by the Chakra Ley, generally oriented north/south, bisecting all three triangles, and giving a geologically derived center line to our emerging geometry. This line parallels the Connecticut River Valley and bisects the Base Ley at Shelburne Falls.

Extended with our classic "Sacred Geometry" progression with Shelburne Falls as the center point, we now scribe a circle using the diameter measure of the Grand Trine base. This circle touches four points of the water trines -- Boston, Canajoharie, Lake Champlain, and Lake Winnipesaukee. Two additional points are marked where the Chakra Ley bisects the circle: at West Fairlee, Vermont, and the rivers' confluence in Derby, Connecticut.

Thus drawn, six of twelve equally spaced points are positioned on the circle, filling in the points of the geometry. This follows the dynamic principles of harmonic growth. A circle scribing the original hexagram is marked by six equidistant points. The larger circle is twice the diameter of the smaller with twice as many points. All of the harmonic proportions are related one to two.

The Circle of Twelve creates a "community enclosure" which brings to mind the Twelve Tribes of Israel (the lost thirteenth at center point), twelve signs of the Zodiac, twelve months, and time itself. The identification and place dialogue of these twelve zones or points would be a book in itself. This book's intention is to establish rather than detail the theory that sacred space on this scale exists, and that we as a species interact with it on a subliminal level.

Two primary points of the twelve are Boston MA and Canajoharie NY, as they are the base points of our Grand Trine and Base Ley. The other ten locales bring into focus the diversity of this community structure. All of the twelve points are on water features infolding the element of Water into this biologic geometry.

The twelve sites by name are from the east in a clockwise sequence: Boston MA / Providence RI / New London CT / Derby CT / Poughkeepsie NY / Arkville NY / Canajoharie NY / Oregon NY / Middlebury VT / West Fairlee VT / Meredith NH / Epping NH. Each of these points represent a larger field of influence. For example, Arkville NY is central to a zone which makes up the Catskill Mountains.

This circle geo-positions Harvard, Yale, Vassar, The Coast Guard Academy, ports and industrial complexes, confluences of rivers, the Catskills, as well as the Adironadack, Green, and White mountains. The

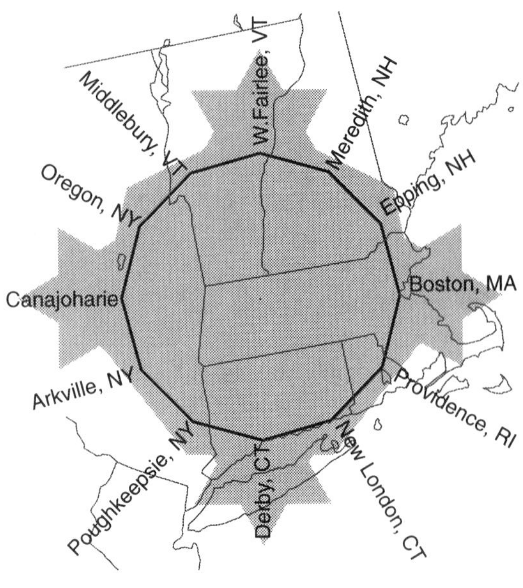

6.2 Twelve Places
These place names mark the points and communities of the stabilizing Circle of Twelve.

twelve encompass the passage of the Merrimack, Connecticut, Hudson, Housatonic, Mohawk, Thames, and Charles rivers. The tangle of these arterial waters is the blood stream of human settlement. Within these twelve zones one finds the highest concentration of Early Sites, those mysterious markers of a long past culture.

It is nearly impossible to piece together the actual tribal landscape of precolonial New England. All records died with the people as a result of the genocide they met through contact with the Europeans. We do know that they once lived in great numbers around places such as New London and Boston. The tribal lands and common grounds are geographically based, responding to the same pattern of the Gaia Matrix.

This is all about geography. A sacred geography. A geography through which the hands of God and Gaia have passed. A geography which reveals an unseen spiritual force at work that underpins the demographic, strategic positioning, and layers of settlement patterns. The combined stories of these twelve places are a vignette of modern North American civilization. For instance, the Providence/ Narragansett site centered on Slaters Mill is where mass production and the Labor Movement had its start. The Shawmut site in Boston, where Bell called Watson on the first telephone, is at the exact point where the Grand Trine's two sides meet at Boston's City Hall Plaza. Each one of these sites has seed-thoughts associated with their sense of place. Explore them for yourself, as a family or a community enterprise.

These twelve pillared zones can be seen as a Grail cup of 'American' spirit, invention and enterprise. This array is a stable form from which power can grow. If Spain had settled New England, this book would be written in Spanish. But this region demanded the hardscrabble ingenuity that spawned invention and nontraditional thinking to adapt to its harsh Northern conditions, traits missing from the 16th- and 17th- century Spanish monarchist rules of conduct.

Here we all dance round the central pole of our continental tent; the core form of a community structure, a tent covering all, its twelve poles give shelter and dimension to the inner spirit of this Ark. A new ark for the Narragansett, African, or New Yorker, a home for all of us, an Ark Home.

The sunset fades in the west, families embrace, and all is well in the garden. But what is going on in that garden?

7: The Power of Seven

In the esoteric world of sacred geometry, the power of seven as expressed in the heptagon is seen as a potent template of spiritual power. It is the geometry behind the 51.51 degree angular construct of the Great Pyramid of Egypt. Similarly, a circle divided into seven equal parts yields a 51 degree angle of separation.

The 51.51 degree angle is also found in the geometry derived from the "squared circle", in which a square's perimeters are the same length as a circle's circumference. With the circle as symbol of the heavens and the square the symbol of the earth, further importance can be attributed this interactive dynamic. Similar in esoteric function to the hexagon, the squared circle unites the worlds with the dynamic unity of seven.

51.51°
Heptagon
Great Pyramid
Keystone

7.1 Seven Squared
Hidden within the heptagon, seven sides is -- the pyramid, the squared circle, and the key stone.

Seven symbolizes the fullness of the universe in motion. Seven speaks of the colors of a rainbow and the notes of the diatonic scale. Hippocrates is credited with stating that through its hidden properties the number seven maintained all things in being, bestowing life and motion, and that its influence extended to heavenly beings. Seven alludes to the seven virtues of faith, hope, charity, prudence, temperance, justice, and fortitude. Seven is clearly a worldwide symbol of dynamic wholeness (fullness both of space and of time, marriage of opposites, resolution of duality) used by Christian, Jew, Muslim, Hindu, Maya, Zuni, Dogon, Buddhist, and Taoist alike. In each tradition, seven is associated with the processes of spiritual evolution, wholeness, action, completion, and the attainment of perfection.

Another aspect of the heptagon's life-giving potentialities is the proportion of phi (1:1.618...). As discussed earlier, it is a 'signature of life'. It has been speculated throughout the ages that God is a mathematician and that phi is the Creator's main equation. Using this proportion in the design and construction of our third skins (homes, offices) would positively affect human health.

The heptagon represents the symbol of the Holy or Great Spirit, embodying God's manifesting power. Seven is the first "perfect number", an abiding force of creation from which all life flows. Seven has been used in religious texts for the number of heavens, hierarchy of angels, and the days it took to create the universe. Similarly there are seven geographical points of the Gaia Matrix which make it an active, creative engine of wholeness and spirit. This heptagon is singularly the most important geometry in our study, for

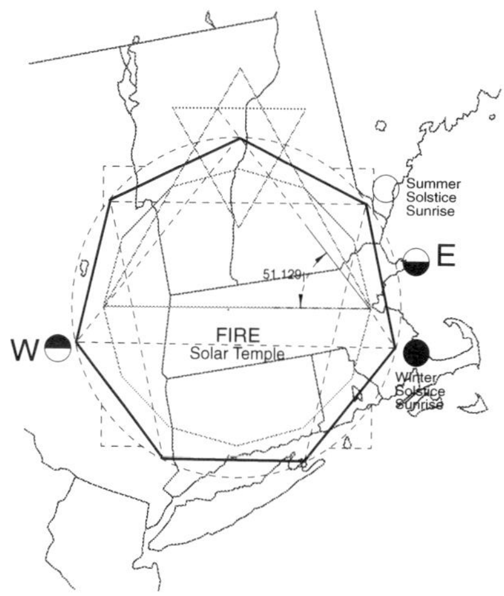

7.2 Fire / Solar Temple
These sunrise lines of the Summer and Winter Solstice reveal the geometry of Arkhom's Solar Temple.

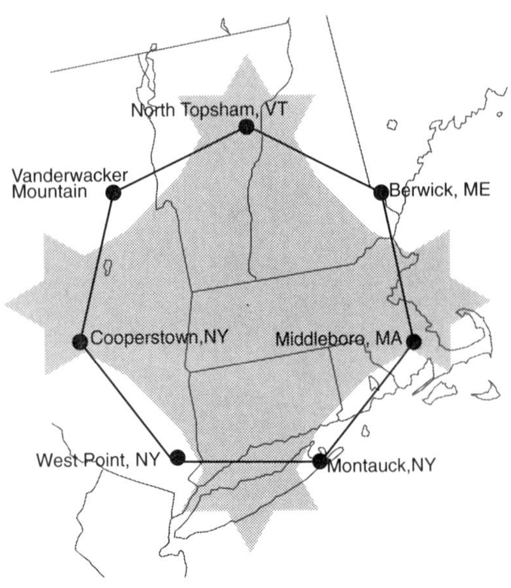

7.3 The Heptagram
These sites key the heptagon's Power of Seven.

reasons which will be evident in its expanded form described in the chapter "A Tale of Three Democracies".

The existence of the Arkhom heptagon was first discerned in a search for solar alignments. Solar orientation is one of the most essential components in creating traditional sacred space. One universally established purpose for ancient constructions was to tell time. The transom light over front doors in early American homes was often intentionally aligned to act as a sundial into the front hall or great room. Solar orientation of buildings is discarded in modern times (except as regard to solar power) in favor of other concerns such as a more convenient orientation to and from the street for entry, or to present the most imposing profile to the passing public.

Arkhom's equinox sunrise and sunset path lays due east and west of its center at Shelburne Falls (the valley of the town also bends to this opening, east / west). The equinox sun rises over Cape Ann MA, specifically Halibut Point State Park (the name actually derived from the nautical phrase "haul-about", as this was where sailboats would tack from to head for Boston). The park is the site of an abandoned granite quarry. The equinox sun sets over Cooperstown NY (Illustration 7.4, facing page). The equinoxes are on or about the 21st day of March and September. Cooperstown, one of the seven points of our heptagon, is similarly the home of the Baseball Hall of Fame for the season of the "Boys of Summer", extending between the two equinoxes.

Summer and winter solstice sunrises at this latitude are 56 degrees apart, or 28 degrees northeast and southeast from the equinox point of due east (or west). This also closely references the orientations to points of the heptagon. The inclusion of these solar orientations introduces the element of *Fire* to our biologic geometry. With the inclusion of the heptagon in our geomatrix, a solar temple is created, imbued with the life-giving fire of the Holy Spirit, a dynamic radiance spinning outward into the greater continental biology.

Seven points denote this field. The northern most one is located very near the center of our initial hexagram, in Topsham VT. It falls on the Chakra Ley, where it energizes the second chakra of the Arkhom spine (discussed in more detail later in the 'Chakara' chapter). Moving clockwise, the summer solstice point at Berwick ME lent momentum to the sewing industry-- a sign of the Three Graces. Middleboro MA the winter solstice point, was in Wampanoag Indian territory and is the present-day location of the New England Archaeology Association. Continuing the spin, the New York State points are Montauk, Long Island / West Point / Cooperstown (the "Great Council Rock" on Glimmerglass Lake, headwaters of the Susquehanna River-- a tributary of Delaware) / Vanderwacker Mountain in the Adirondacks, where the nation's largest titanium deposit is found.

Taken by themselves these sites are significant to the folks who live and work there; together they paint an energetic picture of a vitally expressive place, space, and grace. Where the ring of twelve is static like a foundation, the heptagon is all motion. Gestures such as the arm of Cape Cod (Illustration 2.4)and the sweep of Long Island-- mimic a clockwise motion.

This "spin field" is the demarcation ring (bringing with it change). Beyond it one finds the highest mountain ranges, the largest fisheries, the greatest energy. This ring is what puts the geometry in motion, just as the generative power of phi puts life in motion. As with any spin field, the greatest action is on the wall of the eye, as in a hurricane.

The base of the heptagon is anchored by West Point and Montauk. West Point is of course the well known military school. The water gap for which the college is named is a dramatic escarpment that was strategically used to keep the English in check during the American Revolution, and is the beginning of the Hudson River's outlet estuary to the sea. West Point is also central to an area of the highest concentration of Early Sites in the Northeast.

The activities at Montauk were not as overt. The object of many conspiracies, Montauk is considered to be one of the main research facilities of the "Philadelphia Experiment", where time/space experiments went awry.

Spinning about the stable pillars of the circle of twelve, the seven-sided heptagon acts as an electric generating coil for the geomatrix. The power that is generated within this spin field fuels the creativity and grace which flow out from this Gaia Matrix. Especially evident and expressed in New York City, Boston, and Montreal, this power has been to some degree subverted and polluted by the wars and genocide carried out against Native populations. This has created a collective karmic black cloud which obscures our vision as a culture.

The heptagon also serves to anchor the Arkhom nest into the Unified Vector Geometry (UVG), a planetary energy framework based on "Platonic Geometry". Acting as a kind of support structure, the Gaia Matrix geometries span and connect these UVG branches like a spider's web. Keying off the heptagon -- the UVG also keys into the Chakra Ley, and parallels the Base Ley.

7.4 The Great Council Rock

This boulder in Lake Otsego, at the mouth of the Susquehanna River in Cooperstown NY, was a traditional council site for the Native peoples of the region prior to the routing of the Iroquois by General Clinton in 1779.

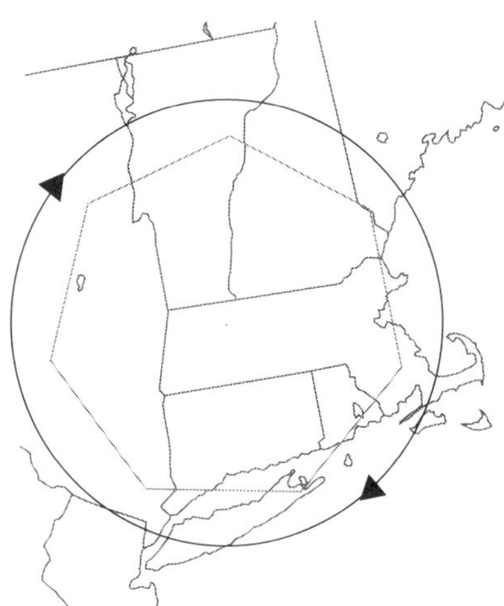

7.5 Spin Field

The clockwise spin set by the seven points is reflected in the visualized spin of the North American Continent.

8: Compass Rose

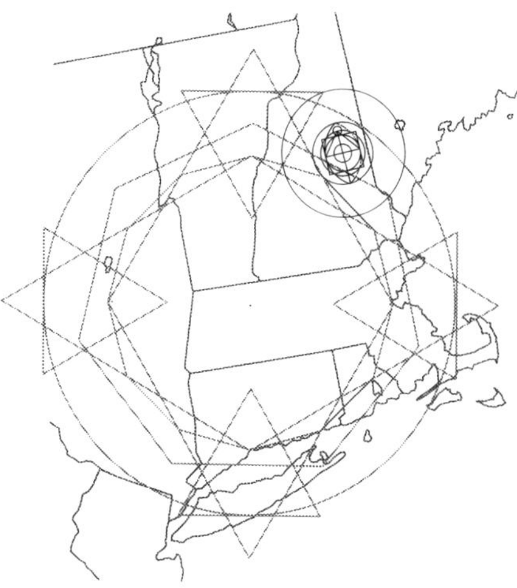

8.1 Winnipesaukee 'Compass Rose'
The position of the Compass Rose is shown in relation to the greater core dynamics of the Gaia Matrix

Every map has an orienting 'compass rose' to identify North relative to the body of the map. Generally speaking the rose is as artistically complex as the map it is imprinted on. Antique nautical maps have sea serpents, whales, and tall ships entwined around their four directional stars. Some are ornate and others are a simple arrow. In the austerity and efficiency of modern culture, the compass rose uses as little ink and time in creation as possible. Arkhom's Compass Rose is one and the same with its geometry, and was created through geologic time in a pattern of intricate beauty. Would nature be any other way?

Integral to Arkhom's landscape, the Compass Rose is centered around the Ossipee Mountains near Lake Winnipesaukee in New Hampshire. It bridges the area where the original Hexagon mixes with the *Circle of Twelve* and the Heptagon. The volcanic rock which makes up the core of this Compass Rose geometry gives the impression of a whirlpool generated by the spin fields of the six, twelve, and seven pointed stars of the Arkhom geometry, with all converging in the Winnipesaukee Lake District. The layout of our compass is, as it should be, a replica of the greater core geometry of Arkhom. It is one of the more inter relational landscape geometries, place names and geography interplay in ways classic to Feng Shui, the design school all the rage with architects, interior designers, and home owners of the 1990's.

8.2 Winnipesaukee Lake Panorama
The smile of the Great Spirit, looking east from the slopes of the Ossipee Mountains.

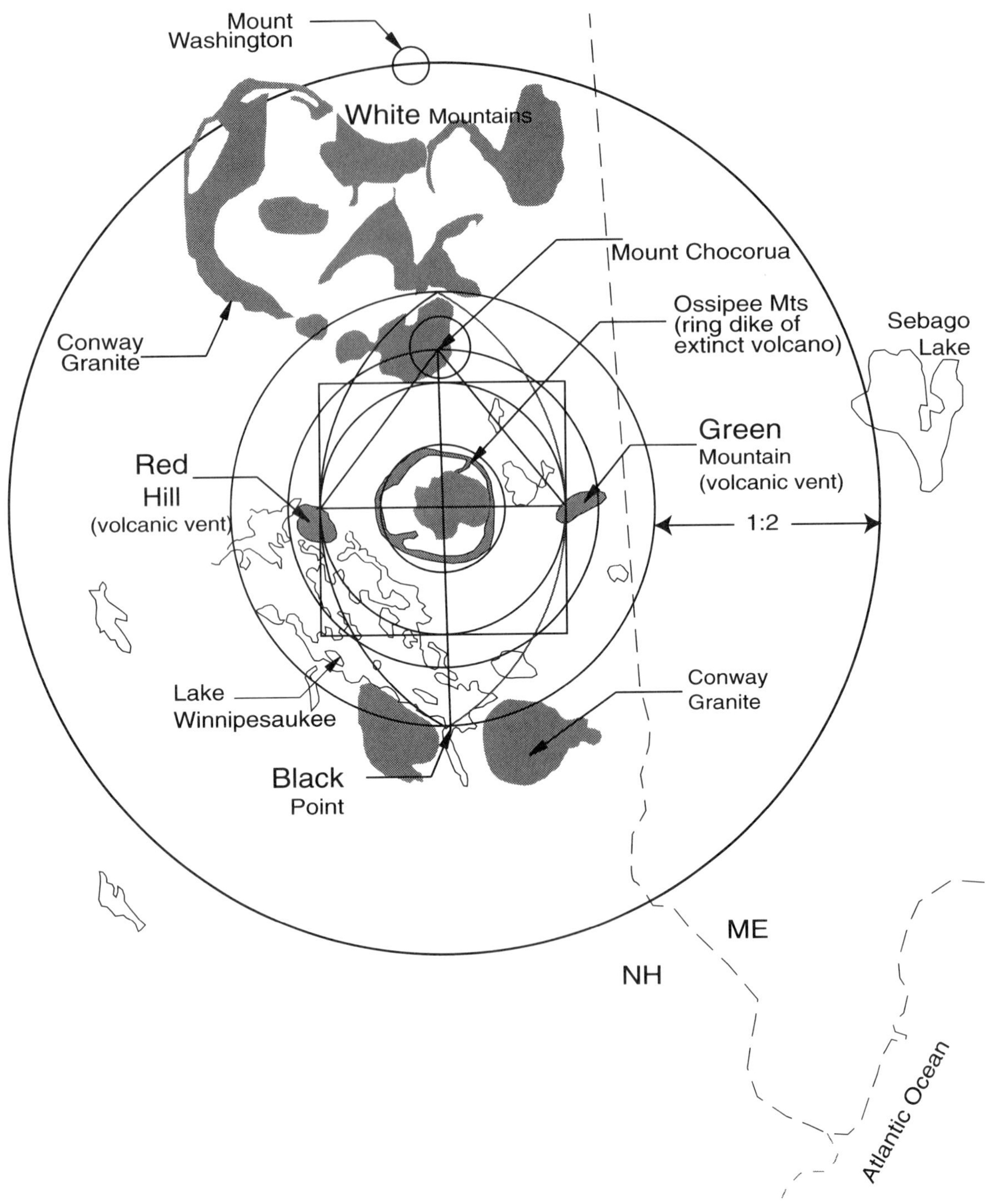

8.3 Ossipee Geology

This geologic rendering illustrates this micro form of the macro matrix. Notice the features of the wise owl (upper portion of illustration) emerging from the White Mountain Granite.

Lake Winnipesaukee in the tongue of the Pennacook is understood to mean "the smile of the Great Spirit". This smile speaks of the Vesica Piscis, the Vessel of the Fish. Winnipesaukee is in fact part of a landscape vesica.

Centered within this "vessel of the fish" is a long - extinct volcano. Geologists estimate that this volcano was originally four miles high. What remains today is the lava vent once buried deep in the original mountain. Because the core igneous rock was more resilient than the surrounding matrix, it is all that remains of the once great mountain, known today as Ossipee.

The Ossipee Mountains, positioned northeast of the lake, generate the orientation, size, and geometry of the Compass Rose. They are a circular range of mountains that in geologic terms are called a *ring dike*, the plug of an extinct volcano. When the lava cooled below ground level it formed granite and shrank as it cooled, allowing quartzite (which melts at a lower temperature than granite) to fill the gaps, creating the dike. It is a powerhouse of piezoelectric energy! The side vents of this volcano, by a coincidence of nature, arrayed themselves in the cardinal directions, forming the foundation of our Compass Rose.

Placed at the two radius points of the Vesica Piscis, the side vents set the geometry at Green Hill and Red Mountain. Mount Chocorua, a pyramid of a mountain on the southern edge of the White Mountains, is the north point of our Compass Rose. Relating back to the squared circle geometry, Mount Chocorua correlates to the great pyramid point of the heptagon. North of this point, and related harmonically, is Mount Washington.

To complete the four directions of the compass we look south to Black Point at the southern tip of Lake Winnipesaukee. This point is framed by undulating hills of the same Conway Granite that is at the center of the Ossipee Mountains vented by the same ancient volcano. The cross formed by these four points on the landscape generate with relation to their lengths-- a phi ratio between the east-west line of Green Hill to Red Mountain and the north-south line from Mount Chocorua to Black Point.

Identifying these directions with color starts to build associative place names for the Lake District. In turn each of these mountains have shapes which reference them to the five elements of the Feng Shui pantheon of space. They are however, arranged in reverse of their exalted positions in relation to classical Feng Shui.

To the north is Mount Chocorua, the color white and the White Mountains -- the white-hot Fire. To the east is Green Hill and the element of Wood. To the west Red Mountain speaks of Metal. Black Point in the south symbolizes Water. The fifth element, Earth, is represented by the shape of the Ossipee

8.4 Mount Chocorua

This cap stone of the Ossipee pyramid has a point which speak to its position. Locally considered a portal to unseen worlds, Chocorua shows us its southern face across Lake Chocorua.

Mountains and this volcano's link to the depths of the planet. Each of these directional Chi relationships are further reinforced by place names that speak to the five elements.

Blending the five elements in a whirling dance, our Compass Rose is a replica of the mother geometry of Arkhom. Caught in a whirlpool of great wheels of bio-geometry, the rose as temple and template directs the traveler north towards Mount Washington-- towards basic elemental cycles and proportions of life. The unity of matter and spirit makes this a portal through which Cosmic Christ consciousness can enter our own. It is something to contemplate while on board the cruise ship M.S. Washington sailing these sacred waters within this sacred space, this smile of the Great Spirit.

9: The Four Directions

Mother geometries like Arkhom's call for integration at all levels. As it is a living geometry we take guidance from nature. A microcosm or fractal form of the continental body, the geometry is beginning to resemble the physical attributes of the Turtle. Native peoples see the continent as Turtle Island (a concept brought to a wider audience by ecospirit poetry of Gary Snyder). The continental Turtle can be seen in two ways, with its head either to the north or south. Head to the south, places the Yucatan Peninsula as the snout of this turtle. Turned around, Greenland is the head, and the Yucatan becomes a newly hatched egg. Its four legs are Florida, Baja, Alaska, and the Maritimes. The tail is Central America or Greenland respectively. As is, our central matrix geometry resembles a turtle without legs, tail, or offspring. The full form of this centric fractal Gaia Matrix is brought to completion.

So far our geo-matrix is fundamentally a large circle, with another circle roughly half the size embedded on the north-northeast side of its circumference. The circle is bisected by two leys, Chakra and Base, neatly cutting it into four pie-shaped pieces. To complete the geometry we replicate the initial hexagram, or six-pointed star, at Boston, Canajoharie, and the confluence of rivers in Derby CT. With this, the four directions or four winds are included to create a basic template for sacred space, bringing the element of Air to our biologic geometry. To be an addition to our study, these newly drawn hexagrams need to highlight geographically significant locales. With the addition of the remaining three hexagrams the geometry brings together Northern Vermont, Cape Cod and Boston, the New York City metropolitan area, and the Mohawk River / Erie Canal / Oneida Lake zone into a foursquare interplay.

As we have seen, the geomatrix appears to have a clockwise spin attributed to the Heptagon and evidenced by the land patterns of Cape Cod and Long Island. By spinning the initial hexagram clockwise, it first clicks into the eastern axis of the Base Ley. Points of the star indicate Hyannis MA and the whale grounds off the tip of Cape Cod. Continuing southwesterly the next critical rotational position locks it into the Chakra Ley, placing the point that was originally at Mount Washington smack on Manhattan Island. This dynamic geometrically illustrates how the earth energy generated by the northern mountains fuels the psyches of Wall Street. A curious correlation between the two is the quick change of weather in these locales, one atmospheric and the other economic.

9.1 Turtle Island

The zoo-morphic shape of the continent suggests the shape of a turtle with its neck (Mexico) stretching south and mouth (Yucatan) open wide feeding on the rising sun (Cuba).

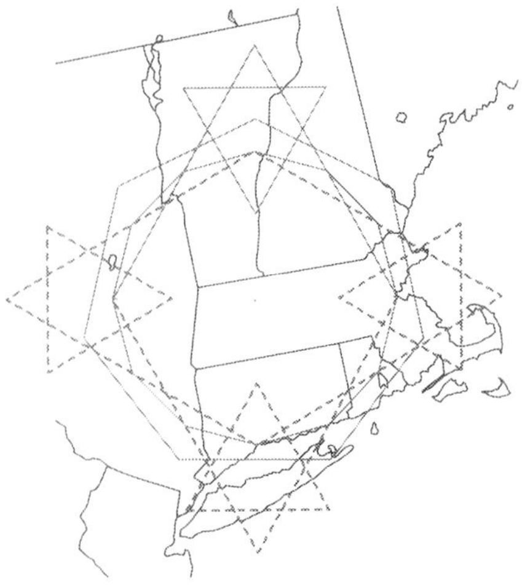

9.2 Four Winds

Replicating the Hexagon/ Grand Trine in the three quadrants of the Arkhom geometry brings New York City, Cape Cod and the Mohawk Valley into play with this geo-matrix. Especially note how the Mount Washington point spins around to become NYC.

If this Gaia Matrix has attributes of a biology, then it is also a sexual being. Greater New York City depicts its sexual organs. Manhattan resembles a phallus penetrating the Hudson River Estuary, which may be seen as the vagina of this Gaia Matrix. The Palisades represent the vaginal wall, with "Queens" being the clitoris. Staten Island has a classic uterine shape. With the Statue of Liberty in the birth canal, some really potent symbolism comes to mind. New York City is a climax experience! It is a dynamic cultural expression, one that is struck in the sexual nature of experience. What of the Heart? What of the higher mind and spirituality?

Turning our arrow to the west, it circles into the Base Ley again, pointing "westward young 'hu'man" along the Mohawk River Valley to Lake Oneida. In subsequent chapters you will see how this seed-point grows fractally into the Great Lakes Biome. The synchronisms continue from here. These four directions point to a greater historical cycle illustrating the significant impact of the Gaia Matrix on our collective life.

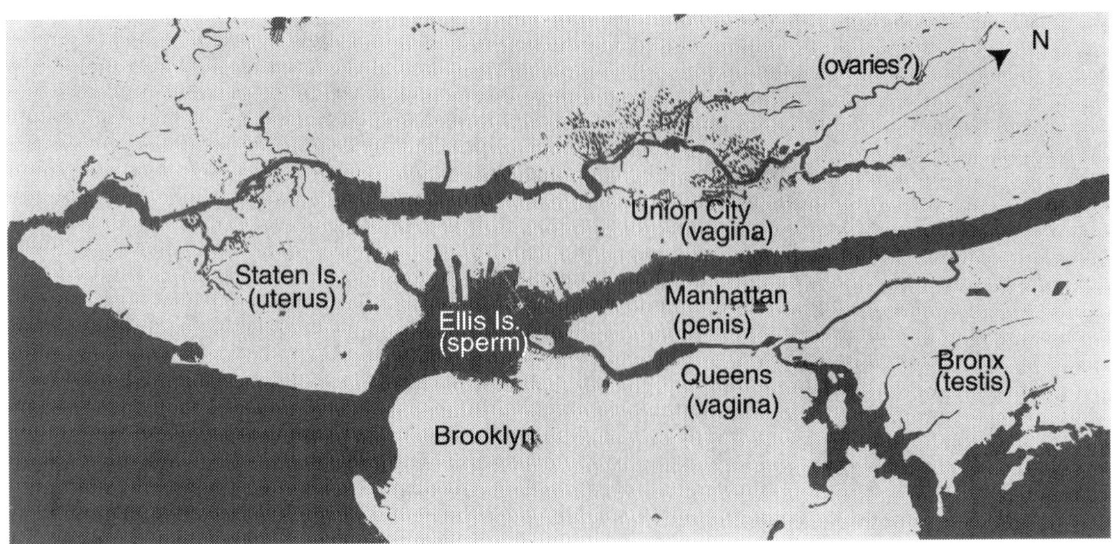

9.3 Gaian Inter-Course
A geographic illustration--
of the gaian biology's sexual organs is full of potent metaphors, including the birth of Liberty, the male control of Wall Street, and the world peoples who seeded the nation from this seaport. Apologies are extended to anyone who might find this distasteful.

10: Chakra System

Places of power have a support system which feeds, energizes, and holds a current through the flux of sun and moon cycles. The megalithic builders of old England tried to formulate this into a system to modulate and focus these known energies at appropriate times. Like any attempt to control nature it was bound to have some problems.

The English system was comprised of calendar sites or henges, menhirs (standing stones), dolmens (3 upright/ 1 cap stone), long barrows, and straight tracks. This system's components required maintenance and periodic adjustments in the arrangement to accommodate both subtle and powerful changes in Nature's ebb and flow. After a time this science was lost and the system ceased its effects. One can see the evidence of the power in excavated earthen mounds whose consecutive layering of piezoelectrically charged soils replicate a kind of battery. One such mound revealed a melted surface on a buried dolmen. Stone starts to melt at 5000+ degrees Fahrenheit. The theory is that earth energies were gathered via a network of menhirs, stored in long barrows, and released by ceremonies resembling May Day festivals. The appropriate times for these interactions with the Earth were determined by the calendar sites which kept track of the seasons. Particularly fine tuned, the 11+ year solar flare cycles were incorporated into the mix, so as to plan for the time when extra mojo is pumped in.

Similarly, a place like New York City requires a network of piezoelectric feeders to sustain itself. This is not to suggest that an artificial system was constructed, as in England, to control telluric energies. It is instead part of New York's interaction with place, space, and grace. Manhattan's bedrock is granite, a highly charged piezoelectric material. When granite is subjected to pressure it increases its electrical signature and thus the power of electro-magnetic attraction. Rock, quarried hundreds of miles from Stonehenge, was used in its construction because of its ability to hold current. In the case of New York, the weight of towering buildings adds this kind of pressure. The network of telluric currents which are drawn to it are the Berkshire, Liberty, and City Leys, as well as the Taconic Ley. These leys in turn cross the Appalachian Ley which serves as another source of telluric power for the warlords of commerce, whose daily priestly rituals, on the Floor of the Wall Street Exchange, control and modulate a modern form of Earth Magic.

Mammalian biological models similarly have a networked neurovascular system which feeds, and is controlled by, centers along the spinal axis. We have all felt that light go off in our heads, the twang on our heart strings, the stirring of our gonads, and that knot in the pit of our stomachs. All life responds in this way. The biology of our Gaia Matrix also has such a neurovascular system.

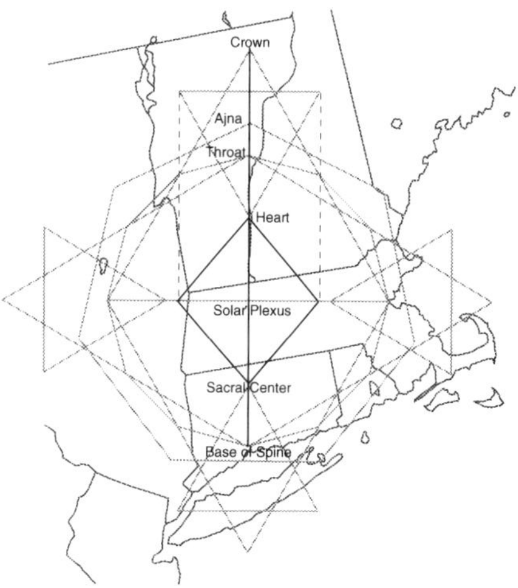

10.1 The Chakra System

This figure depicts the relative positions of the Chakras integrated into the Gaia Matrix.

10.2 Willoughby Panorama
The Crown of the Matrix, Lake Willoughby has many secrets locked in its depths.
Looking southwest the mountains Pisgah and Hor are seen at the far reaches of the lake.

In the case of Arkhom's biological geomatrix, the central spine is the Chakra Ley. This ley courses through New England and the central Arkhom complex from the confluence of the Naugatuck and Housatonic Rivers at Derby CT to Lake Willoughby near Newark VT.

Visioning the spinal system oriented towards Northern Vermont, we proceed with our discussion based on the chakra centers made mainstream by the American actor Shirley Maclaine. These chakras are: Crown, Third Eye (Ajna), Throat, Heart, Solar Plexus, Spleen, and Base or Root. Much has been written about this system from Hindu to New Age perspectives. In a nutshell, the *Crown* relates to cosmic consciousness, the *Third Eye* to clairvoyance and spiritual vision, the *Throat* to communication, and, of course, the *Heart* to love. The *Solar Plexus* is associated with the fire of the intellect, the *Spleen*, or second chakra, with emotion and sexuality, and the *Base* chakra with our basic life force or kundalini, source of our essential vitality. A useful discussion of the chakras may be found in *Sacred Sounds -- Transformation through Music and Word*, by Ted Andrews. The element of *Ether* is brought to our biologic geometry through the Chakra Ley.

The *Crown* of the Gaia Matrix is Lake Willoughby. It is called the "Lucerne" of North America (after the one in Switzerland) because of the dramatic inclines rising around it. Shaped like the pineal gland of the higher mind, this lake's great depths (350+ ft.) suggest the deep well of cosmic consciousness from which we all may drink. Like two halves of a brain, mounts Pisgah and Hor hold the lake in their embrace. Mount Pisgah is a common name used in New England and is more often than not-- a spot with a vista. Pisgah, you bible scholars may recall, was the mountain from which Moses saw the Promised Land. Mount Hor was the burial spot of Aaron, the brother and spokesman for the stuttering Moses. Lake Willoughby is thought to be named by two brothers who were early settlers to the area, Moses and Aaron Willoughby. From these heights, on a warm summer's day, the 'promised' land is plain to see. Opening to the north, this U-shaped glacial-trough funnels the wisdom of the north through this spark gap to Ascutney and into collective consciousness.

The power that fuels this life force coursing up one's spine is called kundalini energy by the yogis of the east. Symbolized by the entwined serpents seen on the physician's caduceus-- this force is associated with snakes, dragons, and water serpents. There have in fact been sightings of a large 'nessie'-like lake monster rising out of the deep waters of Willoughby, like kundalini energy emerging from the crown. In fact a water snake was killed in 1886 by a twelve-year-old lad who boldly severed its body with a sickle. On actual measurement the two pieces were found to be 23 feet in length. These legends are common to the places of northern lakes. Lake Champlain has "Champ", Lake Memphremagog has "Memphre", and Lake Willoughby has "Willy" or "Willa" as symbols of the deep ecology of primordial supra-consciousness.

The alignment of Mount Washington and Mount Mansfield crosses the spine between the Crown and the Third Eye. Situated at this balance point like the pivot of a scale is Danville VT, the national headquarters of the American Society of Dowsers. Dowsers access information from the higher mind with their intuition to find water, minerals, and answers to questions, often related to healing. Nearby St. Johnsbury is home to the invention and manufacture of modern scales. (Previous to this invention the technology for weights and measures had been essentially the same since the time of Jesus.) Qualities of place such as this and other examples of balance found in the Gaia Matrix suggest that it has the power to restore balance to the land. This type of consistent synchronistic reinforcement of the geometry gives one pause as to the power of the Creator's intent.

The *Third Eye* is the point where the heptagon meets the spine of the Chakra Ley. This point, referring back to Sacred Geometry 101, is the crowning point of the Great Pyramid. It is central to the Mountain Triangle. Look at the pyramid on the US one dollar bill to see where this is taking us. Located at the northern border of North Topsham, this Third Eye's geographical zone includes the granite deposits of the "Rock of Ages" quarries, whose main products are funeral monuments. This again links us to the analogy of the Great Pyramid and the mysterious power of the intuition.

On a site visit to the hamlet of North Topsham we were greeted by posters with Day-Glo Third Eye symbols. In this case they were used by the State of Vermont to identify its Artist-in-Residence tour. The symbol was an equilateral triangular "V" shape for Vermont, and a spiral which spun from the center of the "V", matching the geometry of the three mountains to which it is central. For the trained eye these messages are everywhere.

Central to a large granite deposit in the middle of the Three Mountains, the Third Eye activates the Power of Seven that generates the spin of the dynamic heptagonal field. Many of the chakra points of our landscape biology are punctuated by granite outcropping.

Located in the metal deposit of Vermont, the *Throat* Chakra is centered on the town of West Fairlee. This chakra is associated with clairaudience, telepathy, and communication. Scattered in the hills around West Fairlee are many "channels" attracted to the area. Lightgate, the brainchild of Tippi Halsey, is an educational center communicating the emerging ideas of a holistic culture. A healer and educator, Tippi facilitated the development of the Arkhom harmonic structure in a workshop given at Lightgate, when, with her facilitation we came to understand how the power of the Gaia Matrix is broadcast to the greater continental body.

10.3 Vermont Artist in Residence
Logo is reminiscent of the three mountains focus on the Ajna third eye chakra center.

Nearby Thetford is also home to the DNA house, the onetime headquarters of the World Institute of Social Architecture. It was through WISA that Arkhom was first given voice at the Creative Problem Solving Institute in Buffalo, New York in June, 1994 (winning an Earth Art award). In nearby Vershire is an abandoned copper mine, its gaping gash on the landscape looking like a tracheotomy. Copper, known as an excellent conductor of current, energy, and heat is used extensively in communication and electrical technologies. The

10.4 From the Heart
Reminiscent of paintings by Maxfield Parrish, this photo of the author speaks to the sentiment of the heart that prevails in the shadow of Mount Ascutney.

Throat Chakra corresponds to communication, thus the voice box of this Gaia Matrix. It is also a central point in the combined geographies of Vermont and New Hampshire. Together, the two states form a rectangle of phi proportions. Like two halves of a brain, they are opposites in most things, and live to be so.

Maxfield Parrish, an artist and central figure in the Illuminist School, is known for his mythical heart-felt illustrations. Mount Ascutney, the Heart Chakra of our system, was often the object of his art. A participant in the Saint Gaudens art colony of the early twentieth century, located across the Connecticut River from Mount Ascutney, Parrish communicated the rosy daydream of lovers through his art form.

Near Ascutney, many streams flow into the Connecticut River, the main artery of our landscape biology's vascular system. A most striking resemblance to a spinal form is laid plain in the ridge line which connects Mount Ascutney to Putney Mountain. This ridge runs dead straight along the Arkhom spine or Chakra Ley, accentuated by bumps which look like so many vertebrae. Terminating at Putney Mountain, it connects the heart chakra of Ascutney to the Inner Life of Arkhom. Putney Mountain is the mountain at the northern border of this Inner Life and the place called home by many cultural creatives. Of note are the "Seven Pillars", a series of laid stone cairns five to seven feet high, aligned along this ridge. They are thought to be pre-Colonial in origin-- more Early Sites. An extensive survey of the cairns was done by John Martin of Springfield, Vermont. It is likely that the Seven Pillars were used for astronomical measurements showing that quality of place is timeless. Springfield, at the northern end of the ridge, hosts the annual Amateur Astronomers conclave.

As we work our way down the chakra system from the Crown, each center becomes progressively larger. Each of these is a geomantic zones with its own spin field of direct influence. These are not finite points on the land, but rather zones with particular qualities. The Third Eye comprises the circle scribed by the radius between it and the Throat chakra. The Heart chakra is roughly double the size of the Third Eye, encompassing an area set by the radius between Mount Ascutney and Mount Kearsarge in New Hampshire. This radius scribes a circle which includes the historically preserved mansions of Woodstock, Vermont and the old factories of Bellows Falls VT. After all, the heart speaks of warmth and with the lungs restores the blood-- the bellows that kindle the flames of love!

Coming into the core of the geometry, our next chakra is the *Solar Plexus*. The gaian values of Art, Higher Learning, Agriculture, and Spirituality speak of the sensibilities native to this zone. This is discussed in the chapter, "Inner Life". Shelburne Falls is at the center of the North American tectonic plate and the Solar Plexus of this Gaia Matrix. It is also a place that many internationally known, influential people call home.

This central Solar Plexus is a zone of power, marked by numerous nuclear, hydro, and fossil fuel electric power generating plants. The Deerfield River which runs through the Shelburne Valley has headwaters which mark the outer reaches of this zone. Known as "The Hardest Working River" due to the gradual but marked drops in elevation allowing for many power plants, the Deerfield has had a long history of water power use. Some of the early plants supplied power to the town they were in; now that power, handled by the New England Power Pool, can be sent outside of the area.

Working our way southward, the system expands to encompass ever greater geographical zones. The Spleen and Base chakras, respectively identified as Barkhamstead Reservoir and Derby, Connecticut, are part of the greater megalopolis stretching from Washington DC to Boston. This area south of the Base Ley is where one finds contaminated rivers and Superfund sites. The activities of these zones are for the most part focused on the lowest expression of these chakra energies, those of greed, control, lust, and not dealing conscionably with one's waste.

In the *Spleen* chakra one finds Hartford, Connecticut and its water supply, Barkhamstead Reservoir. Peoples State Park is here, as well as one of the wealthiest zip codes in the country, Litchfield CT. There are many beautiful places and people in this zone of all models, colors, and economic positions. There is however a preponderance of negative indicators which suggests an unbalanced expression of this chakra's energy. Connecticut is a state of contrasts in which the wealthiest among its population thrive and the least are ignored. There are the many bedroom communities for New York City commuters. These walled ghettos for the rich exist in rarified isolation from the third-world conditions and industrial disease found in the urban and suburban ghettos. Connecticut has great schools in affluent suburbs such as Greenwich, Litchfield, Easton, and Weston in sharp contrast to inner-city schools. This is a disgrace to us all, and points to the fact that in the United States all are created equal, but none are treated as such.

There is a sickness in the lower chakras of Arkhom. We see it manifest in the ever increasing death rates from colon, prostate, and uterine cancers. The garbage is backed up in our collective bowels, highways and landfills. Here Viagra is lauded as the best thing since the birth control pill. Humanity exists to create markets for the warlords of commerce who provide substandard products with planned obsolescence, generating more waste, more money, more greed, more insurance, and more investment-- an unsustainable way of life.

The *Base* Chakra located at the confluence of the Naugatuck and Housatonic Rivers is home to the Kellogg Environmental Center. Kellogg is on a bluff surrounded by some of the most polluted waterways in America. Petroleum-based industries on the shores of the Naugatuck River developed such products as vinyl flooring and "Naugahyde", a kind of fake leather of the 1960's.

One might conclude that the Kellogg Environmental Center reflects a solution to the problems which surround it. The old estate of the Kellogg family was given in trust to the people of Connecticut. A center for environmental training, Kellogg is an example of the positive impact wealth can have on culture, amist the negative impact generated by the same wealth. Juxtaposed against the backdrop of the regional rust belt, Kellogg is the spark that remains of this source of kundalini energy at the base of our Gaia Matrix's spine. Across the river from Kellogg is the site of the tragic story about the unrequited love of two Native Americans. A kind of Romeo and Juliet story, they were from tribes whose history prevented their union. They would secretly meet at the waterfall and it was the site of her demise.

Social and environmental disease are the payment for wealth in the region. Perhaps philanthropy such as the Kellogg's will shift the priorities of the wealthy toward removing the blight on this sacred landscape. Benefactors with talent and/or financial resources could really help to assist non-profits such as Arkhom, Inc. -- formed to turn our collective landscape into Nature's Cathedral.

Significant benefit comes with removing blocks in ones chakra system. Flow of energy clears and cleans so our full potential can be realized with life enhancing results. A closer connectivity to the source of life-giving energy is nourishing and sustaining, elevates the well-being of people and the land.

11: Harmonic Expansion

The Arkhom geomatrix is a microcosm of the nation and continent, generating harmonic growth from coast to coast. The preponderance of invention, social architecture, economic power, education, religion, art, and nature all speak loudly to the sense of place that is the 'American' experience. How does this corner of the world communicate its lexicon of place to the rest of the continental body? The answer is found in the doubling of its size, just as the doubling of the first mountain triangle generated the full Arkhom geometry. Doubling the size of the rotational field incrementally, it reaches to the western shore of California. Each new harmonic generation is locked into place, describing historical periods within this ever-expanding field. Of course this doesn't stop at the West Coast. The next harmonic expansion brings Hawaii, Alaska, and Western Europe into its embrace. The harmonics then contract as they continue around the globe, ending in a point off the southwestern coast of Australia. This point is the polar opposite of the center of the core geometry 'Arkhom'.

Like poles of the world, these two places are homes of aboriginal cultures whose land remained unknown to Europeans for centuries, and who held the Earth in reverence as a manifestation of the Creator. Perhaps it is time for the American and Australian governments to encourage, document, preserve, and implement the practices of these Native peoples, before we as a human species lose this knowledge -- and are denied its benefit for another seven generations.

Harmonic expansion has keyed the growth and influence of the United States from the Revolution to the present. The Louisiana purchase of 1803 opened the vast land between the western Arkhom harmonics, from the Mississippi to the West Coast. The War of 1812 then solidified American continental gains, while the Monroe Doctrine of 1823 expanded the US influence into hemispheric politics.

In the Mexican War of 1846 - 1848, most of the present-day Southwest became American territory, including the Four Corners region and California. During the war, US troops captured Mexico City, which sits on the edge of a harmonic ring centered on the Yucatan. This ring also keys into New Orleans and the Mississippi Delta, the southern focal points of the Louisiana Purchase. With this victory, America had reached the outer continental harmonic of the Gaia Matrix. The United States became the dominant power from the Atlantic to the Pacific.

The following years brought the Gold Rush and ethnic cleansing of the Native peoples of the western United States. The Spanish American War of 1898 concluded a century of expansion

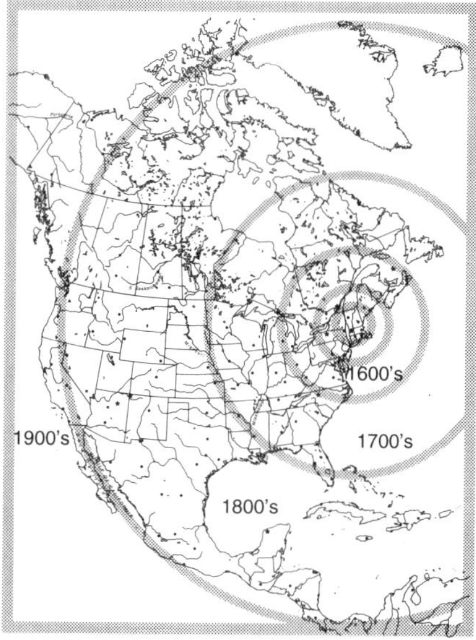

11.1 North American Cycles

From its seed point in the Gaia Matrix, western culture in the Americas has experienced an exponential geographical expansion over the past 400 years. Its influence became global in the 1900's.

corresponding to America's adolescent drive toward national identity. It also marked the beginning of the next harmonic expansion -- America's rise to world power. This phase has seen the projection of US military, economic, and cultural power throughout the world, and the entry of Alaska and Hawaii as states in 1959.

Now as a global power, the expansion can no longer be geographic. We must also recognize that this growth has come at great cost, especially to Native peoples and the environment. For the next phase we must return to the center and grow towards wisdom.

Circling the North American tectonic plate, the continental harmonic speaks to the destiny of all it contains. As illustrated, the tectonic plate is expressed as half land and half water, a form which replicates the Yin -Yang symbol. With an eye on the Bermuda Triangle and one on Hudson Bay, this spinning form is all about the balance of forces and action. In so many words, the American continental karma or fate is to bring balance to the world -- a quality of place which carries with it a great responsibility.

The Constitution of the United States of America was inspired by and roughly based upon the "Great Law" of the Peacemaker, practiced by the Six Nations of the Iroquois Confederacy. Benjamin Franklin was the most vocal advocate for this form of government, and to a great degree the precepts of the Six Nations were included in the US Constitution. There are, however, two glaring exceptions. One is that no decision be made that negatively impacts the well-being of the seven generations to follow. The second is that a council of Grandmothers have the final say in all major decisions, be it in war or peace. To a group of merchants with a morality of maximized profits, from a culture with little appreciation for female sensibilities, there was no choice but to exclude these fundamental precepts. Now that the world is teetering on the edge of envi-

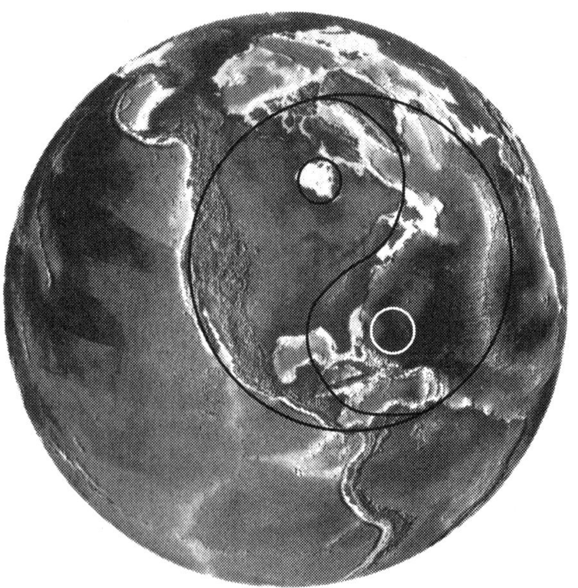

11.2 North American Tectonic Plate Yin Yang

In total the North American tectonic plate is depicted as being half land and half water. The yin yang symbol of balance speaks of North America's destiny of bringing balance to the world.

It holds within its body the Spirit of the Earth.

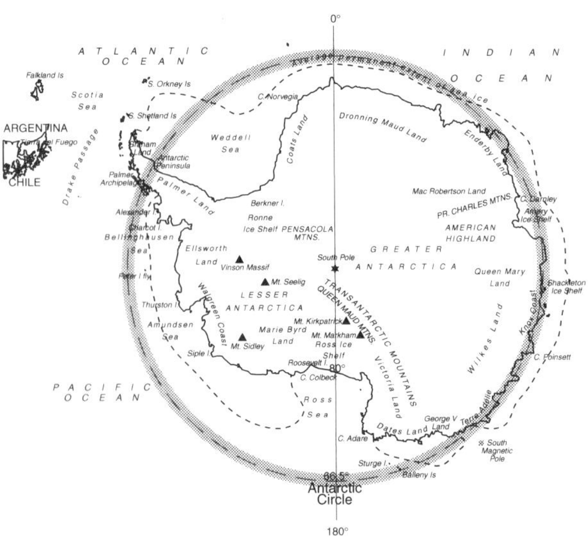

11.3 Antarctica

The diameter of Antarctica is proportionate to the circumference of the Earth. In polarity with its opposite pole, Antarctica holds the Spirit of the cosmos as governor of polar orientation to the greater solar and stellar systems.

11.4 India, Center of Eurasia

Centered on Bangalore, India, this seed point of religions hold the Spirit of the Mind Of God as incarnated in the many world spiritual teachers who have lived there. Bangalore is central to Eurasia and the largest populations on Earth. Its opposite pole is Easter Island, one of the most isolated and least populated places on the globe, known for its enigmatic heads of stone.

ronmental collapse and women are included in decision-making processes, it is high time these important, fundamental maxims be included in constitutional law.

The Arkhom Gaia Matrix is but one of these harmonic generators that make up global dynamic space. Another is centered on the South Pole in Antarctica. The initial field is a circle following the continent's curving edge, centered on the pole. The harmonic doubling of this circle locks into the equator. The next zeros out at the North pole. Thus the size of the Antarctic continent is a fractal of the Earth's circumference. These positive and negative poles are portals for the magnetosphere, and mark the axis on which

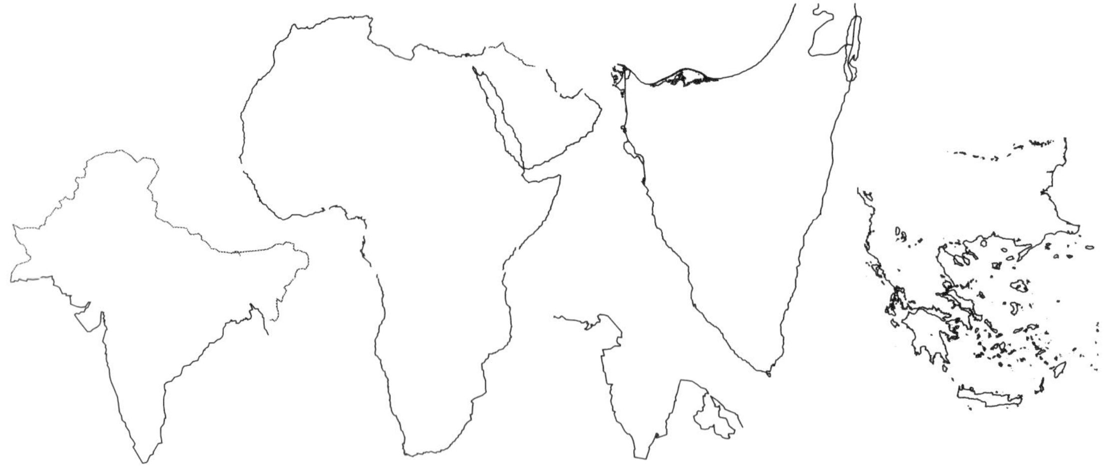

11.5 Fractals of India

Repeated in the forms of land within Eurasia, the shape of India is seen in Africa, Istria, Sinai, and to some degree Greece.

the Earth spins. As the axis of North America and Australia exemplifies the Spirit of the Earth, this axis holds the polarity and spirit of the spinning cosmos.

The third pole is centered on Bangalor, India and zeroes out on the opposite side of the Earth at Easter Island. Centered in the midst of the highest population on Earth, Bangalor and the teachings of the Indian mystics have instilled in the racial / collective mind a discipline or the control of matter through spiritual practice. Thus India holds the Spirit of the Mind of God for the world.

It is with profound connection to the energetics of the Earth that a world teacher like Sai Baba would locate himself central to the greatest concentration of souls on the planet. In a similar way, the American market-driven economy is central to an area with the greatest natural resources to exploit, and Antarctica is central to the greatest focus of gravitational magnetism. Here we see the axiom that the center is the control while the periphery manifests, or radiates out, the potential.

These planetary control mechanisms are also manifestations of fractals in nature. Fractal geometry is a relatively new study of mathematics. As noted earlier, a typical example of fractal geometry is evident in the leaf and stem structure of many ferns, in which is the smallest leaf segment is a replica of the whole fern plume. The Arkhom regional geometry has a fractal shape signature mimicking the continent. Certainly not as completely as a fern mimics and replicates itself, but it nonetheless has patterns which reflect the whole. One can see this fractal relation between Cape Cod / Central America (Fig. 2.4) and Cape Ann / Florida. Globally, the shape of India reflects the shapes of Africa, the Sinai, Greece, and Istria (a peninsula off the coast of Croatia). The circumference of Antarctica is a fractal of the circumference of the Earth.

These simplified examples deserve more study by trained professionals in the field of fractal mathematics. I mention this to stimulate dialogue about the nature of our mechanistic universe. Stone masons will attest to the fact that each stone has a signature angle. Work with this fractal and the pieces fit with ease. Force a different angle and you have one bad day. Similarly, if one works in concert with the central fractal of these planetary harmonics, all will be well with the world. Sai Baba never leaves India yet reaches the

11.6 Sathya Sai Baba

The Holy Man of Puttaparti, India, Sai Baba is positioned near Bangalore. Considered the incarnation of God by millions worldwide, Sai Baba likely uses this point to enter into the minds of humanity, teaching them to "love all, serve all".

Creating free hospitals and water systems in an otherwise impoverished region, Sathya Sai Baba is an Avatar, miracle worker, and stabilizing pole for this seed point of the Spirit of the Mind of God.

11.7 Easter Island

At the opposite point on the Earth from Bangalore, India, are the Easter Island stone heads whose facial features are similar to those of Sai Baba.

whole world from there. By simply setting a harmonic in motion, a fractal of himself, he is able to radiate the mind of God into the racial mind. Similarly, America sets a fractal pattern that affects the world with its market-dominated democratic system, which has profited at the expense of the environment, third-world peoples, and the sovereignty of nations.

These control structures can be used to free or enslave. Whatever fractal form is projected from these regions of earthly power will manifest within its native expression. With Arkhom host to an imperialistic, corporate social structure, the Spirit of the Earth will be a fractal representation of this morality. With Sai Baba the dominant force in southern India, the spirit he embodies of the Mind of God will find its expression in a way that reflects him. The theme of the unity of religions prevails, and is expressed in the New Age movement. The presence of Sai Baba likewise brings religious sectarian issues into focus. These analogies can perhaps be endlessly explored. Suffice it to say that the power that is inherent in Arkhom is a gift and responsibility that must be taken seriously. Our actions, morality, and integrity affect the world. Bad actions will be brought back upon us, spiraling negatively out of control. Good actions, on the other hand, will gather intent into positive, growth-filled identity. The laws that govern nature, particularly as seen in whirlpools and galaxies, govern the Arkhom Gaia Matrix. Develop a sustainable "green" culture in this locale and the world will also-- in turn sustaining the people of Arkhom for centuries, just as it did for the Native peoples who live in balance and abundance with our blue green dot in space.

12: Inner Life

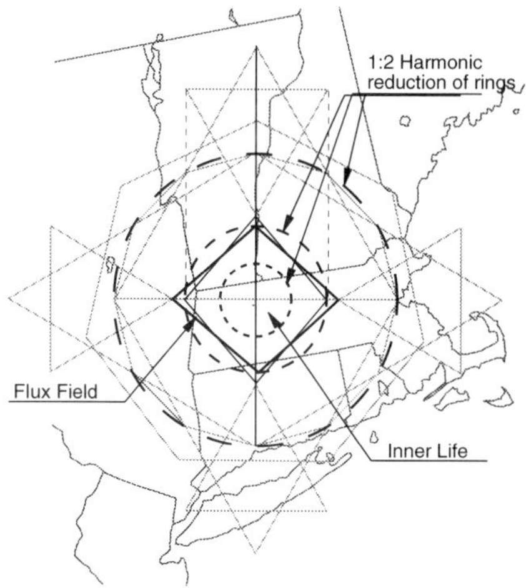

12.1 Inner Geometry Proof

A harmonic contraction of the Ring of Twelve, the flux field, draws the piezoelectric power of the mountain triangle into the core of the matrix. Geometrically related to both forms, the inner flux field combines/ projects the energy and stability of them both.

Another level of interrelationship is found nested within the Circle of Twelve. Just as harmonics are created by doubling, they are created by halving. Applying this contraction to the Circle of Twelve, we come to what can be considered a flux field. Its inner circles encompass three primary points discussed previously: Mount Ascutney, Peebles Island in Troy NY, and Mount Wachusett. These sites in turn set the points for an inner rhombus, or diamond shape. The Monadnock Ley is the basis for determining this rhombus. The fourth point of the rhombus is opposite Mount Ascutney in a glacial and river trough, presently known as the Barkhamstead Reservoir, a place that is unearthly when the water is low.

A flux field suggests a state of being caught between two forms, two worlds, something in the state of becoming and un-becoming. This energetic field doesn't know if it's a circle or a rhombus. It seems to want to be both. A similar condition exists in the layout of Stonehenge. The large Sarsen Circle of Stonehenge creates an energetic between the outer world and the inner sanctum, and broadcasts the buzz and the glow generated by the ceremonies enacted within. In the accompanying diagram you can clearly compare the Arkhom Gaia Matrix geometry with the layout of Stonehenge. Where Stonehenge has the summer solstice sun enlivening it, the Inner Life of this geometry has the three Mountains to the north enlivening its inner sanctum-- holy of holies.

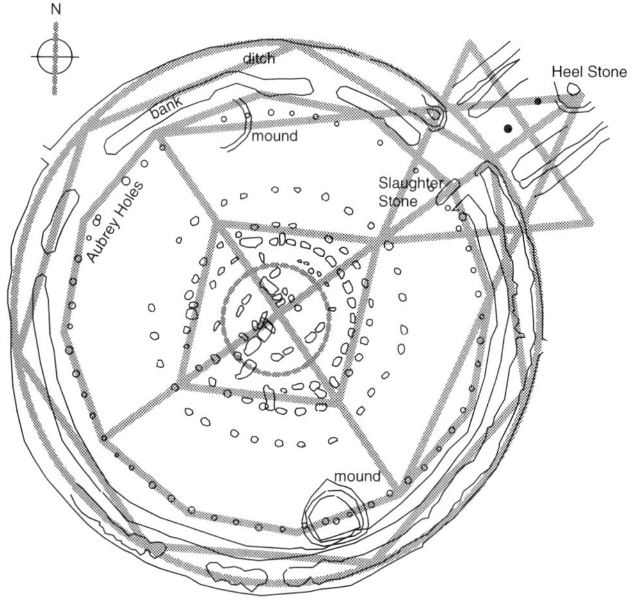

12.2 Stonehenge Geometry

The Inner Circle of the Gaia Matrix is geometrically linked with the megalithic Sarsen Circle. The summer solstice sun illumines the inner life of Stonehenge, while the light of the mountains illumines the Inner Life of the Gaia Matrix.

As you will recall, the Monadnock Ley is the alignment of Mounts Wachusett, Monadnock, and Ascutney on which Mount Monadnock marks the phi proportion of the ley. The other three lines of the inner rhombus are struck by mirroring angle and point from the initializing Monadnock Ley. Each of these equal and opposite sides are manifest in balanced expressions in the landscape. For instance, the NW rhombus side opposite the NE Monadnock side has water features along its course with a large watershed basin and headwater swamp area balancing the Monadnock position along the NW side of the rhombus. Similarly, when the SW and SE sides of the rhombus are mirrored to the northern half, the southern point is at Peoples State Park in Barkhamsted, Connecticut. This deep valley and reservoir is the balance point to Mount Ascutney in the north. Peoples Park was the site of a camp for runaway slaves, renegade Indians (non-reservation), and outcast whites. This camp had a perpetual fire burning and as such was identified as a lighthouse for travelers in the early American wilderness.

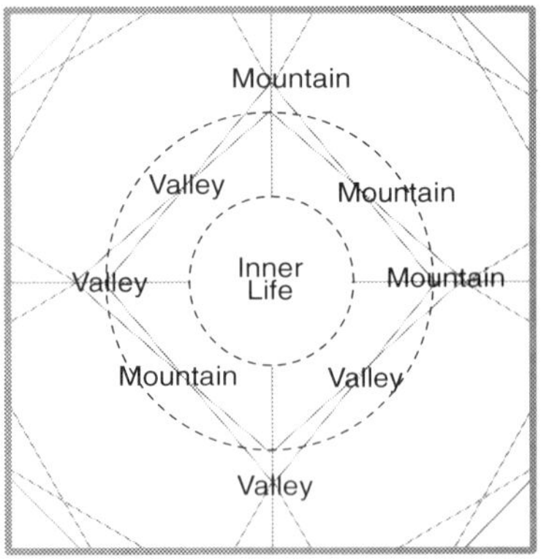

12.3 Balancing Polar Opposites
The interplay between mountains and valleys generates a flux field of balanced opposites whirling around the center point of the continent.

Thus we have seen the mirroring of high point and low point, Earth and Water, in a flux field that alludes to those generated by very large outputs of electromagnetic energy. A warping of space. The ring encompassing this rhombus area marks the three-state (CT/MA/NY) point Mount Everett / the confluence of rivers at Troy NY / the site of British General John Burgoyne's surrender to American forces during the Revolutionary War / the historic early industrial corridor of the Blackstone Valley bordering Worcester in eastern Massachusetts. This ring's diameter is referenced to original mountain and water trines since its length is equal to a side of the Mountain triangle. In this way the inner rhomboid and circle draw the initializing hexagram into the inner core of the Gaia Matrix.

Geometrically there are two interpenetrating rhomboids connected to the four arrayed points of Ascutney, Wachusett, Barkhampstead, and Peebles Island. Circles inscribed to touch the inner and outer points of the two rhomboids show the dynamism of the converging forces on the Inner Life of the Gaia Matrix. The innermost circle is one quarter the size of the Ring of Twelve.

As this inner zone corresponds to the Solar Plexus of our regional biology, its core values should be reflected in its local qualities of place. One would think that a Gaia Matrix would have feminine, or gaian values. What are gaian values? Perhaps you have some idea! In her book *The First Sex*, Elizabeth Gould Davis described matriarchal culture as being focused on the Arts, Higher Learning, Agriculture, and Spirituality, all characteristic of the Mother ethos. A culture which values these pursuits could be considered a gaian culture. Thus it is concluded that for this to be the Gaia Matrix of North America these cultural attributes must be present, and indeed they are in abundance within these inner rings of Arkhom.

Higher learning is very well represented by the "Five Colleges" group of the University of Massachusetts, Smith, Mount Holyoke, Hampshire, and Amherst Colleges, as well as Williams College, Bennington College, Russell Sage, Rensselaer Polytechnic Institute, Marlboro College, and innumerable specialty, state, and community colleges. There are also prep schools such as the Putney School, Deerfield Academy, Williston-Northampton, and Northfield-Mount Hermon. There are so many schools that one might say that education is the area's main industry. The life blood of the inner circle or Solar Plexus of our gaian biology, these schools manifest the qualities of intellect, wisdom, and inspiration native to this chakra.

Focusing on the feminine qualities of higher education expressed in this locale's sense of place one looks to Mount Holyoke and Smith College, the first women's colleges in America. Mount Holyoke was founded by Mary Lyons, who you will recall grew up in the Buckland / Shelburne Falls area. Mount Holyoke is also on the Peacemaker Ley, which is a matriarchal geomantic corridor originating in Seneca Falls, the home of the National Women's Museum, the Women's Convention of 1848, and their signing of the Declaration of Sentiments. In fact the Inner Life of this gaian consciousness was home to such feminists as the poet Emily Dickenson and the abolitionist Sojourner Truth. Northampton has long been associated with a strong feminist community and is known contemporarily for the town's lesbian population, the Arts, and innovative/ creative thinking.

12.4 Sojourner Truth

A personification of Gaian values, Sojourner Truth was an African noble, freed slave, radical abolitionist and feminist, teacher, spiritualist, communitarian, matriarch, and craftsperson. She could well be considered the patron saint of the Gaia Matrix.

National Portrait Gallery, Smithsonian Institute

Sojourner Truth is a great example of gaian values. She lived in Florence, Massachusetts (town next to Northampton) in the 1840's. There she was referred to as "that stately African lady". Active in the utopian community of the Northampton Education and Industry Association, Truth was an outspoken early feminist, and was central to interracial efforts to abolish slavery and win equal rights for women. A statue in her honor is planned in Florence. Truth could be seen as an icon of gaian values. In Nell Irvin Painter's book *Sojourner Truth, A Life, A Symbol,* Truth's life is documented as promoting such values in her travels through 19th-century America. Freed from servitude by the State of New York in 1828, Truth was a central figure to all of the enlightened movements of the day. From Seneca Falls suffragism to the Millerites, from the Kingdom of Matthias to churches throughout the Gaia Matrix, she "sold the shadow to support the substance". Her mission was to win the freedom of Africans and all peoples from the tyranny of slavery and illiteracy, and she accomplished her work with a demeanor befitting her native royalty. An agriculturalist, educator, matriarch, spiritualist, craftsperson, communitarian, and freedom fighter, Sojourner Truth imbued the Gaia Matrix with values that personified truth in action.

Turn over a stump in the hills around this region and out pops a painter, musician, playwright, writer, or dancer. These hills and valleys are alive with the arts of the Mother. Many paintings of the Hudson

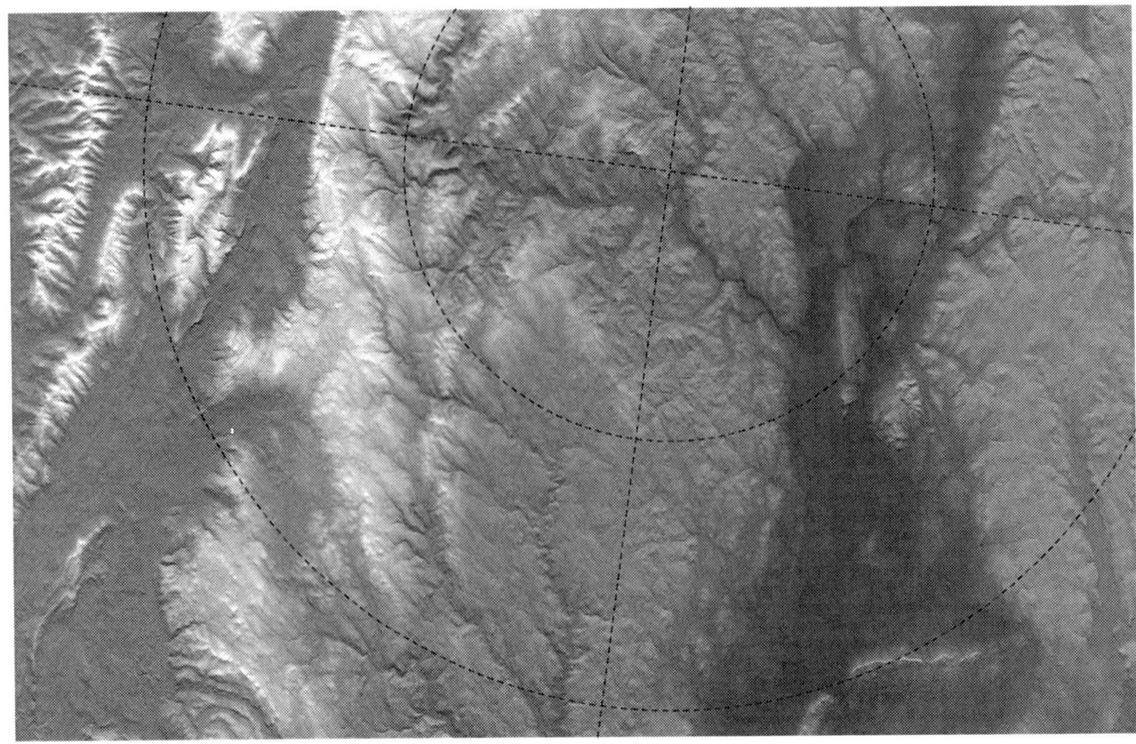

12.5 Shelburne Falls Center Point
Shelburne Falls, at the confluence of rivers in the northwest corner of Massachusetts, is the center point of Arkhom. The outer harmonic ring of the Inner Life touches on Mount Greylock in the upper left, and the gap in the basaltic dike of Mount Tom; and the Holyoke Range in the lower right.

River School were of Pioneer Valley vistas and the valley. The area still hosts many nationally known artists. Berkshire County is home to the Tanglewood Music Center, the Jacob's Pillow Dance Festival and School, the home and studio of "Saint" Norman Rockwell, Clark Art Institute, and the recently opened Massachusetts Museum of Contemporary Art (MassMoCA). Artist collectives include the Leverett Arts Center and the Shelburne Falls Art Bank, and artists such as H.P. Lovecraft, Leonard Bernstein, Herman Melville, Emily Dickinson, Nathaniel Hawthorne, and many of the Transcendentalist writers were inspired within the womb of this Gaia Matrix.

Elsewhere there are more intensively productive areas, but the quality of agriculture practiced here honors values and preserves this limited resource for the sustainable future. In a recent landmark example of development versus farming, a Greenfield farmer sold his prime agricultural land for one dollar to a land trust to prevent the City of Greenfield from developing a commercial district there. After Mother Nature spent 50,000 years creating some of the finest alluvial soils in the world, it seemed shortsighted to the farmer to have this community resource forever despoiled for the sake of short term profits. The Connecticut River Valley was the breadbasket of New England for both the Colonials and Native peoples. Story has it that the settlement of New Haven was saved by the generosity of the Nonotuck Indians who, hearing that the newcomers were near starvation, sent thirty canoe-loads of corn grown in the fields

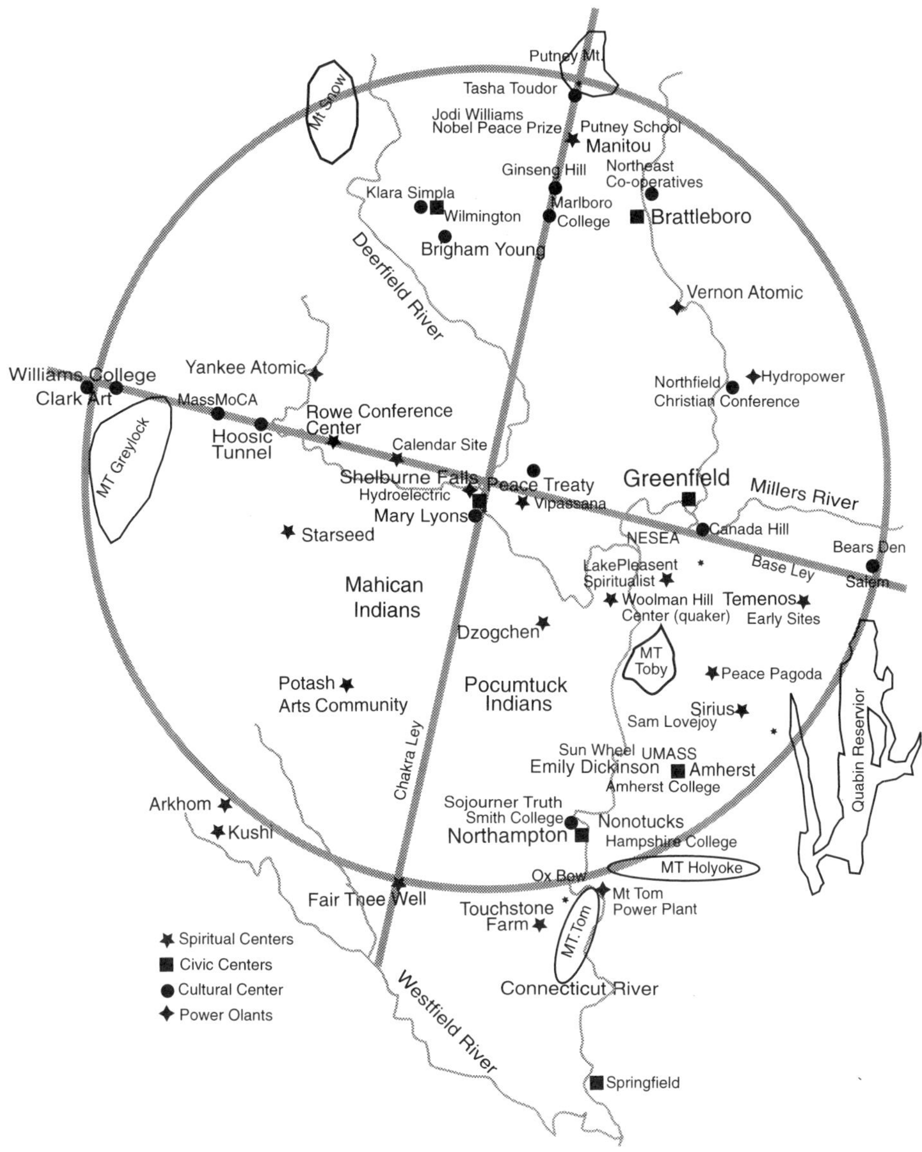

12.6 Inner Names
Universities, spiritual centers, and the Arts spark the inner life of the Gaia Matrix, effecting positive change within the core of the geometry that embodies the Spirit of the Earth.

around present-day Northampton. The tragedy of it was that the Colonials, seeing this abundance, attacked the Nonotucks the following summer and took possession of this collective resource from which they had most recently benefited. The altruism exhibited by the Nonotucks would be considered a gaian value.

Organic farming has returned to this region, educating and being a model for sustainable and healthy futures. One has to wonder to what degree chemical fertilizers, hormones and other additives 'necessi-

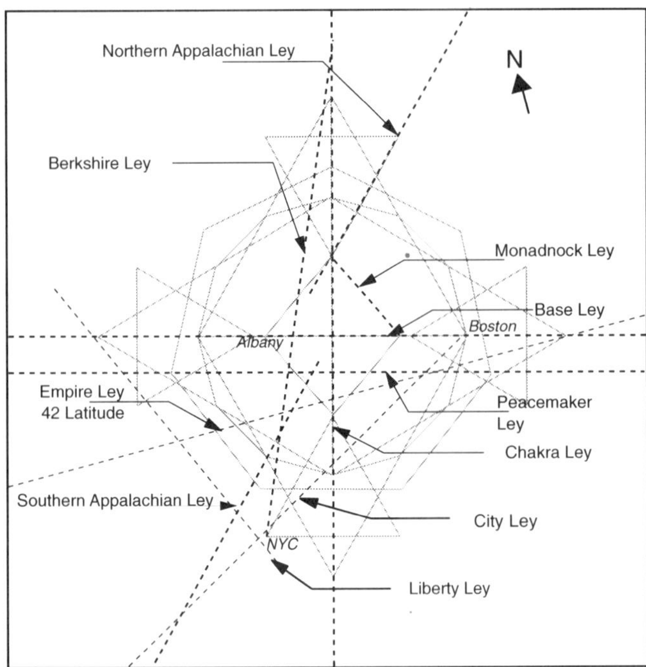

12.7 Arkhom Inner Leys
These Geomantic Ley Corridors frame and penetrate the inner geometry, enlivening and powering this engine of culture.

tated' for high volume food production and proven to contribute to the rise in cancer rates, destroys the soil. Force-feeding the soil destroys its natural processes-- lacking the micro health the dependence on chemical supplements is increased. Rather source minerals and direct regard to soil nutritional regeneration, amplifies its vitality and that of the food produced.

Integral to the Inner Life of Arkhom are food and dairy co-ops, Community Supported Agriculture (CSA), and that nectar of the gods, maple syrup. One finds herbal schools and farms, a lavender cooperative, and the inspirational, responsible, and sensitive gardens of Tasha Tudor. There are several schools of landscape sciences in this area and a longheld closeness to the land. There is also a solid land preservation movement afoot in this inner zone, as well as community action to preserve the watersheds. These are all expressions of gaian values!

Spirituality is another gaian value prolifically expressed in the Inner Life of this Gaia Matrix. Here you will find paganism and monotheism being practiced with acceptance of their diversity. Even the University of Massachusetts exhibited the gaian spirit by constructing a calendar site called the Sun Wheel as an "astronomy" study. In the hills around this core one finds a high occurrence of Early Sites which were likely used by the Native peoples for vision questing and celestial time keeping. Among many conference and retreat centers in the Inner Life, there are Rowe Camp and Conference Center (interfaith/Unitarian Universalist), Woolman Hill (a Quaker center), StarSeed (retreat center with focus on earth energy), Fare-Thee-Well (non-denominational healing center), The Sirius Community (emphasizing sustainability and the Findhorn model), Touchstone Farm (dance focus), and Temenos (healing springs and retreat center).

Spiritual traditions are well represented by The Abode of the Message (Sufi Order of the West), The Threshold Society (also in the Sufi tradition), The Leverett and Grafton Peace Pagodas, the Dzogchen Community in America, the Vispassana Meditation Society, monasteries, churches, temples, and many more. The Kripalu Yoga Center and the Kushi Institute (macrobiotics) add to the mix and stimulates the Inner Life geomantically. There is also a plethora of alternative healers who use food, bodywork, holistic medicine, art, and spirituality to bring their clients and themselves to equilibrium and health.

Suffice it to say that the Inner Life is strong in the Gaia Matrix. Or is it? Located within the Inner Life's geobiology are the Yankee Rowe and Vernon nuclear power plants. A study has found a direct relationship between the high incidence of both birth defects and cancers to the Rowe plant's venting of

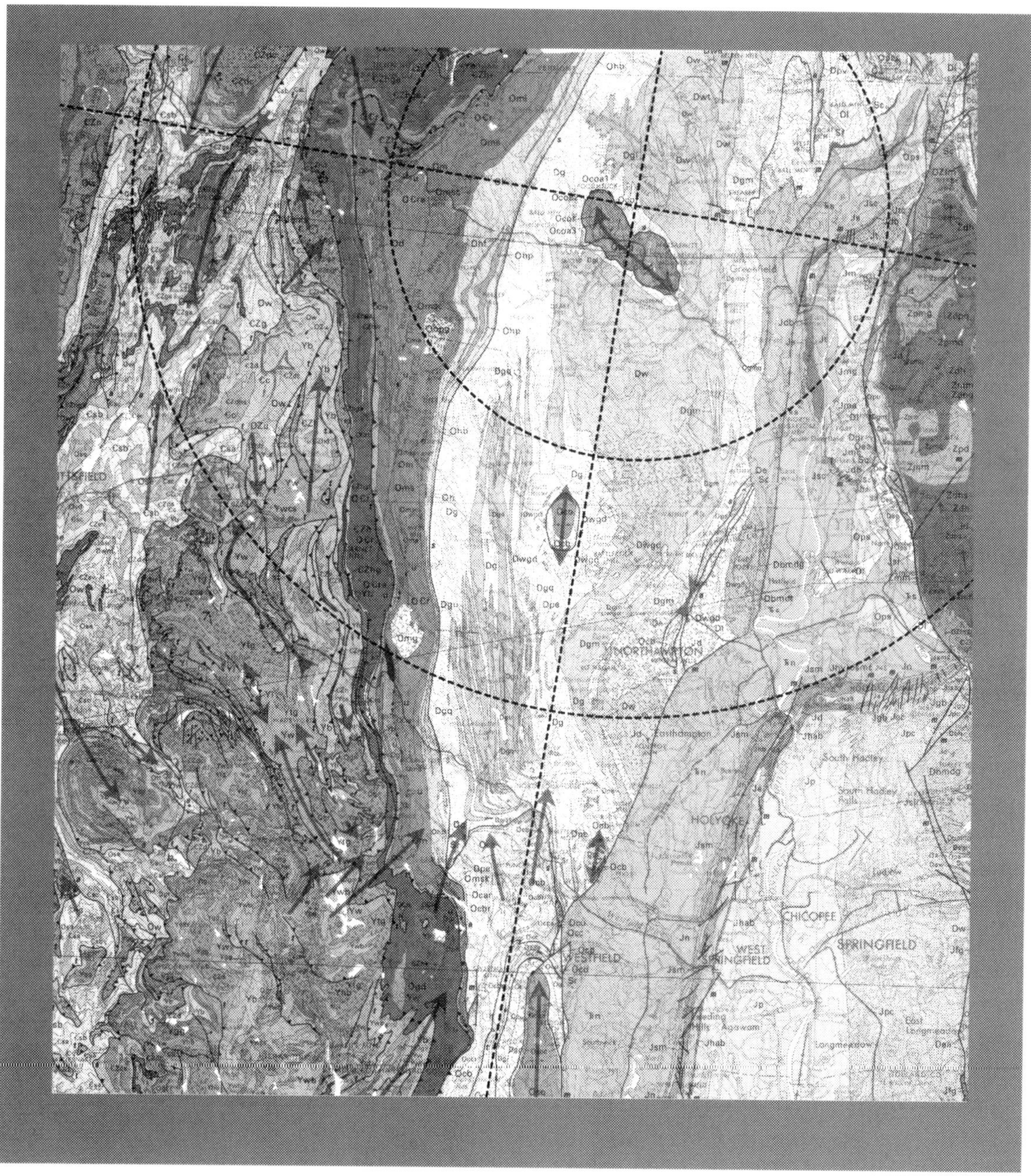

12.8 Inner Geology

The cross in this map locates Shelburne Falls within the geology of Western Massachusetts. Embedded in a river of metamorphic rock called mica schist, granite domes mark the Chakra Ley. The largest of these, the Shelburne Dome, resembles a potato-shaped seed in the mouth of the Mother. This granite intrusion is the center point of the North American tectonic plate. The arrows depict geologic movements, while lines show faults in the Earth. Mount Tom and Mount Holyoke define the L-shaped structure in the lower right.

"acceptable" levels of radioactive gases. This inner circle is the power plant for the continent, and while both the Rowe and Vernon nuclear plants speak of this quality and power of place, they do not bode well for the residents who find themselves downwind. The Rowe plant was closed in 1991 by a management vote.

This center point of our sacred circle is what is projected outward, the inner zone is the center point of the continental sacred circle. In the case of nuclear power the core of our circle splits the atom, an act antithetical to life itself. Robert Oppenheimer quoted from the Bhagavad-Gita (11:12) after witnessing the first nuclear explosion: "I am become Death-- destroyer of worlds. If the radiance of one thousand suns were to burst forth at once in the sky, that would be like the mighty One, Krishna".

A quality of place is not per se a gaian quality, but is a direct output of her power, her electricity expressed through place. Earth energy can simply be thought of as an electrical current or vibrational resonance. The Government project HAARP (*High-frequency Active Aural Research Program*) uses this same current to transmit high-energy signals through the Earth instead of around it (not good) as a weapons and communications device. The electric body of the Earth is seen most obviously in the Van Allen Belt which acts as a protective shield from solar radiation. Earth energy is all about electricity, and the Inner Life has plenty of it. Analogous to an electrical generator, Arkhom's outer rings and hexagons are its generating coils, the inner circle its static conducting pole. The fire in your belly, if you will.

Within the Inner Life are the two nuclear power plants, and also hydroelectric plants on the Deerfield and Connecticut Rivers. Great Barrington was the first town in the country to be electrified. General Electric supplied the transformers for the first community electrification of the world from Pittsfield, and Sprague Electric of North Adams MA supplied the cable and capacitors. Light is light, but the electric industry can be seen as the shadow side of the inner spiritual light, judging from the issues of nuclear waste removal and PCB-- poisoning our habitat. In the 1970's a plan to build a nuclear plant near Amherst turned into a national anti-nuke case when Sam Lovejoy toppled the test tower of the plant. Significant citizen action also played a role in the decommissioning of the Rowe plant. The center of the Mother Matrix is an area of fire ce activism, whose conscience has always been in the driver's seat.

In recent years the area has been the site of experimental wind generation plants, far more appropriate to the gaian values within our central flux field. The *North East Sustainable Energy Association* (NESEA) of Greenfield has long been a leader in educating, promoting, and lobbying for sustainable practices especially in the generation of electricity. To this end they sponsor a yearly electric car race, the Tour de Sol, and conferences on sustainable, energy-efficient construction at locations in and around the Gaia Matrix.

This type of sense-of-place analysis speaks volumes about the inherent qualities of the land. Gaia speaks of her will in this manner. The core zone or Inner Life is crisscrossed with a number of geomantic corridors which feed its vitality. At the center of it all is the historic village and peace treaty site of Shelburne Falls. Emblematic of the centric energy and whirl of this continent are the glacial potholes there, whose swirling, colored patterns in the rock speak of the dynamism of this Inner Life. Here the Shelburne Dome -- a granite plug -- locks deeply into the mantle of the planet and acts as a spindle around which the Gaia Matrix spins out its graces.

On a closing note, it must be stated that the gaian culture of the past is not necessarily what the author proposes we return to. With the objectivity of patriarchal sciences we can see our blue-green home with a space-based perspective, allowing us to experience the body of Gaia. How are gaian values translated from myth to application in the high-tech present? Many of the advances we consider part of everyday life are the result of a patriarchy on the loose. Each war has created a new technology, and each genocide has given humanity a better understanding of our self-destructive nature. The ideal values of gaian culture are common-unity based and ultimately matriarchal in spirit and action. A question remains as to whether or not we are any closer to God as a result of the wars, ethnic cleansings, inquisitions, and polarizations that have been justified over the past millennia by men acting independently of the wisdom of a Council of Grandmothers.

You may have noticed that the weather is out of whack nowadays, and so is the distribution of collective resources-- exampling the unity of life. --"*The King and the Land are one.*"-- We are the king, and both we and the land are sick. In a western myth of spirituality, King Arthur sent the Knights of the Round Table to search for the Holy Grail, the cup Jesus used at his last supper. This Grail quest is a symbolic quest for salvation and/or illumination. Central to the myth is a king with a terrible wound and a devastated land. To heal the wounded monarch, and ultimately the land, the hero, Percival, had to answer the question: "*Whom does the Grail serve?*" A similar question arises around this Gaia Matrix. Whom does it serve? GE? The Illuminati? Strip-development, anywhere USA? Whites only? The Economy? The Bottom Line? Or might this grail/ark/drum template of consciousness serve to elevate humanity towards a closer relationship with 'God' and true freedom?

The answer is, "*We and the Land are One.*" The revelation of this unity begins the healing of both the land and humanity. Every act affects the whole. Respect each individual. Do unto Gaia as you would want done unto yourself. Healing the disease between land and people will ultimately heal the sickness of disconnection we all experience.

Our evolving Gaia Matrix is a Grail vessel. When we remember we are one with it, we may share in its abundance by exhibiting our own uniqueness and individual talents while behaving responsibly. *The Sovereign Self and Gaian Consciousness are one!*

13: The Universal Ark

The geometry we have described has all the components that make up sacred space, bringing together classical religious architecture and an otherwise unconnected community. The location is chosen by Grace, but this form has yet to be widely recognized by the community it serves.

In our modern lives we experience an ever decreasing community circle. In fact this community in many cases is a community of one. Our relationship to the sacred has become decentralized and marginalized. This is bad news for the soul. We humans are a social species. In the absence of real community we make due with what Scott Peck's Foundation for Community Encouragement refers to as "pseudo community". Feeling a part of a community, no matter how dysfunctional, is necessary for human health. Since the 1950's and 1960's the western world has experienced the growing chaos brought on by individualism. Encouraged by industrial and information societies, widespread use of birth control, and the absence of mothers and fathers in the 'hom': individualism has become an ingrained phenomenon. What a shock this is to the human psyche, to have 500,000 years of social evolution and interrelationship suddenly removed. We are starved for a sense of connection and community.

Churches, temples, and mosques are empty compared to 100 years ago. In a futile attempt to replace the collective experience of grace and divinity, this culture creates temples for individual worship in the form of shopping malls, mirrored gyms, and homes rivaling that of Zeus himself. Yet our lives are still missing a sense of connection. We come together as cults, in stadiums for religion with sports-like zeal, as bereavement groups, as alcoholics, or even groups as specific as Entrepreneur Small Business MS Windows Users for a Virus Free/ Crash Free Operating System Future (ESBMSWUVFCFOSF). Yes, community exists, but in ever more narrow and exclusionary circles. Faced with the prospects of a global society, what is this cult of the individual to do? We seem to want community, but only on our own terms or in terms that directly relate to our personal worldview. As a Catholic Sufi Heterosexual Techno Peasant for Geo Sacral Sustainable Egalitarian Futures (CSHTPGSSEF) I am not one to point fingers! We sail the great ocean of spirit in the same ship. We must look objectively at ourselves, our futures, and our cultures, making conscious choices about our future. After all, this is what the gift of millennialism is all about, a gift to evaluate the past and present, and our potential futures.

Short of advocating a return to Victorian values or forcing women back to the 12th- century, our culture needs moral and community values as underpinnings which transcend the divisiveness of individualism, while preserving liberty and freedom, and allowing for a new expression of spirituality within a community context that is non-exclusionary, universally accessible, and a natural outgrowth of our evolving society and planet. In short, a Universal Ark. The revelation experience at the eureka moment of Arkhom's discovery was entwined with a mandate to create such an Ark.

This Arkhom geometry, the center of the Gaia Matrix, is a Universal Ark. Up to now this Ark has existed behind the scenes as an instrument of Grace through which the agencies of Light and Darkness have affected and controlled humanity. The Universal Ark as an ideal has been given to the modern world by Baha'u'llah in 1852, and his call for the Bahi' to unite the world and create a peaceful equally shared,

13.1 Hazrat Inayat Khan's Universel
Courtesy of Sufi Order International

borderless home out of the planet. The morality espoused by the Bahi' is found in the actions of the Peacemaker and the women of Seneca Falls. Another Avatar by the name of 'Sai Baba', alive in 1999, has a similar message and unity ideal. Other voices of this pulse are Rudolf Steiner's embodied in the form of the Goetheanum, and Hazrat Inayat Khan's call to build the Universel, a temple for all religions. Inayat Khan, a Sufi mystic who brought Sufism to the west in the 1920's, saw this temple as the single most important means to achieve this unity. His son Vilyat Inayat Khan fulfilled this mandate with the construction of the "Universel" in the garden of the family home in Suresnes, in the suburbs of Paris. The first Goetheanum designed by Steiner (and associates) was destroyed by the Nazis. It was rebuilt in Dornach, and its wood structure was replaced by concrete.

The ideal of the Universal Ark is one held by many faiths and schools of thought. These places of universal worship and unity of human ideals, however, all have different practices prescribed by their builders. If we were all of one religion or political persuasion we would (theoretically, at least) be a world at peace. What a Universal Ark provides is a structure to fulfill this ideal and still preserve and honor our diversity as an expression of spiritual liberty and unity.

The Arkhom geometry is a sacred form that expresses this movement towards universality. As our institutions fail to meet our social and spiritual needs, new forms appropriate to our evolving planetary culture are needed. Cultures clash in this age of instant communication. Is global culture to be homogenized into a western model of democratic, market-based hedonism? A prudent response is to offer a community-based model for spiritual unity that preserves and honors religious diversity, provides the underpinnings of ethics, morality, and conscientious behavior-- with respect and unity of the world's peoples as a planet with compassion and peace.

The very center of the North American tectonic plate is located in Shelburne Falls MA. This same center point is the center of Arkhom and the entire Gaia Matrix. It is known locally to be a treaty site between Native tribes and Colonial people. From this epicenter the treaty agreement insured a day's peaceful travel passage in every direction. Taking this at face value and applying it to contemporary travel methods creates a place of peace out of the entire world. The Gaia Matrix is a sanctuary for all. This is the mandate of the American matriarch, Liberty.

Arrayed multidirectionally around this center pole, one finds symbols of the world's major religions, a universal geometry of religious iconography. Calling this an Ark of course immediately puts this notion of unity in jeopardy, as the term has specific religious connotations. In truth this geometry is an expression of the Christian Holy Grail, the Jewish Ark, the Muslim Kaba, the Mormon Golden Tablets, and the Native American Drum. It is a universal symbol of sacred space. As stated earlier, the letters A-R-K, translated from Runic, one of the original geometrically depicted languages, mean *"the transmission of knowledge through light"*. This is the spirit in which the gift of a Universal Ark is offered. It is offered to the world at this critical point in human evolution as an *Ark of Peace*.

13.2 Steiner's Goetheanum
*Photo by Thomas Spalinger, * Rafael-Verlag*

This *Ark of Light* is not a physical church, temple, mosque, or lodge. No walls, no holy of holies, or bones of particular saints are present. It is a *'place'* of light. A place of imagination and myth, a place of rivers, mountains, and teeming humanity. Its existence is demonstrated in our daily lives, yet its physical presence is somewhere between the worlds of flesh and spirit, like the world teachers who have graced humanity with windows to perfection, to see God and Goddess. The universal Ark, Arkhom, our Gaia Matrix, is an etheric temple of light. A network of the collective emotions and actions of individuals, groups, and the hand of the Creator has coalesced into an emerging truth that covers all. This Ark is a Home for all, a place to experience the unity and vital place for all beliefs, natures, and peoples.

Over the centuries, places of spiritual power have been the result of a world teacher's direct revelation and communication of ideals of divinity. The crash of a meteor, a miraculous spring, a site of a great sacrifice have all been signs leading us to believe a place is sacred. The tops of mountains and the bowels of canyons have also become places of pilgrimage. With so many places worldwide, both natural and human-made, having attributes of the sacred ascribed to them, the message is clear that *we live on a sacred planet.*

World teachers have gifted us with the knowledge that we were all given life to come to God through free will, making it much more significant than a forced march to heaven would be. This Universal Ark is a temple of free will. With neither doctrine to support it nor revelation to inspire its construction, this sacred space is non-sectarian, yet rooted in the sacred, the result of a collaboration of spirit, free will, and biology between Divinity, Humanity, and Nature.

In the previous chapter on Harmonic Expansion we learned that the North American tectonic plate, shaped like a Yin-Yang symbol of balance, is a pole of the Spirit of the Earth. With the placement of this

Gaia Matrix or Universal Ark at the center of this plate-- the impact on the Earth follows logically. The world is out of balance because life within the Gaia Matrix is out of balance. Create conscious unity at the center of this matrix of balance on a scale suggested by this model, and there will be peace on Earth. Presently this temple is abundantly full of various forms of deceit, corruption, falseness, and self-motivated action. This makes the Peacemaker's message all the more powerful for this time of awareness and transformation. What better message do we want emanating from the center of this planetary mechanism of balance?

The result of a long period of evolution, this emerging landscape temple has coalesced to a point where its presence is known. The dynamic seat of western world power fully shifted from Europe to the Americas, but it lacks the moral authority and community cohesion to assume this mantle with a spiritual dimension to back its action. A nation of self-interested, self-serving corporations and individuals are in control of this powerhouse of spiritual dynamism. The world's greatest leaders have been humbled by the responsibility of their leadership. We "Yanks" need to do the same if we would lead the world into a respectful, peaceful, and sustainable future. This idea is foreign to many seeking the bottom line, but it is necessary for our survival and must be embraced and acted on with free will.

The Universal Ark presently exists primarily as an element of ether rather than one of fire or earth, even though these elements are also present.As yet but a skeleton of itself, it has been slowly materializing over the millennia and requires humanity to actualize it as the work of architecture it is: a '*Cathedral of Nature*'. What exists now is just a blueprint of a structure, something to be visualized or imagined in its fullest expression and form. As individuals we tend to view the universe egocentrically. Our reference points are from our bodies outwards. To *see* this blueprint requires a considerably expanded vantage point.

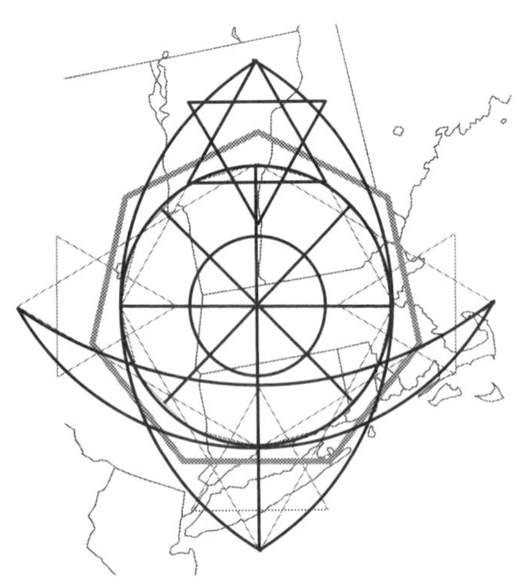

13.3 Universal Symbol

The symbols of many world religions, components of sacred geometry, can all be drawn from the Arkhom geometry. These include the Star and Crescent of Islam, the Star of David of Judaism, the eight-spoked Wheel of Dharma of Buddhism, the Cross of Christianity, the Lingam and Yoni of Hinduism, and the Vesica whose origin is the Goddess worship of the Great Mother. Uniting all is the seven-sided life affirming geometry of the heptagon.

The initial impulse of course is to identify a specific spot, create a model, and ground it. Shelburne Falls would be the logical place to receive such an impulse. Individuals relate to individual locales. In a sense this area of 110,000 square miles is just a tiny spot compared to the size of the Earth, solar system, or galaxy. Building an Ark at the center point would symbolize the whole but only serve to reinforce the ego point. Instead, the ego point needs to step up to the scale of all humanity for it to be universal. An Ark built at the center point is like saying the center point of a circle is "the" circle.

We have departed from sharing the same air and other natural resources. Working inside individually controlled environments, many rarely see the sun and in fact fear it. Pure, fresh, clean nature is alien to many. Our food is mostly pre-prepared and packaged. We look to reliable connection with nature such as pets -- never more popular -- with their unconditional love. Yet many pets are abused. Our environment cannot keep up with the runaway pace of pollution and abuse, nor can we create artificial environments to accommodate all.

Coming into focus with the land and cultural features still allows one to reclaim some clarity of vision. Exploring these aspects of our surroundings, as illustrated in this book, brings an intimacy with the planet we live on. As each person takes responsibility for his or her own interaction with others, community relationships can be imagined, and we can begin to address the despair.

The Universal Ark could be a great panacea. Located at the confluence of many global earth grid, meridian, and ley alignments, it is in a position to receive the grace manifested in the New Jerusalem, the Hopi Ark, and Avalon; and to serve as a unifying form of human and divine interaction on the sacred Earth. The Universal Ark is envisioned as a renewed Ark, Grail, Drum, Jerusalem, and Avalon, a new home of evolving western spirituality at a balance point of the world. A Universal Ark, an Arkhom.

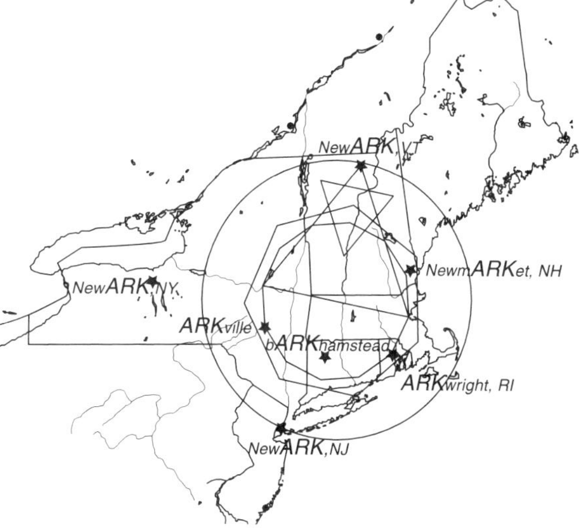

13.4 NewArk

Through the hand of Grace the location of "ark" place names combine to point to the existence of a New Ark in the landscape of the Northeastern United States.

13.5 Shelburne Falls-- Temple Obelisk

A memorial in the town cemetery, this monument is one of many markers which point to Arkhom as a new temple which has been built by many over the millennia.

14: Cycles of American Destiny

Thus far we have identified component parts that speak of the building blocks of nature, stability, dynamism, community, continuity, and the life-giving force of creation. With all these elements of sentience and mobility-- the existence and recognition of a lifeform follows logically. Looking at geological maps one is struck by the river-like flows of bedrock. The universe is in motion, but some elements are slower than others. Rock is one such slow-moving viscous element. When examining American history similar patterns of flow emerge in roughly 100-year cycles.

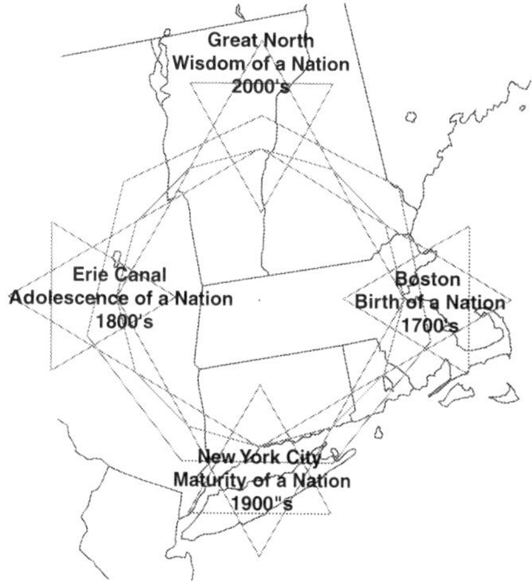

14.1 The Life of a Nation

The Cycles of American Destiny chronicle the birth, growth, maturity, and old age of a biology. Birthed from Boston, the nation expanded via the Erie Canal, and came to adult power with New York City. The 100-years following the millennium point to a time of wisdom for the United States, reflected in its aging population.

The spin field of the Gaia Matrix has a four-directional orientation. The radial edge of this field extends to Lake Willoughby in the north. As described in the chapter on the *Four Directions*, the four quadrants are arrayed into four equal quadrants by rotating the Grand Trine and the complementary hexagram. The four quadrants of this cyclical field are keyed into Boston, the Erie Canal (Mohawk River corridor), the New York City metropolitan area, and Lake Willoughby's Northeast Kingdom. Defining these areas as such by no means limits them. They represent symbolic zones of the prevailing issues articulated in cycles of history. These historic cycles are analogous to the cycles of one's life: childhood, youth, maturity, and old age. Just as these phases of one's life have issues that predominate, so too, the cycles of history in the American experience. The influence of the four quadrants is further accentuated by radiating landscape features that carry their sine waves both into and out of the eye of our cultural hurricane. The conduits that carry these cyclic intentions are ley corridors, river systems, and landmass orientations.

Each conduit additionally has a quality of being' which speaks to the carrier signal of its representative cycle. In the 1700's Boston was the seedbed of the American Revolution. Here a coalition of intellectuals, merchants, farmers, and fishermen sacrificed to create a country free from the tyranny of the English Monarchy. The carrier-signals originating in Europe-- spurred Boston on. Crossing the Atlantic on the 42nd parallel of latitude is the Empire Ley, and with the extended City Ley (as it connects to the Ley of Conflict in Europe) these wave forms combined to seed western civilization in the fertile womb of the Gaia Matrix. The spark point of two drifting continents-- Boston's ancient volcanic caldera, was once a volcanic island between these continents. Here one finds Pudding Stone native of Africa in Roxbury MA, mixed with the native rocks of Boston. There is potent symbolic relationship in this geology-- the first death of the American Revolution was a Black Man and the race riots by the 'southies', all point to Boston being an ignition point for the pulse of freedom in the body of the American continent. Freedom for all-- but the Indians. The carrier wave of this cultural current took form in the tectonic plate, expanding along the Base Ley alignment with westward expansion.

Boston's history is full of new beginnings, from the Sons of Liberty who started the American Revolution to the Secret Six who supported John Brown's crusade against slavery. New thinkers such as the Transcendentalists Thoreau and Emerson, flourished in Boston. Today Boston is the seedbed for technological advances in the laboratories of MIT and associated medical, and technical research facilities... Another one, of many examples, is the creative group of architects and planners wanting to turn the Boston City Hall into a showcase of sustainable technologies. (See chapter by Henry MacLean.) Many such seedbeds exist throughout New England, but none with Boston's prodigious history of experimentation in both thought and action.

The second cycle of American history is the one which defined the American spirit. Analogous to our cultural youth, the 1800's had us pushing westward. The alignment of the Erie Canal and the Mohawk River system has the look of a bolt of lighting coursing toward the heart of the continent. Following its birth, the youthful nation expanded via this Canal and river valley. In its search for national identity, the youthful nation grew into an industrial power during the Civil War. The young 'America' "won" the west, gathering to itself resources unheard of in the history of the world. Sadly, this was done at the expense of the original inhabitants, who have yet to be acknowledged by this arrogant European youth. This period fostered the "pioneer" mentality and the search for wealth, exemplified by the Gold Rush. With its personal power and identity in place, complete with an education from the school of hardknocks-- the nation was set ready to emerge into the full power of adulthood in the 1900's.

During the 1900's the New York City quadrant locked in. The culture became a mature power embracing its responsibility as a parent, provider, and protector. The island of Manhattan illustrates this sentiment quite graphically in its physical representation of a fully-developed sexual being. Once again, we find the orientation of the land mass pointing out from the center of our geometry. In fact, Lower Broadway projected northward, points directly to the center-- Shelburne Falls. This orientation remains a mystery. Is it there by design or synchronicity? In any event New York City was well worth the 24 wampum rental price paid the Native landlords for it.

During this period of maturity, democracy was projected to the world at large by the male-dominated power of capitalism propagating the emerging global economy. New York City to this day acts as the world's big daddy of trade and economic power. Potent symbols of power, Wall Street, The Fed, the World Trade Center, the Empire State Building, and the Statue of Liberty combine to create a sense of place that has become an icon of both the greatest good and the greedy worst.

Secure as a nation, culture, and emerging civilization, we rest squarely on the cusp of a new cycle as we enter the 2000's. Just coming into our cultural field of view, this new cycle will -- without a doubt -- be like no other. Following the life pulse of the Gaia Matrix, the next wave focused on the crowning point of the geometry, will return to the wisdom of the elders symbolized by the mountains of the north. Traditionally, the wisdom of the elders assured the continuity of the generations. Could Ben & Jerry's ice cream company in the mountains of Vermont be one indicator of this new wave-form lapping at the shore of our collective consciousness? With 1% for peace as a corporate credo, it exemplifies emerging "green" or gaian values. Vermont's policies of sustainable energy, land preservation, a ban on billboards, tax levied on land developers based on the period of time property is held (to prevent speculation), farm protection, and its numerous spiritual centers are indicators of what is in store. Other signs that speak of Vermont's sense of place are the milk cow and snow. The white color of milk and snow speaks to the qualities of visible light, spiritual light, and the wisdom of our elders, all coinciding with an aging population profile. Could this herald the end of the 'Pepsi Generation'? The cow is a longtime symbol of the Mother. Vermont's sense of place is inseparable from the nurturing embrace of this Mother symbol.

Landscape indicators of this emerging cycle include the Connecticut River system, the spine of our landscape biology, and the merging forks of mountain and river all pointing towards the center of Shelburne Falls. With this preponderance of telluric forces, focused and backed by conscientious action, an entirely new cultural form is coming on-line in North America. A recent example is Jodi Williams of Putney, who won the Nobel Peace Prize for her work to ban land mines, all done via the Internet. For the first time in its history, the United States' cycle of destiny will match the exalted position of these majestic mountains and engines of Gaia.

With the parenthood of the culture defined and entrenched, with a few zillion dollars in the collective bank account, with the kids grown and living comfortably, our collective body, heart, and soul is wondering what's next. With the benefits of fiscal security the elders look to God, to wisdom, to continuity. Coinciding with the advent of this wisdom-culture is the dawn of a new millennium. There is no telling how it will shake down. With the billions at our collective disposal, perhaps philosophies and policies will be instituted to steward the country (and the world) towards balance, in harmony with the privilege of our remarkable biology.

Missing from this discussion so far is the French factor. With the next critical position aligning with the north and wisdom, this cycle points to what was the position of the first European interface with the Gaia Matrix-- Montreal, Quebec. In a sense, an orientation towards the north is a return to the beginning. Discovered in 1535 and established in 1642, Montreal was one of the first large scale settlements in the Gaia Matrix. To this onetime seat of power for the majority of the North American landmass, the French Canadians of Montreal brought Christ-consciousness to the land. The return north is a return to Ville-Marie. The City of Mary. The City of the Mother.

Its location at the confluence of three rivers gives Montreal a geometry of life-giving Grace. You will see in the following chapter on *Three Democracies* that of the three, Montreal is poised to be restored to its position of rulership in this next phase of the evolving American Revolution.

15: A Tale of Three Democracies

In previous chapters we saw how outward expansions are generated by the doubling of the outer ring of the Gaia Matrix. The next evolution of our geometry is nested within the first of the harmonics rings. This first level harmonic is marked by Niagara Falls/ Mount Katahdin/ Baltimore/ and the edge of the continental shelf out in the Atlantic Ocean.

Within this first harmonic is a smaller ring created by the doubling of the Arkhom core heptagon. Embedded on the circumference of this ring are the centers from which three American democracies have sprung: The United States of America in Philadelphia in 1776, the Dominion of Canada in Montreal in 1867, and the Iroquois Confederacy in the 1400's in Seneca Falls. All are equidistant from the center of geologic North America, radiating out from the center of the Gaia Matrix and the Arkhom geometry. This quite remarkable pattern is yet just another documentation of this geometry's direct impact on the social, political, economic, and environmental biologies of North America. This ring-- more than any -- attests to the validity of the Arkhom theory that human culture is in a state of common union with this landscape biology. Each of the three points on this harmonic circumference have unique geometries that reference Arkhom. This second generation of the seven-pointed field of spirit is marked most clearly on the landscape by the border of New York and Canada along the St. Lawrence River.

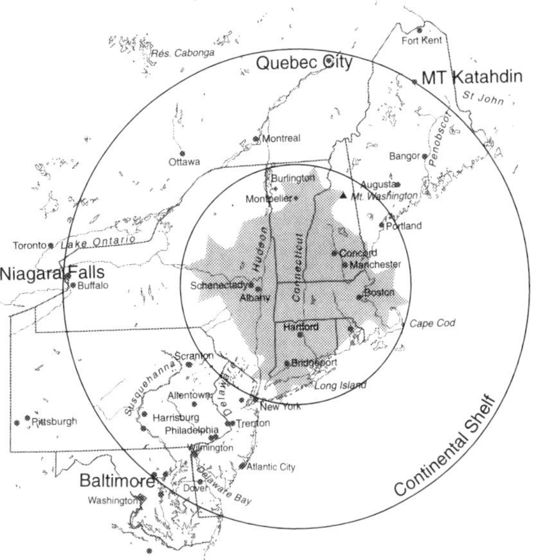

15.1 First Harmonic

Expanding from the temple grounds of the Arkhom Gaia Matrix, the first level harmonic creates a field which locks into such geographic features as the upper reaches of the Chesapeake Bay, the edge of the continental shelf, Niagara Falls, and the outlet of the Saint Lawrence River at Quebec City.

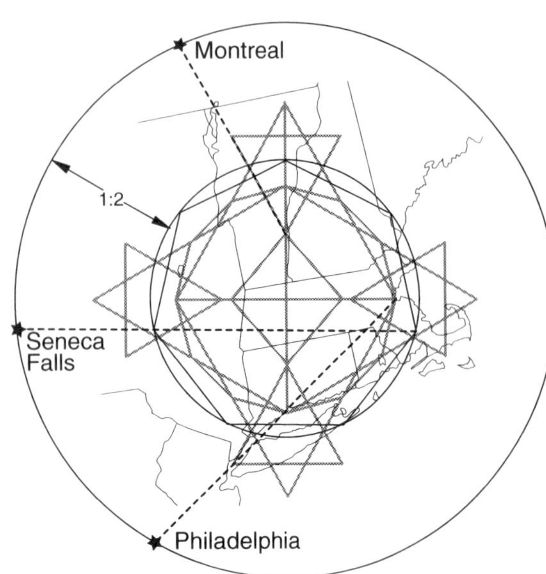

15.2 Three Democracies

Doubling the ring of the heptagon reveals a key harmonic identified with three portals that birthed democratic governments. Each of the three governments has drawn power from the Gaia Matrix to accomplish its mandate, in geometric relationship to this central engine of culture, reflecting an evolving human consciousness.

Seneca Falls, New York

Seneca Falls is located at the northern end of Cayuga, the largest of the Finger Lakes, and the middle finger of this handprint of the Great Spirit. Not specifically acknowledged as the center of the Iroquois Confederacy-- it is so geographically. The actual central fire of this democratic league was either Onondaga Castle or Onondaga Lake, both ceremonial centers for the Tadodaho or Firekeeper of the Confederacy, where present-day Syracuse is located. The harmonic ring of the Arkhom core heptagon passes through Seneca Falls at the convergence point of numerous planetary grid lines of the Unified Vector Geometry.

Within the field of Seneca Falls are numerous integral leys which speak to this portal's potential. The Seneca spin field encompasses the Finger Lake region from the whale nose of Lake Oneida (the Thumb) in the east, to the Genessee River in the west. Directly south, on this circumference, is the confluence of the Empire Ley and the Washington Ley. Located at the edge of the Arkhom geometry and the end point of the Base Ley at Lake Oneida, the Seneca spin field is the originating point of both the Peacemaker and Liberty Leys. To encompass the entire Iroquois Confederacy, the field is expanded by one harmonic.

The eastern door of the Iroquois Confederacy is at Canajoharie (Mohawk). The western door of the confederacy is Niagara Falls (Tuskarora). Both doors are equidistant from the center point of Seneca Falls. Expanding this second-level harmonic field to the third-level harmonic, the cities of Philadelphia and Montreal are linked in a single spin field with Mount Ascutney and Mount Wachusett. Interpenetrating at this multidimensional level, Seneca Falls projected the Great Law of the Iroquois into the collective consciousness of the Gaia Matrix, affecting the minds and morality of the Colonial peoples.

The location of the National Women's Hall of Fame, Seneca Falls honors the beginning of the struggle for women's right to vote, out of which arose the American feminist movement. As was the fashion of the day, the writers of the American Constitution made no provision for the political participation of women. Finally in 1848, in Seneca Falls, Elizabeth Cady Stanton, Susan B. Anthony and Lucretia Mott convened the first official Womens' Rights Convention, where the Declaration of Sentiments was publicly presented and signed.

Declaration of Sentiments and Resolutions

Seneca Falls Convention, 1848
prepared by Elizabeth Cady Stanton

When, in the course of human events, it becomes necessary for one portion of the family of man to assume among the people of the earth a position different from that which they have hitherto occupied, but one to which the laws of nature and of nature's God entitle them, a decent respect to the opinions of mankind requires that they should declare the causes that impel them to such a course.

We hold these truths to be self-evident: that all men and women are created equal; that they are endowed by their Creator with certain inalienable rights; that among these are life, liberty, and the pursuit of happiness; that to secure these rights governments are instituted, deriving their just powers from the consent of the governed. Whenever any form of government becomes destructive of these ends, it is the right of those who suffer from it to refuse allegiance to it, and to insist upon the institution of a new government, laying its foundation on such principles, and organizing its powers in such form, as to them shall seem most likely to effect their safety and happiness. Prudence indeed, will dictate that governments long established should not be changed for light and transient causes and accordingly all experience hath shown that mankind are more disposed to suffer, while evils are sufferable, than to right themselves by abolishing the forms to which they were accustomed. But when a long train of abuses and usurpations, pursuing invariably the same object evinces a design to reduce them under absolute despotism, it is their duty to throw off such government, and to provide new guards for their future security. Such has been the patient sufferance of the women under this government, and such is now the necessity which constrains them to demand the equal station to which they are entitled.

The history of mankind is a history of repeated injuries and usurpations on the part of man toward woman, having in direct object the establishment of an absolute tyranny over her. To prove this, let facts be submitted to a candid world.

He has never permitted her to exercise her inalienable right to the elective franchise. He has compelled her to submit to laws, in the formation of which she had no voice.

He has withheld from her rights which are given to the most ignorant and degraded men--both natives and foreigners. Having deprived her of this first right of a citizen, the elective franchise, thereby leaving her without representation in the halls of legislation, he has oppressed her on all sides.

He has made her, if married, in the eye of the law, civilly dead.

He has taken from her all right in property, even to the wages she earns.

He has made her, morally, an irresponsible being, as she can commit many crimes with impunity, provided they be done in the presence of her husband. In the covenant of marriage, she is compelled to promise obedience to her husband, he becoming, to all intents and purposes, her master -- the law giving him power to deprive her of her liberty, and to administer chastisement.

He has so framed the laws of divorce, as to what shall be the proper causes, and in case of separation, to whom the guardianship of the children shall be given, as to be wholly regardless of the happiness of women - -the law, in all cases, going upon a false supposition of the supremacy of man, and giving all power into his hands.

After depriving her of all rights as a married woman, if single, and the owner of property, he has taxed her to support a government which recognizes her only when her property can be profitable to it.

He has monopolized nearly all the profitable employments, and from those she is permitted to follow, she receives but a scanty remuneration. He closes against her all the avenues to wealth and distinction which he considers most honorable to himself. As a teacher of theology, medicine, or law, she is not known.

He has denied her the facilities for obtaining a thorough education, all colleges being closed against her.

He allows her in Church, as well as State, but a subordinate position, claiming Apostolic authority for her exclusion from the ministry, and, with some exceptions, from any public participation in the affairs of the Church.

He has created a false public sentiment by giving to the world a different code of morals for men and women, by which moral delinquencies which exclude women from society, are not only tolerated, but deemed of little account in man.

He has usurped the prerogative of Jehovah himself, claiming it as his right to assign for a sphere of action, when that belongs to conscience and to her God.

He has endeavored, in every way that he could, to destroy her confidence in her own powers, to lessen her self-respect, and to make willing to lead a dependent and abject life. Now, in view of this entire disfranchisement one-half the people of this country, their social and religious degradation -- in view of the unjust laws above mentioned, and because women do feel themselves aggrieved, oppressed, and fraudulently deprived of their most sacred rights, we insist that they have immediate admission to all the rights and privileges which belong to them as citizens of the United States.

In entering upon the great work before us, we anticipate no small amount of misconception, misrepresentation, and ridicule; but we shall use every instrumentality within our power to effect our object. We shall employ agents, circulate tracts, petition the State and National legislatures, and endeavor to enlist the pulpit and the press in our behalf. We hope this Convention will be followed by a series of Conventions embracing every part of the country.

Lucretia Mott, Harriet Cady Eaton, Margaret Pryor, Elizabeth Cady Stanton, Eunice Newton Foote, Mary Ann McClintock, Margaret Schooley, Martha C. Wright, Jane C. Hunt, Amy Post, Catharine F. Stebbins, Mary Ann Frink, Lydia Mount, Delia Mathews, Catharine C. Paine, Elizabeth W. McClintock, Malvina Seymour, Phebe Mosher, Catharine Shaw, Deborah Scott, Sarah Hallowell, Mary McClintock, Mary Gilbert, Sophrone Taylor, Cynthia Davis, Hannah Plant, Lucy Jones, Sarah Whitney, Mary H. Hallowell, Elizabeth Conklin, Sally Pitcher, Mary Conklin, Susan Quinn, Mary S. Mirror, Phebe King, Julia Ann Drake, Charlotte Woodward, Martha Underhill, Dorothy Mathews, Eunice Barker, Sarah R. Woods, Lydia Gild, Sarah Hoffman, Elizabeth Leslie, Martha Ridley, Rachel D. Bonnel, Betsy Tewksbury, Rhoda Palmer, Margaret Jenkins, Cynthia Fuller, Mary Martin, P. A. Culvert, Susan R. Doty, Rebecca Race, Sarah A. Mosher, Mary E. Vail, Lucy Spalding, Lavinia Latham, Sarah Smith, Eliza Martin, Maria E. Wilbur, Elizabeth D. Smith, Caroline Barker, Ann Porter, Experience Gibbs, Antoinette E. Segur, Hannah J. Latham, Sarah Sisson

The following are the names of the gentlemen present in favor of the movement:

Richard P. Hunt, Samuel D. Tillman, Justin Williams, Elisha Foote. Frederick Douglass, Henry Seymour, Henry W. Seymour, David Spalding, William G. Barker, Elias J. Doty, John Jones, William S. Dell, James Mott, William Burroughs, Robert Smallbridge, Jacob Mathews, Charles L. Hoskins, Thomas McClintock, Saron Phillips, Jacob P. Chamberlain, Jonathan Metcalf, Nathan J. Milliken, S.E. Woodworth, Edward F. Underhill, George W. Pryor, Joel D. Bunker, Isaac Van Tassel, Thomas Dell, E. W. Capron, Stephen Shear, Henry Hatley, Azaliah Schooley

The Women's Convention of 1848 gave form, definition, and geomantic power to the women's suffrage movement. It was seventy-two years before women were given their rights as voters and humans, unlike their local examples of women of power, the Iroquois women. These ideals were projected into the life energy of the nation, changing the very nature of this latter-day democracy and culture of the United States. It is curious that place names of the Greek democracy, such as Syracuse, Ithaca, and Utica were used in the naming of towns and cities in the Seneca Falls area. The Haudenosaunee (Iroquois) Confederacy, a matriarchal culture, was a democratic form of government in which final decisions rested with the women. It was a powerful nation which was the equal of the Colonial governments of the 17th and 18th centuries. The lake waters, the matriarchy, the women's movement, and the compassionate values of the Great Law of the Peacemaker all speak of the power and balance of the divine feminine.

15.3 Longhouse
This reconstruction of a traditional Iroquois dwelling at the James Fennimore Cooper Museum in Cooperstown NY is unusual for its pitched roof and vertical walls. The rounded roofs of bent pole construction were more typical of the Longhouse tradition.

In a book called *Forgotten Founders* by Bruce E. Johansen (1982), it is detailed from historical documents that Benjamin Franklin and Thomas Jefferson both had a great deal of contact with the Iroquois. They highly respected the political unity of the Iroquois federation of nations and patterned the fledgling US system after it. The author points out numerous parallels between the two. We have been taught that the US system of governance was a "great experiment" devised by the Founding Fathers out of their discontent with the systems of Europe. It appears, however, that the US system is actually an outgrowth of the influence of Deganawidah--The Peacemaker. This is particularly interesting in light of the importance placed in the 1990's on the US role in establishing world peace.

Francis Jennings, in *History and Culture of Iroquois Diplomacy,* writes the following about the Iroquois League of Nations:

> The Deganawidah epic is the story of an Iroquois prophet, who supposedly lived during the Stone Age of North America and who brought a message of peace -- that all men should be kindred and should stop hunting, killing, and scalping one another. He preached the principles of "righteousness, civil authority, and peace", which together constitute "The Great Law". He persuaded the local chiefs of settlements scattered in the forests of what is now upstate New York to abandon their feuds, reform their minds, and unite. He formed the Iroquois Confederacy, endowed it with symbols, and supported it with ritual sanctions.

In *The League of Nations,* Lewis Morgan tells of other principles attributed to Deganawidah-- reverence for the aged, the care of orphans, strong family ties, and common brotherhood. We may recognize these as cornerstones of the world's great religions, compassion, and any truly civil society.

Seneca Falls, a world grid point, is all about democracy-- its modern origin, its continuing evolution, and its "Great Law" as a sustainable model for the future. Two of the lines radiating from this point were identified earlier as the Peacemaker Ley and the Washington Ley. From this you can see how the pulse generated by the Haudenosaunee feeds thoughtforms directly into our central geometry and that of the District of Columbia. Over the past 300 years there has been a continuing suppression of this pulse. The ethnic cleansing campaigns of Generals Sullivan and Clinton in 1779 destroyed the political and economic viability of the tribes of the Finger Lakes. At key points are stockpiles of life-destroying nuclear weapons, coupled with prisons along this primary pole of power. A curious footnote of history is that Cazenovia NY, a point within the Seneca Falls spin field, was an alternate site for the federal capital of the United States of America. It was as if early planners secured it so that in the event the experiment in Philadelphia didn't work or the nation was invaded, the culture could fall back on the original center of the "League of Nations".

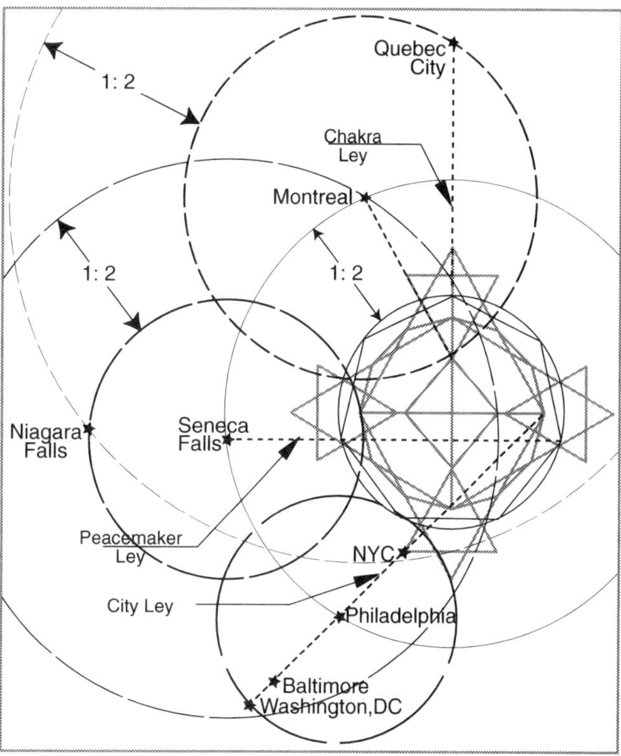

15.4 Democracy Spin Fields

The harmonic expansion of the three portals of political power reveals their historical/ geographical interconnection. Of the three, Montreal and Seneca Falls have the strongest geomantic ties with the central matrix. The Iroquois form of government at Seneca Falls had a dynamic influence on the governments of Montreal and Philadelphia.

Journals of soldiers in the Sullivan-Clinton Campaign described the area as a "veritable Eden," an "earthly Paradise". The Native Peoples attributed the creation of a "Heaven on Earth" to the imprint of the benevolent hand of the Great Spirit (hence the Finger Lakes).

Seneca Falls is a place of fire and water. Fire-fighting water pumps, iron water pipes, and clothes irons are manufactured there. Yearly, in the fall of the year, the reed beds in the great swamp called Montezuma Marsh would burn, and people would suffer from the malarial fever borne by the mosquitos of the marsh. The Wesleyan Chapel called "The Great Lighthouse" was the only church that welcomed all the reformers of the time. The Abolitionist, Suffrage, and Temperance movements all worked there to extinguish the fires of tyranny with the waters of knowledge. Here one finds makers of globes, alphabet blocks, socks, and bells -- ringing in the warmth of knowledge. From here milled flour and corn were shipped via the Erie Canal to feed the masses. Central to the bread basket of the Iroquois Confederacy and the crossroads of grid lines, rail-lines, roadways, and flyways is Seneca Falls, the small town that changed the world.

Philadelphia, Pennsylvania

Philadelphia was the locus of the developing democracy of the United States. The Declaration of Independence was signed in Philadelphia on July 4, 1776. It was the site of the Constitutional Convention, and was also the capital of the United States from 1790 to 1800. Of the three cities in this tale, this module of power personifies the Western industrial, mechanistic, business-focused culture. Philadelphia, founded on Quaker principles of religious tolerance, was a city of liberty, even before liberty was popularized. Slavery was outlawed there from the start. Today Philadelphia is adjacent to oil refineries (in New Jersey) which service the Pennsylvania oil industry. A center for printing personified by its famous resident (and founder of libraries) Ben Franklin-- Philadelphia was in the forefront of the popular press, the educator of the masses.

15.5 High Point, New Jersey
This obelisk marks the edge of the Philadelphia spin field. Other points include West Point, Annapolis, and Washington DC.

Names have much to say about quality of place. In Greek, *philadelphia* means "brotherly love". Plato, Euclid, Archimedes, Homer, and Helen, all Greeks who set the mechanistic model of industrial society, are at home in this city. The United States is a kind of epitome of their planetary pulse as played out in the American mythos of battle, adventure, science, trade, philosophy, and male-dominated political power.

As is the case with any analysis of a landscape geometry's dynamic zone of influence, the center is determined by the surrounding geographic features. The defining point of the Philadelphia geometry is Port Jervis and its accompanying High Point NJ. At High Point there is an obelisk that inscribes the Philadelphia spin field, while Port Jervis marks the passage of the Liberty Ley. The City Ley halves this circle with the alignment of Baltimore, Philadelphia, and New York City. The course of this ley traces the final stretch of the Delaware River as it empties into Delaware Bay. The Philadelphia circle describes New Jersey's northern border with New York and the southern boundary of Delaware and Maryland, embraces New York City and Baltimore, and is a dynamo for Washington DC. And just as West Point is an important site on the core Arkhom heptagram, the Naval Academy at Annapolis MD falls on the Philadelphia harmonic, as does Gettysburg PA.

The preponderance of monuments, the Army and Navy schools, and the layout of state borders suggests a deliberate design. Could this layout be of Masonic origin? Was Gettysburg chosen as a battlefield because of its strategic placement on this array? This is fertile ground for speculation, conspiracy theories, God's Grace, and the actions of a Sentient Earth. These sites, all with physical land-based underpinnings, shape the historic democratic development of the United States. The Philadelphia portal, powered by the Arkhom Gaia Matrix, has unfortunately (or perhaps necessarily so) dominated the North American continent at the expense of other portals, cultures, and peoples. The United States' cultural-centric worldview and morality of maximized profit has its role to play without a doubt. However, this does not a whole world make. In fact a monolithic culture such as this would eventually expire from a poisoned environment, finite markets, and moral corruption. The limitations of this portal are seen in the perimeters of its dynamic geometry. While it does link key points of the Gaia Matrix to the greater body of the continent-- it lacks harmonic connections. If we double its diameter the Philadelphia spin field does not lock in at this next harmonic level. Its link with ley currents and the Arkhom heptagram are its main sources of power. While this is significant, the inability of this field to expand harmonically limits the long-term strength and stability of this Philadelphia experiment.

Montreal, Canada

The island of Montreal is the seat of Canadian power and culture in the Americas. The island's first settlement was called Ville Marie, dedicated to Saint Mary, Mother of Jesus. Montreal, if any Canadian

15.6 Montreal Panorama
Looking east from Mount Royal, cosmopolitan Montreal is seen as an island city amidst a plain of plenty.

city, is at the center of Canada's history and its fight for sovereignty and national identity. A fortress city in the middle of the St. Lawrence River, Montreal is multinational. In fact, Montreal's flag includes four symbols displayed equally-- French Fleur-de-lys, the English Rose, the Scottish Thistle, and the Irish Shamrock embossed on it. The location of Montreal is at the apex of three water features, the St. Lawrence River, the Ottawa River, and Lake Champlain or the Richelieu River. The places marked by the Montreal spin field (like all spin fields) speaks to its nature, history, resources, and political potentials.

This third-portal zone on the heptagon harmonic is defined by Montreal at the center, with Quebec City, the outlet of Lake Ontario into the St. Lawrence River, and Mount Ascutney at its periphery. A breadbasket surrounded by farmland, Montreal's sphere of influence is bounded by the Green, Adirondack, and Laurentian mountain ranges. Reaching the southern shore of Lake George, the Montreal field touches on Mt. Ascutney and encompasses the formative equilateral mountain triangle of Mansfield / Washington / Ascutney. Montreal accesses the generative power of the Arkhom engine to power this pole of Canadian culture via this 300-mile-wide spin field. Expanding the initial Montreal field by dou-

15.7 Biosphere
A geodesic dome designed by Buckminster Fuller for Expo 6, the onetime American pavilion houses the biologies of four climate zones. A kind of biological ark, the Biosphere is one of many balanced artificial environments propagated by the City of Mary.

bling its diameter harmonically, the next field keys into Niagara Falls / New York City / the arc of Cape Cod / the coastal border of Maine and Canada. Beyond this harmonic there are no further levels of this type of progression which lock into landscape features. By Montreal's radiant field accessing the Arkhom geometry in its entirety, the Canadian culture engages to key into and grow from this source of power at the core of the tectonic plate. This geometric dynamism supports Canada's continuing sovereignty and cultural identity separate from the domination of Hollywood and Wall Street, and separate from the control of the English establishment.

Of the three seed centers of democracy, Montreal has the most auspicious and strategic position of the Gaia Matrix geometries. Historically, Canada has had one hand tied with the conflict between the English and French cultures. With this conflict resolved, potential exists for Canada, through Montreal, to come into its own as the main portal into the collective continental consciousness. If Quebec were to secede from the Dominion of Canada it would no doubt cut off the rest of Canada from the engine which allows for its very existence. To identify how this pulse might manifest, we need to look at Montreal's qualities of place.

It is possible that Montreal has been able to hold onto its distinct French culture and language because of its dynamic geographic connection to the land, despite being surrounded by an English culture which willed to suppress it. The city itself has a distinctive feel of Europe and expresses itself with the independent exuberance found only in multicultural countries. Being an island city, it has many bridges to other worlds, bridges to the 21st century if you will. Bridges which at this time are used beyond their limits, resulting in daily traffic jams.

Montreal recently completed the BioDome, housing four environments from around the world, a kind of biological Noah's Ark. It is an example of adaptive sustainability, created when the original geodesic dome, constructed for the 1967 World's Fair, needed repair after a fire. Here the arts are vibrantly supported and integrated into all aspects of life. It is a Catholic city and takes its religion seriously, but Montreal's spiritual life is not so much based on religion as it is on a spirit of united festival. The yearly cycle includes national and provincial holidays, jazz, theater, dance, comedy, French song, film, food, flower, Grand Prix festivals, a fantasy festival, a fire festival, and in the winter Montreal's underground city is so popular, it boasts over 2,000 establishments and over a half-million visitors daily.

Montreal is a place of true civilization/ community unlike any other on the continent. All aspects of culture are participated in and supported there (not just sports). Architectural gems are not neglected but are scrumptiously maintained. Special-interest exhibits, museums, and education programs flourish. It is a place that respects people enough to give them universal health care, freeing them from the games of the

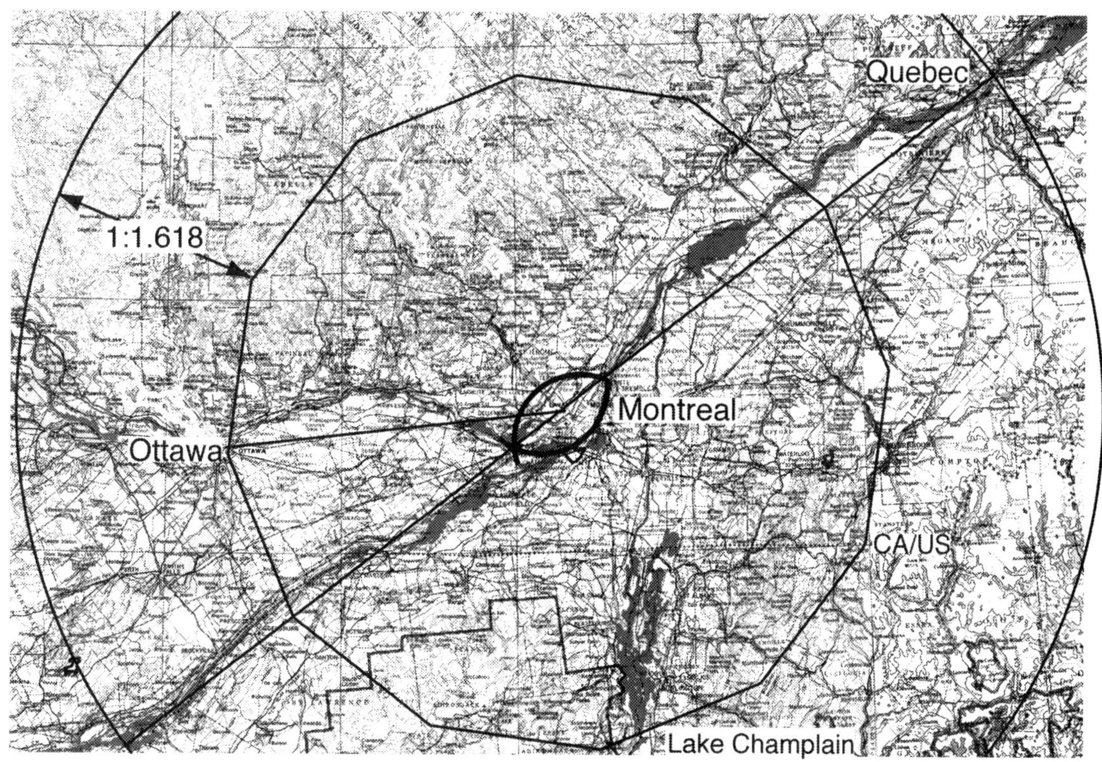

15.8 Montreal Regional Geometry

Reducing the size of the Montreal field by phi (1:1.618) reveals a twelve-pointed geometry generated by the relative positions of Ottawa, Montreal, and Quebec City. Other points include the Canadian -- US border/ Lake Champlain/ asbestos deposits.

hospital mergers/ business, HMO's, and the medical insurance industry to live a healthy life in liberty, fulfillment, and happiness. Montreal's diverse population and island nature makes it a city of international cooperation and individual contribution. In this way it is a model for global cooperation. This is the case in spite of the secessionist movement, which has twice failed to gain independence from the Dominion. For Canada to come into its full sustained power, this conflict or split in the group mind needs to be resolved. To succeed in secession would be contrary to the new pulse of green culture stirring in Arkhom. Held back economically by the French secessionist movement, Montreal-- and the province of Quebec in general-- was spared the homogenization of North America by the high rolling economy of the past 200- years. Because the city has been protected from this process, it is poised to take up its position as the focus point of the next 100-year cycle.

In the discussion on Cycles of American Destiny it was suggested that this next phase of cultural evolution would be focused on the north. The closest metropolitan seat of power in this direction is Montreal. In this regard it is a return to power for the island. Montreal was the seat of French control and culture that once encompassed much of North America in the 1600's.

French Canada has place names of all the saints in the book. The first settlement on the island which is today Montreal was called Ville-Marie or the City of Mary. Another of the islands is called the Isle Jesus.

15.9 The Vesica of the Island of Jesus and the City of Mary

Located at the confluence of the Ottawa and Saint Lawrence Rivers, the two Islands of Montreal Metro fit within a Vesica Piscis. The City of Mary (Ville-Marie) is seen as a reclining figure with the Island of Jesus (Ile Jesus) in its lap. This symbolism speaks of the sense of place inherent in the wisdom of the North (Nord). Also see illustration 19-1.

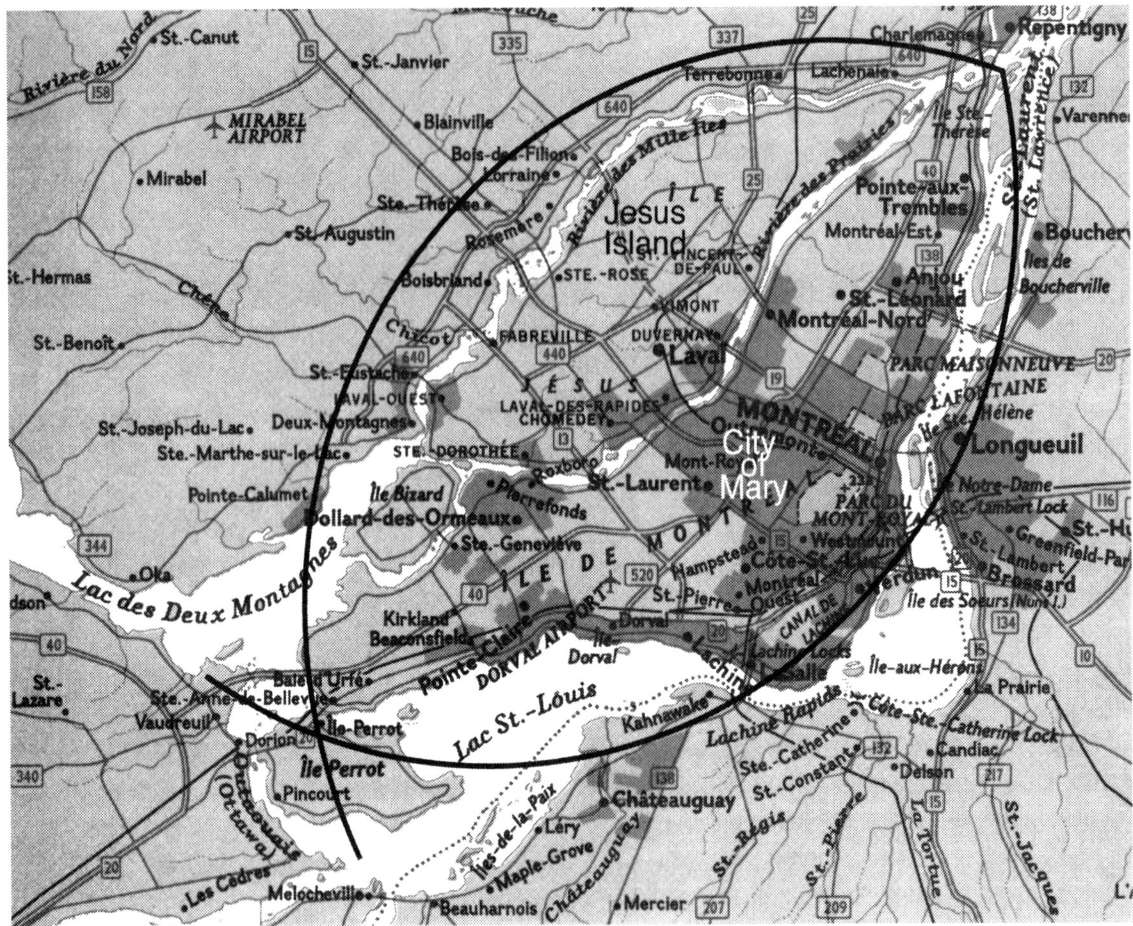

The sense of place alluded to in these names does not mean that the next American culture will be Catholic, but rather that it will play to the sentiment and values of wisdom, compassion, spirituality, self-sacrifice, tolerance, and love. Jesus as a world teacher transcends the shortcomings of the church. A culture which embraces the Cosmic Christ would awaken to the Christ within. The City of Mary could translate (in some languages) to the City of the Mother or the City of Gaia, Earth.

Isolationism has always proved negative to all but the controlling elite. By taking the path of independence from Canada, Quebec would succumb to a paradigm which is having its last gasp around the world. To sustain the world it is necessary to have respect for the common ground of the Earth, open exchange of ideas, liberty, peace, wealth, and resources. For these reasons we theorize that Montreal, as its qualities of place indicate, will become the next cultural center of North America, eclipsing New York City as it keys into the Arkhom Gaia Matrix and brings forth the next century. Vive le Quebec! Its birth waters have broken.

To review, we have identified three portals through which the sentient landscape has interfaced with human culture over the last 600 years or more. Each one of these points has been an experiment in social architecture that to some degree has proven successful and which seems to be building towards another step of democratic development and cultural life. We have seen how one portal has given way to another portal and cycle. As the new government of the people came into Philadelphia, the influence of the Great Law of the Iroquois peoples declined, their lands becoming a virtual prison ground and nuclear stockpile of the Philadelphia experiment in freedom. This was a clear suppression of the feminine impulse by the masculine oligarchies of the City Ley. Similarly, as the next cultural orientation turns to the north and Montreal, the cycle of wisdom will eclipse the light which has shone for the past 300 years on Philadelphia. One might construe this as a call to arms but it is nothing of the sort. It is simply the nature of Nature. "*To every season turn, turn, turn, and a time for every purpose under heaven*". Some day in the not too distant future, the US will know that it is time to empower the next generation of freedom, liberty and democratic evolution.

At the dawning of this *Age of Aquarius* we are seeing the dissolution of nationalism worldwide. Serbia and Quebec are two examples of nationalism's final death throes. Political systems necessary for their times, they are, in a word, *extinct* in the face of a global economy and environmental unity. Human population is at six billion. Population levels this high need new forms of social structure to sail this ship together in peace. Combined in a holistic model, these three portals into our Gaia Matrix can cocreate the next form of government, a kind of biological democracy based on the economics of natural systems.

This new democratic form will be birthed from the union of the Great Law (a feminine pulse) and Western economics (a masculine pulse), birthed out of the waters of the St. Lawrence. No Canadian wants to become a citizen of the States (bad health care), nor do a majority of Native people accept the Western, European (Greek form) worldview as their own. As Quebec resolves its issues of nationalism, as Native American spiritual and environmental values return to their rightful place of honor on the continent, and as the "English" limits are reached, we will come to learn that each portal's expression is a necessary part of an evolving whole society. This new, Aquarian, environmentally based democratic model will ideally bring balance to the world with compassion, order, prosperity, and peace.

16: Three Biomes

A biome is a major regional area classically defined by its distinctive climate, plant communities, and landforms.

The three biomes described in this chapter are center on the second harmonic ring of Arkhom within the field of the third harmonic that encompasses all of eastern North America. Like the three democracies, the Three Biomes each sing to a unique song.

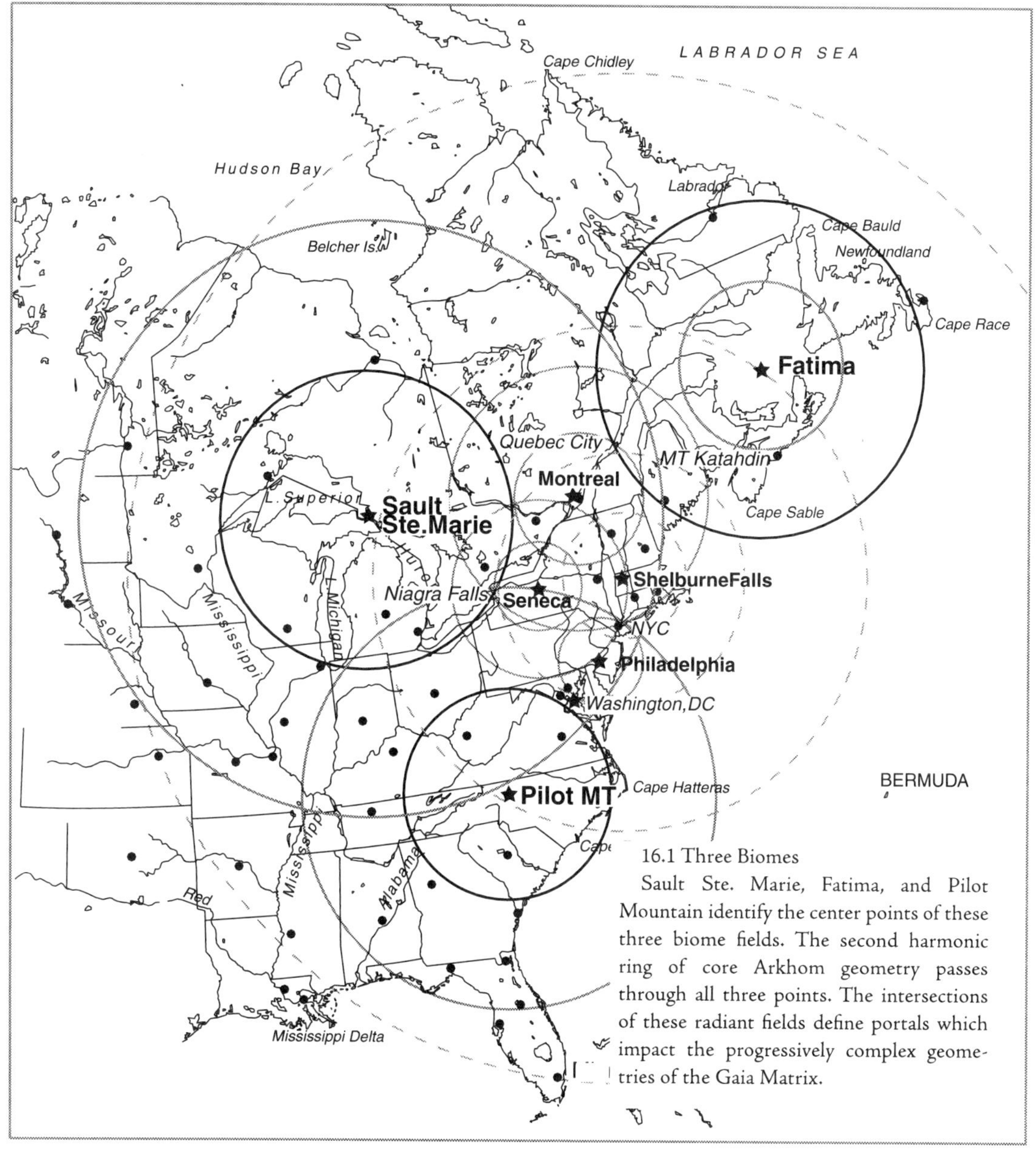

16.1 Three Biomes

Sault Ste. Marie, Fatima, and Pilot Mountain identify the center points of these three biome fields. The second harmonic ring of core Arkhom geometry passes through all three points. The intersections of these radiant fields define portals which impact the progressively complex geometries of the Gaia Matrix.

Waters of Mary

Working our way outward from the center of the Gaia Matrix, our process of discovery brings us to the Waters of Mary, better known as the Maritime Provinces of Canada. The mari of *mari*time, is a root word meaning"sea". Waters of Mary plays on words which have significance for this watery realm.

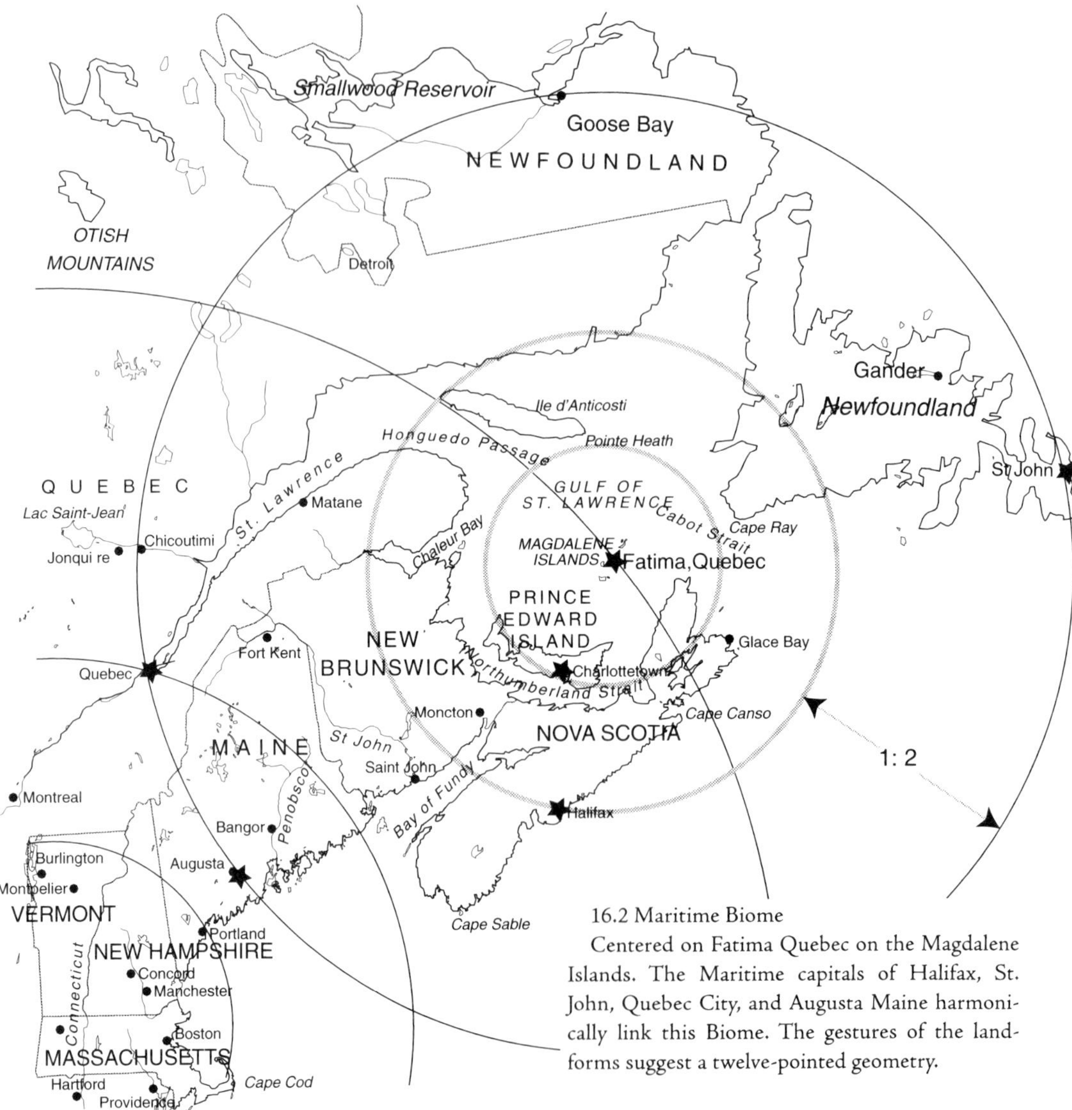

16.2 Maritime Biome
Centered on Fatima Quebec on the Magdalene Islands. The Maritime capitals of Halifax, St. John, Quebec City, and Augusta Maine harmonically link this Biome. The gestures of the landforms suggest a twelve-pointed geometry.

The geometry of the Waters deserves more research to reveal the full scope and complexity of this regional biome. The gestures of the land and waters speak of birds in flight, spirals of current, and stable geometries. This most beautiful and abundant region merits a book unto itself to fully elucidate the historic, social, and environmental dynamics of its islands, straits, waters, and settlement patterns. There is enough evidence to indicate the signature of the Waters in this geomorphic, biomic field.

The Waters of Mary have a clear harmonic pattern which keys into all four of the Maritime provincial capitals, as well as outlets, inlets, and coastal headlands. Quebec City (the capital of Quebec) and Augusta (capital of the State of Maine) mark the circumference of Mary's Biome. With Maine included one might say that it does not belong in the United States. Geographically it does resemble the lake-filled provinces of eastern Canada. Those who have traveled through the state of Maine can attest to its unique sense of place and way of thinking. The state government has considerable respect for and understanding of the importance of Maine's bioregion to maintain and enhance environmental quality. Sponsoring and organizing such resources as www.gulfofmaine.org, advanced computer mapping resources, and in the *Gulf of Maine Times*, is in its third year of publication in 1999. The publication's subtitle in fact is: "promoting cooperation to maintain and enhance environmental quality in the Gulf of Maine".

Central to this biomic field are the "Iles de la Madeleine" (The Islands of the Madeleine). La Madeleine in French refers to Mary Magdalene of New Testament fame. Located in the Gulf of St. Lawrence, the main fishhook-shaped island is the humble center of not only the Maritimes but some of the greatest fisheries in the world.

In addition to Mary Magdalene, an association exists with Mary, the mother of Jesus. The point on the island identified as the center of the Biome's circle is called Fatima. For non-Catholics, Fatima (in Portugal) received a visitation of Mother Mary, and a number of miracles were attributed to her Grace. Mary's son Jesus was also a *fisher-of-men*. All of these associations are appropriate to the Mari-time Provinces. Both qualities speak to the Sea and the Great Mother. A kind of seed thought amidst the fertile water--the fishhook-shaped island of Fatima speaks to the mysteries and faith centered around Jesus and Mary that is the focus of the fisherman's prayers of protection as they work the fisheries of this watery biome of Mary.

The geometry of the Maritime biome of Canada and Maine suggests a twelve-pointed matrix. There is some fine work being done with land geometries in Nova Scotia. We will leave it to those living there to share their discoveries, knowing that at least one book on the subject is in process. We hope that our work will assist and serve as a reference for their research, and that of many other pioneers in this field.

The Great Lakes Pentagon

The Great Lakes Pentagon has to be one of the most glaringly obvious geometries on the continent. It is delineated by the tips of Lakes Superior and Michigan (the sites of Duluth and Chicago respectively), as well as Niagara Falls, located between Lakes Ontario and Erie. The central point of the pentagon is where the lakes converge in Sault Ste. Marie, yet another point that honors the divine Mother. The city of Detroit, located on the southern line of the pentagon, lies midway between Chicago and Niagara Falls, in the passage between Lake Huron and Lake Erie.

This pentagon stands on its own as a naturally generated form, but there is more. Every pentagon has within it a pentagram. You will recall from *Sacred Geometry 101* that the pentagram is a phi ratio geometry in the proportion of water, humanity, and life.

You will note in the accompanying illustration that the lines and form of the pentagram mark coastlines and lake shapes to its proportionate embrace. An equal and opposite pentagon when overlaid brings more water features into this matrix of Gaia.

The Great Lakes geometry interfaces with the Seneca Falls harmonic spin field at Niagara Falls, their common point. Both fields reflect each other in the five Great Lakes and five Finger Lakes, which contain their own *pent* geometry in the Seneca Falls zone. Visually one can see their relationship as the closed fist of Seneca Falls opening into full expansion as the hand in the Great Lakes. Hold a fist to your chest on your Mount Ascutney point, take this heart energy into your clasped fist, and release it into the world as

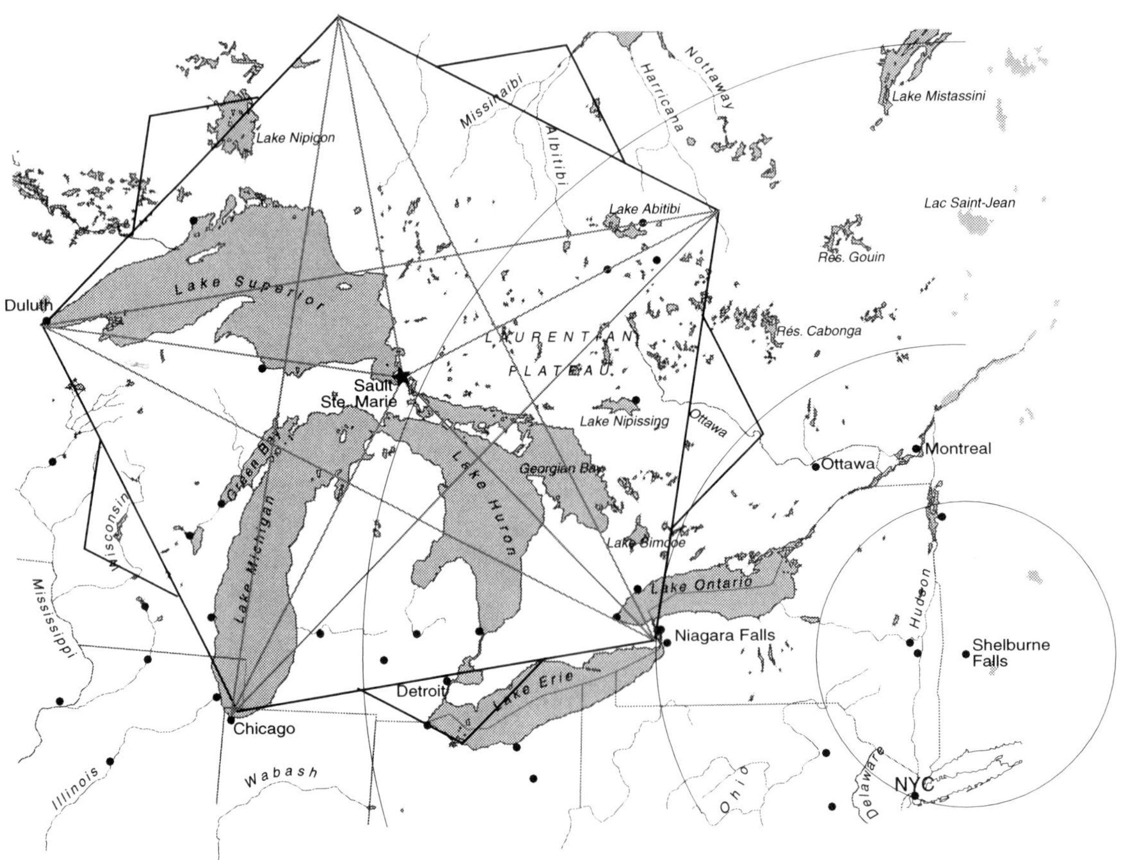

16.3 Great Lakes Biome

The geopositions of Niagara Falls, Chicago, Duluth, and Sault Ste. Marie in relation to the Great Lakes establish the pentagram geometry of this biome. The full geometry further delineates the coastlines and shapes of the lakes. The mirrored pent form in the background points to other water features arrayed around the Great Lakes.

you extend your arm and open your hand into the waters of the Great Lakes. A give away of the Mother's milk, the waters of life --H_2O.

Pilot of the Great Smokies

Pilot Mountain in North Carolina has always been considered a sacred mountain. Early inhabitants of the Piedmont gave it a wide berth. Native peoples dare not tread on sacred peaks for fear of getting on the wrong side of the Creator Gods who inhabited such precincts. It is now a State Park with camping and a road to the summit base. The quartzite cliffs of this ancient volcanic plug bear testimony to a once great mountain long since eroded. With an aviary of vultures, ravens, and hawks, one can almost see fire Devas leaping across the pinnacles of this once liquid furnace. This is the pilot house of the Southern Biome.

Cut nearly in two by the Great Smoky Mountains, the biome's initializing spin field is set by the length of these mountains from Front Royal to Atlanta. The Potomac River from Harpers Ferry to Washington

16.4 Pilot Mountain

The quartzite plug of Pilot Mountain remains the witness to a long extinct volcano. A sentinel of the middle Piedmont and the Blue Ridge Mountains, Pilot is the omphalos of the south. Held sacred by Native peoples, Pilot is home to ravens, buzzards, and the fiery Southern spirit.

DC scribes the generation of the northern arc of this field. Other salient points along its circumference include the Chesapeake Bay/ Charleston SC/ the Outer Banks of North Carolina/ the coastal border point of North Carolina and Virginia/ Mound City National Monument (Ohio)/ and Berkeley Springs WV.

Several points that beg for inclusion in the description of this biome are specific to the War Between the States, the American Civil War. Southern forces launched the Civil War from Charleston with an attack on Fort Sumter on April 12, 1861. Atlanta, opposite Washington DC, marked a turning point when the Northern troops burned it along with the Confederacy's war supply. One finds the Robert E. Lee Memorial on the hill overlooking Arlington National Cemetery at the point of the Pilot Biome's circumference closest to Washington DC.

Not directly connected to a governing portal like those that birthed the three democracies, the Southern Confederacy accesses the central matrix geomantically. The central matrix is necessary for the emergence of the independent nation. Through both subtle and overt means, the Unionists of Boston and Washington DC have held dissension in check by controlling the Gaia Matrix of North America. The question remains as to what degree they were aware of it.

Other sites on the Pilot's circumference also relate to war. Here you will find Yorktown VA, where the surrender of General Cornwallis ended Britain's rule next door in the Jamestown VA site of the English settlement in North America. Others include the Pentagon, the Central Intelligence Agency (CIA) in Langley VA, and the birth places of both General Robert E. Lee and General - President George Washington.

Harmonic expansions of initializing geometries or biomes confirm their validity by locking into places of geographic significance. The harmonic doubling of the Southern Biome illustrates this clearly. It highlights Mound City at the confluence of the Ohio and Mississippi Rivers, Chicago, Seneca Falls, West Point, and Daytona Beach (the current sacred ground -- as entertainment mecca -- for a great many Southern racing fans).

The center point of Pilot Mountain marks a crossing of the City Ley and another previously unmentioned grid line of the UVG, called the PeeDee Ley (named for the River). Coursing out of a primary grid point on Abaco Island in the Bahamas, the UVG grid energy plays heavily into this biome's dynamics. Just as the radiating lines of the Seneca Falls UVG point frame Arkhom, the lines radiating out of the Abaco UVG point-- frame the Pilot Biome. The angle of 60 degrees at which these two leys intersect one another indicates another geometry. This angle generates a hexagonal form suggesting part of the greater hive structure set by the Gaia Matrix. Within the hexagon is a hexagram, a Star of David, inherent to the southern landscape. It speaks of the Southern Biome's inescapable connection to the whole.

Pilot Mountain adjacent to the Great Smoky Mountains is thus shown as the centerpoint of the Confederacy.

The Southern Biome, walking to the beat of a different drummer, is an important sphere of the emerging Gaia mind. Both independent in identity, and part of something greater, it bears more investigation and accurate mapping. Historically, the Mississippian cultures of mound builders fit strategically into this field of plenty, with many of their centers located on the Southern Biome's ring.

These three biome fields are not autonomous. Each have harmonic fields which interpenetrate and rely on each other for energetic support. The places where two or more of these fields converge mark strategic

16.5 Southern Biome

Nested within the planetary Grid lines of the UVG, this biome is traversed by the City Ley setting an angle with the Pee Dee (river) Ley replicating the hexagonal format of the Arkhom geometry. The Harmonic rings of this biome are marked at strategic locations by Civil War and Mound Builders sites.

locales of spirit. One such place is Mount Katahdin in the State of Maine. Abeneki legend has it that the beautiful stone people live in the center of this mountain along with sundry thunder beings and gods, and human souls that the stone people seduced to enter their kingdom. Thought to be the spot where the rising sun first lights the continent, Mount Katahdin anchors the northern end of the Appalachian Trail. Other key points seen in the overlap of multiple harmonics are New York City, Mount Ascutney, and Niagara Falls.

The investigation of these three biomes has just begun. As one might imagine, these structures give parameters for designing sustainable systems of scale. We as individuals recycle or pollute as we choose. Our choices have significant impact on these biological systems no matter how small the act. We must plan now for the health of future generations. The interconnection and relationship with nature that these models present-- give us precisely what we need to design sustainable systems for the next thousand years. The pioneer, conquest/ dominance-at-any-expense attitude without consideration for the health of the land and its people-- is a paradigm no longer possible. The war against Nature must end. As you can see from these regional structures, we and the natural order are indistinguishable. We are a biology responsive and integral to this interconnected Gaia Matrix, Earth.

In the next chapters we will look at how a group of individuals may have worked in concert to impose their will on the land, using these geometries and those of their own invention.

17: The Masonic Age

Any book of this nature posits a human conspiracy theory or two. With the founding merchants of this great country being mostly of the Masonic persuasion, it seems appropriate to attribute some of this social design to their knowledge of sacred geometry and the esoteric arts of geomancy. Known for at least the last 1000 years by Western European intelligentsia, geomancy has been used by commanders in war to choose battlegrounds, and by kings in peace to site castles and churches.

The Americas were the first 'virgin' land on which this intelligentsia could ply their esoteric sciences unhindered by preexisting social architectures. It was a proverbial playground for these politically ambitious gentlemen. They wanted to form a new world order, a new society based on Masonic morality. As the one dollar bill says: "*Annuit coeptis novus ordo seclorum*" (at the beginning of time a new order of the world). They were highly intuitive men who saw in the Iroquois ways the seeds which formed the Constitution of the United States. They knew how to harness the power of nature through geometry. They wanted to break with the old political and economic order of Europe and to replace it with their own. Altruistic ideals, a taste for a new future, and billions of acres of a resource-rich continent to exploit--were the factors which brought this experiment of brotherly love to life in Philadelphia as the *United States of America.*

Citing documented evidence of the Masonic agenda in America would give our conspiracy theory a more scholarly front. However, it is not our intent to chronicle the activities of the early American Masons, but simply to *show their footprints upon the land.* The presence of Masons in American politics and commerce is a known fact. There are paintings of George Washington in full Masonic regalia setting the cornerstone of the Capital Building. Thomas Jefferson used the canons of sacred geometry in his architectural designs. Ben Franklin's magic square of numbers, where any row of numbers add up to the same number, also speaks to Masonic preoccupation with universal laws and the esoteric power of number, form, and sacred canon.

There have been enough tomes written on the subject to say with certainty that these white Anglo-Saxon men knew how to subtly manipulate Nature's forces and humanity's psyche for political ends. They used this knowledge in the battles of the Revolution, in the design of their cities, and in the symbols and monuments of their republic. They left us a rich heritage with a dark side. One need only look historically at the plight of African American and Native American peoples then and now to see the grave mistakes that were made and are still being made for this-experiment-in-brotherly-love to prosper... a sweet drink of success with a very bitter aftertaste. What of this blemish on the soul of America? Do the ends justify the means? What would the world be like if these social architects never invented the United States of America? Let's look at the footprints these Masons left behind.

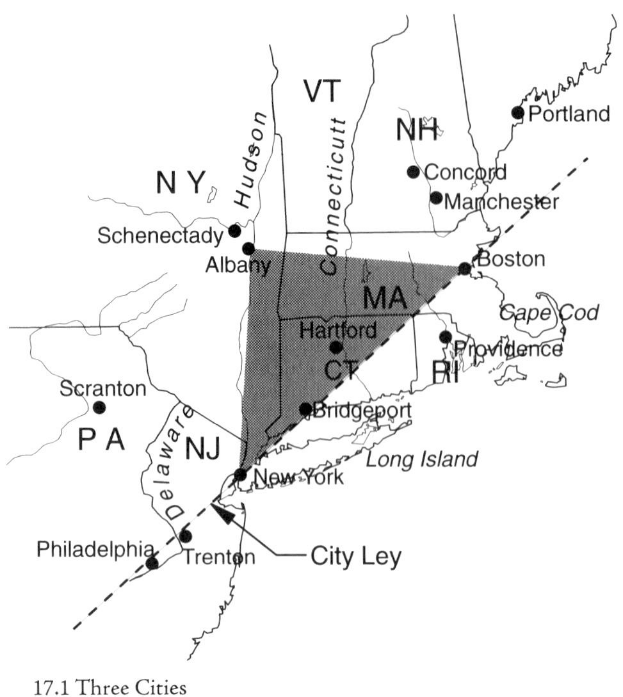

17.1 Three Cities

New York City, Albany, and Boston generate a right triangle, how neatly depends upon the map. With the City Ley as its base, the Boston to Albany side is delineated by Interstate "90" setting Albany at a 90 degree angle to Boston and New York.

The Tale of Three Cities

You have probably noticed by now that things come in threes. Three mountains, three biomes, three democracies, and now three cities. In this chapter our subject cities are Boston MA, Albany NY, and New York NY. Referring to the City Ley in earlier chapters, you will note that New York City and Boston are located on this ley. Using this as a base line you will see that Albany is at a 45 degree angle from the two points of Boston and New York. The location of these three cities creates a builders square, a primary symbol associated with the Masons. Was this just a coincidence? In Freemasonry, the Venerable Master wearing the symbol of a square hanging from the girdle signifies that a Masonic Lodge can only have one resolve, to follow the statutes of the Order, and one course of action, that of good.

Early on in the deliberation over a flag design for this new country, a snake was used as the coil which bound the thirteen original colonies together. It was a symbol of knowledge, alchemy, and telluric power. A good symbol, but one that didn't play very well with the folks who had a thing about snakes, either Biblically or otherwise. This snake however alludes to another serpent, a serpent which in fact did connect all the colonies -- the Appalachian Mountains. The chapter on leys documented how these mountains aligned cities and states (and also battles in the Revolutionary and Civil Wars).

The right triangle generated by the placement of Boston, New York, and Albany lassos this serpent energy, or better yet, creates a head of rulership for control of the Empire (New York State is called the Empire State). The Masons were adept at land surveying; George Washington was among the best. He used his intimate knowledge of the Appalachians for both war and commerce. As in the legend of Arthur and his father, Uther Pendragon, "The King and the Land are One". Pendragon means "head of the dragon" and the dragon is like the serpent. Therefore the triangle becomes the pendragon. This gives another reason for New York's modern dominance. Our Appalachians are thus seen as the backbone of this early country, a caduceus-like entwined snake which was the unifying earth energy for the colonies. The Masons' footsteps are evidenced in this design and in the placement of future cities.

It appears that of these three cities were laid out not only to create this right triangle but for each city to have a unique and sacred geometric pattern as the basis for its design. To top it off, these designs keyed directly into the Gaia Matrix-- preexistent in the New England wilderness. Were these patterns the result of the natural order of things? Was there a Divine hand? Was it the consciousness the Native peoples had instilled in the land that inspired or coerced these social architects? Did it just "feel good" according to intuition, or did the Masonic surveyors know of these natural geometries and design their society accordingly? The answer is most likely all of the above. Let's look at these cities more closely. Perhaps there are secrets yet to be unlocked.

Boston, Massachusetts

Boston's original people were known by the tribal name of Shawmut. The eastern part of present-day Massachusetts was divided into two confederations, the Wampanoag and the Massachusett. The Shawmuts were at different times affiliated with and protected by one or the other of these tribal groupings. The Massachusett people were known as "The People inside the Hills", referring to the Blue Hills which surround the Boston peninsula. A site overlooking the abundant fisheries of the bay and tidal flats, this was a paradise found. Easily defendable, the land of the Shawmut and their confederations was easily conquered with a few well-placed diseases in the Native population. This start of biological warfare in the Americas referred to is the epidemic of 1616 - 1619, probably smallpox, which killed nearly all the native Massachusett peoples.

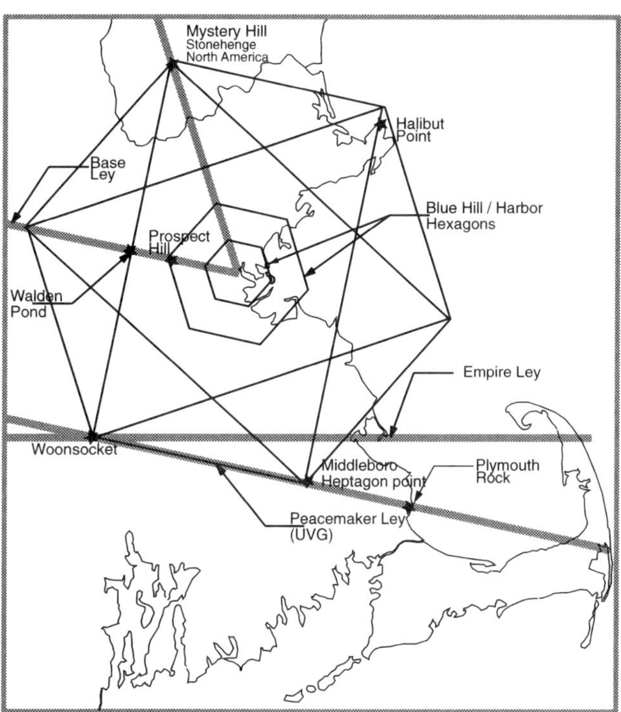

17.2 The Boston Hub

The Boston metro area is known as the "Hub". Encircled by the Blue Hills and curving highways, the city is shown in relation to the geomantic ley corridors which frame the harmonic expansion originating from the city core.

The ring of Blue Hills around Boston has a high point, Prospect Mountain, which marks the passage of the Base Ley to a point at the center of Shawmut tribal lands, the site of present-day City Hall Plaza. The exact point is the sunken garden and inoperable fountain in the plaza. Tracing the history of this auspicious site, as described in our discussion of the Base Ley, one finds the Grand Lodge of American Masons located adjacent to it. From here Paul Revere rode, Bell first telephoned Watson, and the Sons of Liberty (Masons) sparked the Revolution. From here the *voice* of liberty was heard around the world, and continues to resound through Boston's schools, innovation, and

17.3 City Hall and Sunken Garden

City hall rises behind a (temporary) white tent that recalls the Longhouse tradition of the original inhabitants. The sunken garden in the foreground marks the center point of the Boston Hexagon.

socioeconomic power. Boston has communicated the ideals of the Revolution for the past 200 years.

At the apex of Tremont Street's curve is the center point of a city which has grown into the shape of a hexagon. Points of the Boston hexagon reference the Base Ley and the Grand Trine alignment with its high point at Vermont's Lake Willoughby.

Boston over the centuries has filled its bays, swamps, and tidal basins to accommodate its ever burgeoning population. The points of the hexagon are North and South Station/ two points defining the docks/ Boston Common/ and the bridge to Cambridge (Base Ley). Here, since this hexagon was formed over time, it can't be attributed entirely to the early Masons. Hexagonal growth of populations was studied by the demographer and mathematician William Bungie. There is evidence that this is a natural propensity of human populations. The Boston Hexagon, however, keys into the surrounding landscape in such a way as to indicate that Boston had a master plan for development from the early American period.

Harmonically, Boston is nested into a dimensional field which locks into the Blue Hills and other geographical features including Mystery Hill, known as the "Stonehenge of North America", the Peacemaker Ley, and Cape Ann. Illustrating the magnification of the Boston pulse it is clear that the thought patterns set in the landscape radiate into the supra-consciousness of the Gaia Matrix.

17.4 Boston Inner City

A result of infilling the bay of Old Boston, the core hexagon expresses a harmonic fractal of the hexagonal geography which encompasses it. The Grand Trine of the Arkhom geometry shown locking into this shape resulted from both geologic and cultural forces.

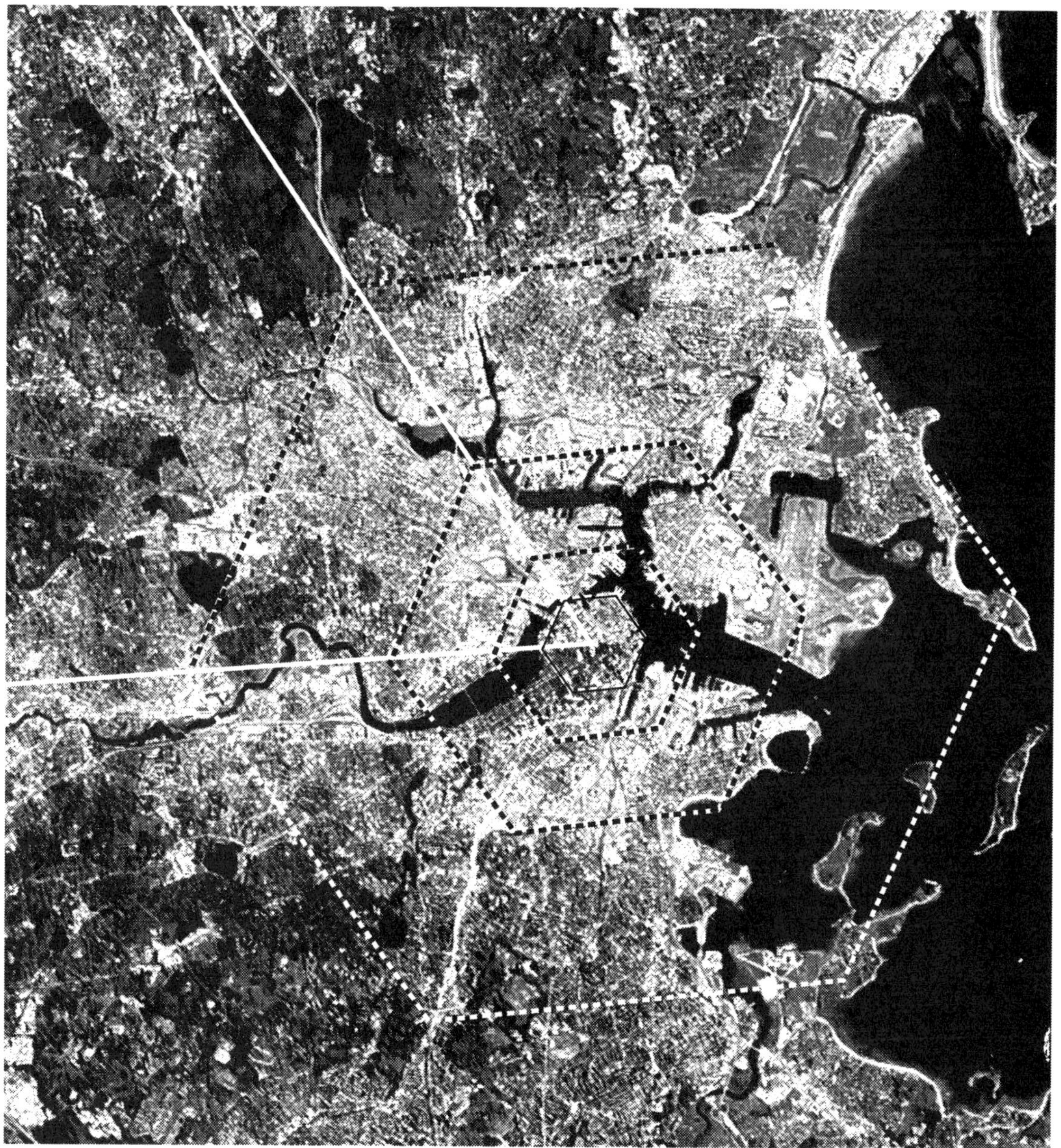

17.5 Boston Hexagon
This satellite photograph shows how the hexagonal geomorphology linking rivers, bays, harbor, airport, and Arkhom to the inner city.

New York, New York

Heading south along the City Ley towards Atlanta, our next city is New York. A Dutch port initially, New York became the center of British power in the Americas. Specifically, Staten Island, the pilot's seat of royal control, was where British royal power planned to have its capital. Remember, Staten Island is analogous to and shaped like a uterus. The Masons over the centuries mostly focused on the business end of Manhattan. All puns intended. At the tip of Manhattan Island is the historic Fort Clinton. From this

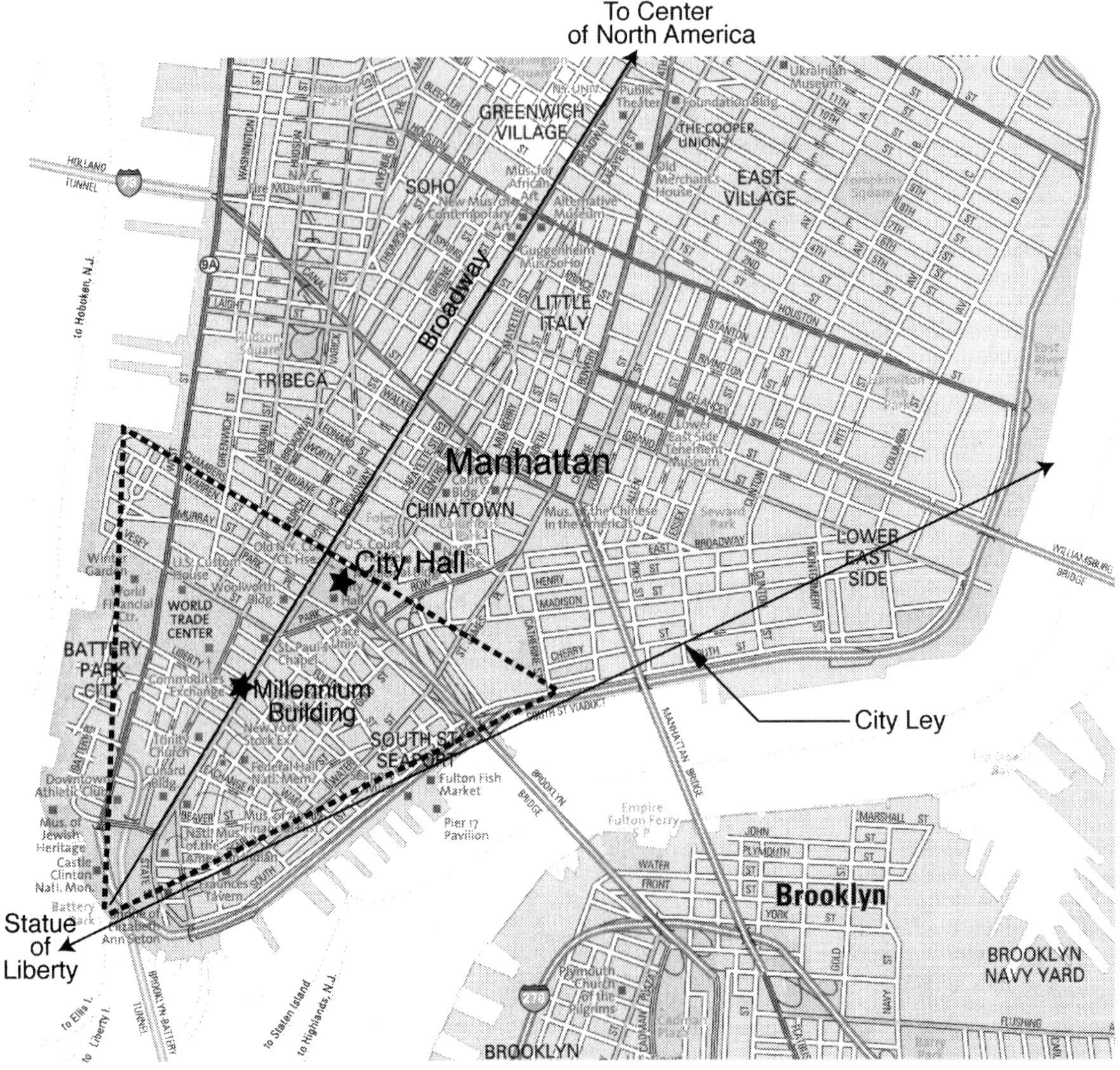

17.6 New York City Arrow

The reference lines of Lower Broadway and the City Ley reveal an equilateral triangle within the city plan. With City Hall at its base, this arrow projects the power of Wall Street from the Center of the Gaia Matrix out across the planet Earth. The black tower of the Millennium Building symbolizes the economic power to which it is central.

point a perfect equilateral triangle has been created over the past 200 years of filling in. Providing land for the World Trade Center's twin towers, this triangle was completed in the early 1990's, with the filling in of the docks along the Hudson River. From Clinton's fort in Battery Park at its southern end, Lower Broadway cuts this triangle in half, with City Hall at the base of this triangle at the intersection of Chambers and Broadway. Broadway points directly to the center of Arkhom at Shelburne Falls. New York City's position relative to the center is exactly opposite Mount Washington NH. The analogy of the windiest mountain with the greatest flux of temperature correlates to Wall Street, sharing this quality of place exhibited by the daily ride of the Stock Market.

With Clinton's Fort at the tip of Manhattan, could President Clinton have been enacting the play of the "King and the Land are One"? Certainly President Clinton and Wall Street are one. A culture expresses itself through its land, cities, and presidents (kings). Because of the entwined matrices designed by our founding Masonic fathers, there is a direct relationship between form and function, land and government. New York City projects its seed of commerce out of the Center of North America, powered by Mount Washington granite and the City Ley. Its focused, stable geometry helps New York City control the economies of America and possibly the world. The invisible handshake of the operative Mason is clearly seen giving the merchants and money-changers a position of kingship and male power in Nature's temple.

Albany, New York

17.7 Albany Skyline

Government is the main industry of the capital of the Empire State. The towers of the New York state bureaucracy dominate the Albany skyline.

Albany, the self proclaimed "All American City", whose name means white, is the capital of the Empire State. At the right angle between Boston and New York City, Albany has hidden in its design the plan of the Great Pyramid of Egypt. The Great Pyramid is a power that is seen on the dollar bill. Implicit in the pyramid is another similar American symbol, the keystone of Pennsylvania. It is the symbol and geometry that is at the core of the Masonic revelation. Just as a keystone is critical to the stability of a stone arch which holds up the building, Philadelphia was the keystone or arch of the Untied States. It possesses the

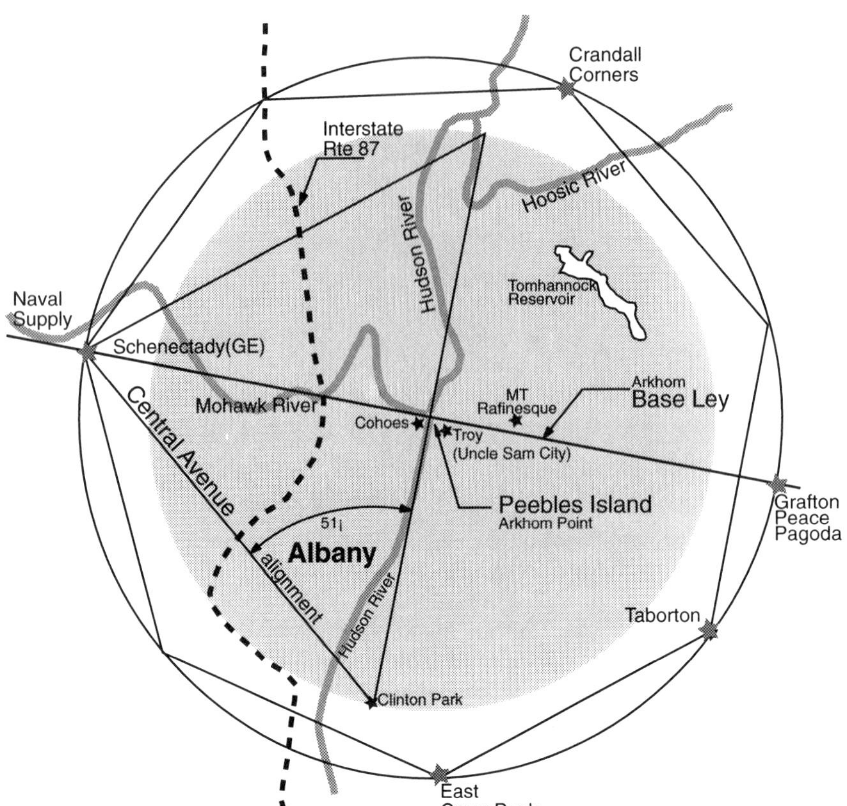

17.8 Albany Pyramid

The Squared Circle geometry is set by the relative position of three rivers, the passage of the Base Ley, and the alignment of Central Avenue. The intersection of Interstate 87 and the Mohawk River marks the relative position of the King's Chamber in the Great Pyramid.

Power of Seven and the life-giving force of the waters of life and the Holy Spirit. It represents the manifesting power of creation.

Nested near the confluence of the Mohawk and Hudson Rivers, Albany uses these same waters to define itself. The confluence of these rivers is at Peebles Island, one of the primary Arkhom sites. A state park and headquarters of New York State's Department of Urban and Historic Parks, Peebles Island is a site well worth visiting. Here one finds an Eden-like environment with native plantings that are self-sustaining, set in sharp contrast to the surrounding chaos of bridges, highways, deteriorating buildings and churches. On the island are Revolutionary War battlements of mounded earth, known by the name that reflects their shape -- breastworks. Once the site of native fisheries, waterfalls are abundant, as are vistas where the rivers come together to merge. Peebles Island is the locus or center point of the base of the Albany pyramid. Another base point is the Port of Albany (oil depot) on the Hudson, which marks one of the angles of the pyramid.

The primary feature of the Albany cityscape is Central Avenue. It begins at the Port of Albany, and defines one side of the pyramid as it makes a beeline through the New York State capital buildings on its way to Scotia NY. There it intersects the Base Ley at the apex of the pyramid. The confluence of the Hoosic and Hudson Rivers marks the third point of the pyramid, opposite the Port of Albany.

The gleaming towers of the state office buildings in Albany reflect the creation of one of the greatest bureaucracies in the world. They stand in stark contrast to the decaying city, oil tank farms, PCB-polluted rivers, and abandoned factories which surround them. The brainchild of Nelson D. Rockefeller, the father of America's war on drugs, the Albany State Offices reflect qualities appropriate to the Empire State.

Symbolic of the capstone of the pyramid, the General Electric Corporation was headquartered for many years at their turbine generator plant in Schenectady NY, next door to Scotia. Have you ever wondered why GE has become a world power unto itself? GE Schenectady is a shell of what it used to be since GE's corporate headquarters moved from the Albany capstone of power (along the culture-generating Base Ley of Arkhom) to its new location-- the omphalos of global commerce, drawing from nearby New York City. The Schenectady plant's main product was electrical turbines, another kind of spin field whose power propels much like the Great Pyramid once propelled the soul of the Pharaoh to the afterlife.

Further evidence of this pyramidal sense of place comes from the Scotia burial mounds of the Red Paint People. As we have seen, every Pyramid has its heptagon and a circle which can be scribed around this centric geometry. Everything within this circle can be considered part of the pyramidal complex or energetic field. Tracking the Base Ley from Scotia to its opposite eastern point on this circle, we find the Grafton Peace Pagoda (over eighty throughout the entire world, two of which are in the inner rhombus of the Arkhom geometry). As you may remember from the Base Ley's story line, this place is also peppered with Early Sites, many of which were likely to have been burial mounds for Native peoples. This forms a curious juxtaposition, with a military- industrial complex on one end, and a Peace Pagoda at the other, with both close to ancient burial sites. Another circumstance worth mentioning here is that the Peace Pagoda was completed around the same time that GE abandoned Schenectady. A natural principle is seen particularly in this case, that opposites attract and repel simultaneously.

The tale of these three cities shows that a conscious hand is at work in their design, their triangular form, and their interaction with the central Gaia

17.9 Albany, New York Towers

The towers constructed during Governor Nelson D. Rockefeller's terms.

17.10 Albany's Egg

The Albany Symphony Orchestra Hall. 'the egg' is evidence of overt ET contact (one for the X-Files).

Matrix of North America and the Appalachian Mountains. Important cities in the scheme of things, are they the product of the Masons? Unless the old boys' fess up, we will be left to wonder whether they are the work of God, the Gaia Matrix, Angels, the Devil, ETs, or indeed the Masons. Whatever the case may be, by understanding of the impact of these places on the health of the whole continent, it is hoped that responsible action will follow. Will it benefit the interests of the stockholders if their company's place of power is abandoned and polluted? Will it matter if Boston chooses to send a message of sustainability from its axis mundi at City Hall, over the greed of developers who want to build another hotel on this sacred ground? What will make a difference? Wall Street will, when it invests in long-term global social gain over short-term maximization of profits.

There are extreme responsibilities associated with these three cities. They were set in the collective mind as a control mechanism for the benefit of Constitutional ideals, not for the benefit of the CEOs, bankers, and the little wills of men. Or were they? With knowledge is freedom, with freedom is responsibility. This powerhouse of culture belongs to the people. Take rightful control of your destiny and rebuild it in light. We need leaders who value the lives of the next seven generations higher than the making of billions in excessive profits from the pain of those same seven generations.

It appears that we have discovered an attempt by whatever social architects to exert influence over the Gaia Matrix to benefit the growth of a new society. Things appear to have gotten a little out of hand, but here we have an opportunity to make things right -- choose Life, Liberty, Happiness, and true equality.

Washington DC

neither here nor there

Why would any government pick a malaria-infested swamp for the capital of their country?

Washington DC was the first fully designed large city in America. Its site placement and layout, designed essentially by Pierre L'Enfant, made it defendable with the placement of arms at the crossings of broad avenues. A maze of circles for any enemy to navigate, it is the same for the unaccustomed traveler, despite the ordered numbers, syllables of alphabetical names, and direction quadrants. There have been many studies of the layout of Washington DC. Some have found embedded pentagons, others the Masons' Square as its primary template. Seemingly unrelated, the branches of government have individual alignments which are autonomous yet part of the whole design. Everything about the city is just slightly out of whack though. The Washington Monument, while on the Capitol axis, is just off the intersection with the White House axis.The center of the District of Columbia diamond is well off (four city blocks) both of these axes. Perhaps it was this designed this way on purpose so that there would be no single place of absolute geomantic power, but rather shared powers-- just like the concept behind the government it houses.

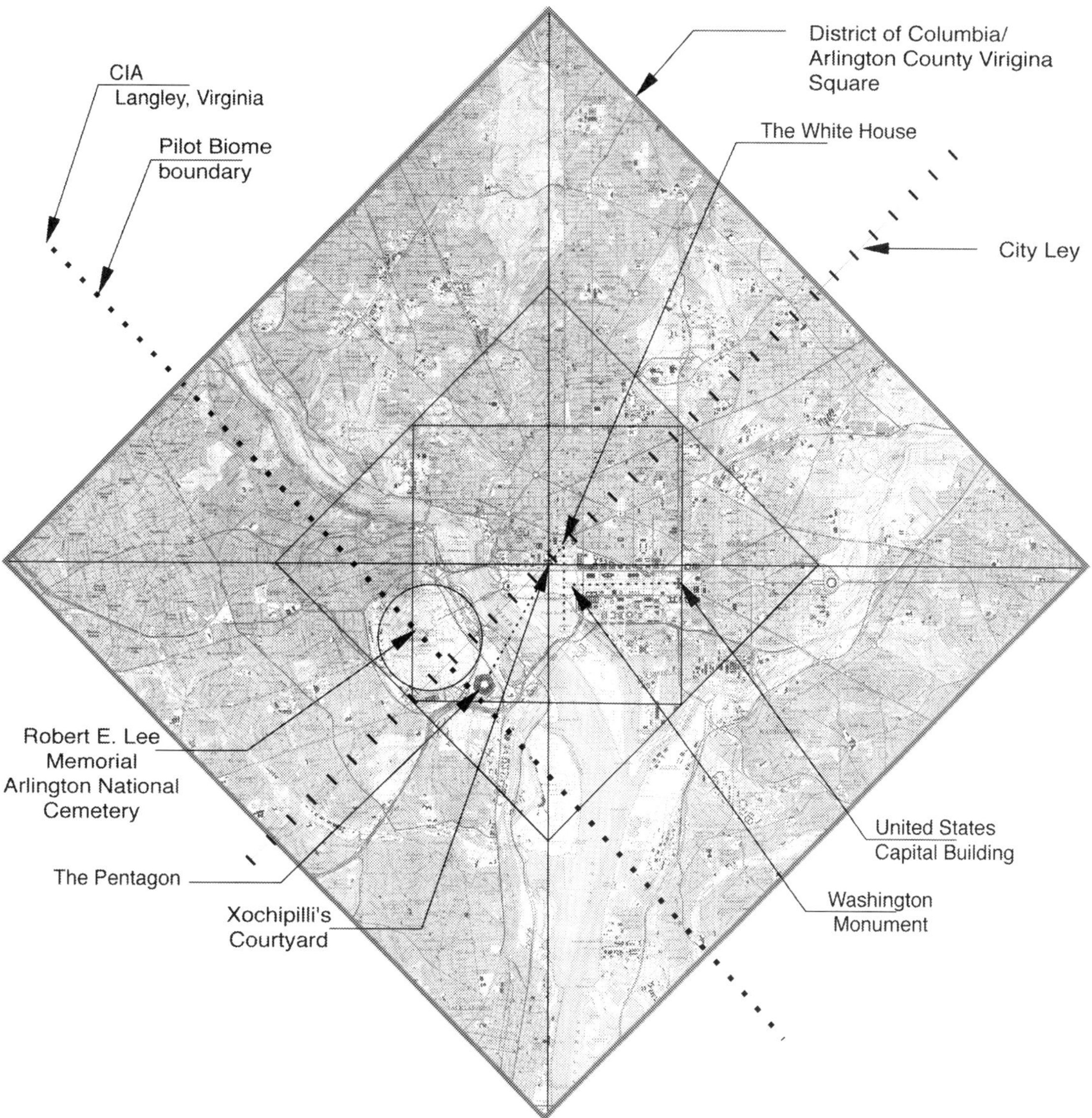

17.11 Washington DC

The District of Columbia Square, as defined by DC and Arlington County Virginia, shows the dynamics of the City Ley and Southern Biome Field penetrating Washington Metro. The central icon Xochipilli resides in the courtyard of the Organization of American States Building. The alignment between the Pentagon and the White House must pass through this statue of the Aztec god of Flowers.

Reports indicate that George Washington chose the site for this first landholding of the Federal government. The selection process for the site was democratic and contentious, with both the North and South wanting the capital. Ultimately, George Washington won the day. The capital was located on the upper crust of the Piedmont Plateau at the lower lip of the coastal plain. Sited between the states of Maryland and Virginia, the new capital is on the spiritual boundary of North and South.

The District of Columbia and the city of Washington were the result of a collaboration (running argument) between L'Enfant, Washington, and Jefferson. L'Enfant quit before completing the design of the District of Columbia as a result of this quarrelsome process. Nonetheless L'Enfant was the primary designer of Washington. In fact, so enraged was L'Enfant that he wouldn't relinquish his plan to the federal government, only upon his death was it given up. At a time before copying machines, this single design plan of the city of Washington was secured to his person at all times in an attempt to make the feds pay up and shut up.

No doubt these were extraordinary men versed in all manner of consideration due such a project. A reference to the exotic crew who laid out the boundaries of the District of Columbia appeared in a March 12, 1790 issue of *The Georgetown Weekly Ledger*:

> Some time last month arrived in this town Mr. Andrew Ellicott, a gentleman of superior astronomical abilities. He was employed by the President of the United States of America, to lay off a tract of land, ten miles square, on the Potowmack, for the use of Congress: is now engaged in this business, and hopes soon to accomplish the object of his mission. He is attended by Benjamin Banniker, an Ethiopian, whose abilities, as a surveyor, and an astronomer, clearly prove that Mr. Jefferson's concluding that race of men were void of mental endowments was without foundation.

Throughout the city are symbols and monuments of Masonic origin. The Washington Monument is one example. At 555 feet, it is 74 feet taller than the Great Pyramid, but still references it. John Michell articulates this relationship in his book *City of Revelation*, in which he states:

> The profile of the Great Pyramid (base angle 51degrees 51minutes) plays an important part in sacred geometry and arithmetic. Its height in feet, 481, is the length of a vesica formed by two circles each of circumference 1746, the number of fusion. Each of these circles has a diameter of 555 which, if measured in feet makes the area of each circle 5.555 acres.

Another is the placement of the Jefferson Memorial (the magician) opposite the White House (the king). Clearly the designers of Washington DC used every symbolic design, form, and strategic plan they could come up with to make this city the capital and 'geomantic center' of the United States of America.

The most obvious geometry of DC is the square of the district itself. Alluding to the squared form of the New Jerusalem as described in the Bible, with rivers coursing through its walls, the District's square points are aligned with the four cardinal directions. Only two-thirds of the 100 square miles is part of the District of Columbia, as it is bisected by the border with Virginia. The other third is scribed by the borders of Arlington County VA.

The center of any geometry holds a certain power over the form's spirit and intent. Relevant to this study, it warrants a look at the center of the DC square, just off the intersection of 17th street and Constitution Avenue, an unlikely center for such a great city.

While not directly linked to the subject of Masons in America, examining this central point is nonetheless salient to our discussion of Washington DC. Closest to the center point of the DC square is the Pan American Building, which houses the Organization of American States. The OAS is one of the world's oldest international organizations. The building itself was designed to symbolize the peaceful spirit that pervades relations among the nations of North, South, and Central America. This unusual building, for Washington, abounds with representative art from the Mayan, Aztec, and Zapotecan cultures. Moreover, in the building's courtyard there is a curious statue of Xochipilli, an Aztec god, which holds the distinction of being the central icon of the District of Columbia.

17.12 Xochipilli

The God of Flowers and thus hallucinogenic drugs, Xochipilli presided as one of the primary gods at Aztec rites of human sacrifice. Also associated with sports, gambling, and lust, Mr. X symbolizes the dark side of America's culture and power.

Xochipilli goes to Washington

Xochipilli, the Aztec god of flowers, has many associative attributes which make for a curious icon, symbol, or archetype for Washington DC. As the god of flowers, Xochipilli was one of the deities called upon in the surgical process of human sacrifice as practiced by the Aztecs. The god of flowers is also the god of hallucinogenic drugs, extracted mainly from the flowers of plants. Another of Mister X's many personas is the god of youth, lust, sport, and gambling. Quite a character profile for Americans to gather around. Recall that the Washington Ley identifies multiple contemporary locations associated with drug culture or production. This plays directly into Xochipilli's negative persona.

The statue of Xochipilli and the Pan Am building were completed in 1907. It was the same period that sports and gambling became national pastimes, and drugs and vaccinations started to be developed in a big way. You may also recall that not long after Xochipilli's installation, the human sacrifice of two World Wars came to plague the country.

Hidden and inaccessible to the general public as he is in the back courtyard behind a building which addresses the political divide of North and South Americas. Xochipilli speaks of a divided America in denial of itself. Granted, the United States has never been as overt as the Aztecs when it comes to human sacrifice. It has, however, participated in it during its entire history. Recounting the major wars and dozen odd skirmishes in this century, one can see how human sacrifice was practiced as war in the name of God and country. Human sacrifice is in this sense integral to America's sense of self, how it defines leadership, patriotism, manhood, and success. Not so different than an Aztec fighting the good fight for gods and country.

As a *Christian* culture, the USA practices a religion centered on the sacrifice of Jesus and celebrating it every Sunday with the ingestion of the symbolic body of Christ. The Aztecs practiced slavery to advance their economic power, just like the USA. America's use of child labor, and its wasting of Indians and immigrants-- Africans, Chinese, Irish, and Mexican populations to support the lavish life-style of the few, is again analogous to Aztec culture.

Now, in the era of multi-national global industrial expansionism, a kind of economic World War III is being waged on countries, environments, and third-world populations.This modern version of Xochipillian culture is drugged into complacency by the hallucinogens of Hollywood, television, Disneyland, and the happiness in every "Happy Meal's" in Everytown, USA. This is an accepted practice bolstered by the morality of maximized profits at any cost. Given this, there couldn't be a more appropriate backyard symbol for Washington DC than Xochipilli at the center of this City of the Sun.

This strange case of Señor X at the center of the Washington DC is something to addressed. Is this really who we want to personify the country's ethos? Who or what would be more appropriate? Do the Daughters of the American Revolution, whose national headquarters is next door, have any suggestions? After a century of wars isn't it time to stop the human sacrifice all ready? Haven't we grown beyond the stage of autocratic warlords with their entourage of heart surgeons, slaves, and pampered athletes? Let's move on and send Xochipilli packing, however slight the chance be-- move him out of that auspicious location!

Washington DC is at the furthest navigable point inland on the Potomac River estuary. The river's course upstream bisects the northwest side of the square. Using Xochipilli as the center point, and the Potomac as an alignment towards the northwest, the river creates a wave form straight to Harpers Ferry, West Virginia. Harpers Ferry marks the passage of the Lower Appalachian Ley closest to DC. Harpers Ferry is also the spark gap between the Pilot Biome (south) and the first harmonic of the Arkhom Gaia Matrix (north). Washington DC is thus placed to bring unity, controlling from afar that critical gap between the Northern and Southern States, via the serpentine spine of the Appalachian Mountains. Washington may be seen as the solar plexus of the national body, the center of national power.

Extending the points of the DC square to connect to the Appalachian Ley, the north point aligns with Gettysburg, a telling site of a decisive Civil War battle that helped return the country to unity. To the west is the northern headland of the Great Smoky mountains at Front Royal. As with most land geometries, harmonic expansion can similarly be applied to Washington. The doubling of Washington's square places points on the Mason-Dixon Line and the Shenandoah ridge line.

It all makes sense, but only geomantically. Why go to such efforts to link with unseen forces? It is clear that the founding Masonic merchants appreciated and used these elemental geomantic powers to bring focus and lasting authority to this budding democracy. Tapping the power of the Appalachian Dragon, DC's northwest side lays parallel to the Appalachian Ley, siting Washington to mirror the telluric power of these mountains. Add to this the perpendicular angle of the Potomac River to the Appalachian Ley and the Masonic Square is generated as a control mechanism of this critical gap or spiritual divide between North and South. That is why the Masonic surveyor George Washington placed Washington DC in a malarial swamp *neither here nor there*, in control of two worlds, but not of either.

John Brown -
God's Madman or Boston's Pawn

17.13 John Brown, Geomancer
The man thought to be the catalyst for the Civil War, Brown accomplished this through his 'suicidal' raid on the Harpers Ferry Armory, at the spark gap between North and South. This visionary murderer was the most radical extremist of the Abolitionist movement.

Any discussion of Harpers Ferry must include the man that made the place infamous. As we have stated, Harpers Ferry is at the spiritual divide between North and South-- Maryland and Virginia. Or perhaps we should we say Mary(land) the Virgin(ia). This confluence of the Potomac and Shenandoah rivers was the gap through the Appalachian mountains that John Brown chose to start his ill-fated slave rebellion.

John Brown was a "Calvinist" whose literal interpretation of the Bible fueled the spirit behind those "Old Testament" eyes (more likely an indicator of a thyroid condition). Funded by abolitionists from Kansas to Boston, he was a man *"on a mission from God"*. On the surface of it there was 'no good reason' to start such a rebellion from the indefensible position of the ravine of Harpers Ferry. Despite 4000 years of military theory to the contrary, Brown insisted to his supporters and fellow abolitionist, Frederick Douglass, that the position was defendable and would in fact spark the great battle that would "purge the nation of its sin of slavery with the blood of its sons". But why Harpers Ferry?

"The Allegheny Mountains", Brown told Frederick Douglass as early as 1847, "are the basis of my plan. God has given the strength of these hills to freedom, they were placed there for the emancipation of the Negro race". Brown spoke of the mountains as God's handmade bastions of liberty, natural homes for the poor, the hated, the despised-- all victims who fled injustice. Brown believed that God had established the Allegheny Mountains from the foundation of the world that they might one day be a refuge for fugitive slaves. Why Harpers Ferry, when other positions were more defendable in the nearby mountainous terrain? It seems Brown was not alone in choosing that site.

Brown, a revolutionary wanted for murder, was supplied with money, weapons, and sanctuary by a group of Boston humanitarians who called themselves the *Secret Six*. The Secret Six included Thomas Wentworth Higginson, editor of *Atlantic Monthly*; Samuel Gridley Howe, world famous physician; Theodore Parker, the Unitarian minister whose rhetoric helped shape Lincoln's *Gettysburg Address*; Franklin Sanborn, educator and close friend of Emerson and Thoreau; and the immensely wealthy Gerrit Smith and George Luther Sterns.

According to Edward J. Renehan's book *The Secret Six*, these gentlemen conspired with Brown in choosing Harpers Ferry to start this second American Revolution, or the completion of the first revolution. It seemed these gentlemen knew about the power of symbol to galvanize a population or group. One meeting they had in Boston to plan this uprising was held at Paul Revere's Inn. Many of them were the sons of men who were the *Sons of Liberty*, the organizers of the first American revolution -- predominantly Masons. The Secret Six supplied Brown with $7,000 for this treasonous endeavor and released him to accomplish "the plan" whose ultimate effect would transform America, fulfilling the mandate of the Bill of Rights; knowing full well that the raid on Harpers Ferry was a suicidal act. Choosing Harpers was a calculated act designed by men who knew that a raid on this site by this man would accomplish their goals. But how? Were they privy to knowledge of Washington DC's esoteric mechanics? Perhaps they envisioned with the spilling of blood into the waters of the Potomac (up river from Washington DC) would symbolically catalyze the issue of slavery in the nation's Capitol.

By all accounts, the raid was bizarre and suicidal. Armed with Frederick the Great's sword, Brown led a group that he believed were to be sent to him without a public notice.The sword had been given to George Washington, passed down to his relative, Colonel Washington, and stolen for Brown by his followers. Thus Brown's raiding party entered the Harpers Ferry Armory firehouse with a wagonload of rifles and ammunition. This attack was in retrospect more about symbol and intention than actual revolt. Brown's vision had the streets of Harpers Ferry filled with "Negroes" fighting the good fight for freedom, when actually only a handful of slaves were even aware of this planned mighty rebellion. The few that did show quickly dispersed upon seeing the suicidal nature of the endeavor. Brown's plan called for the creation of a republic of free slaves within the state of Virginia, another absurd notion given the tenacity with which the gentlemen of Virginia held to their rights as slave owners. His ideas sounded like the ramblings of a "God-intoxicated madman" at the time, but in retrospect his raid did precipitate action on the issue of slavery, and more. It is interesting to note that the commanding officer of the Federal troops sent to put down Brown's rebellion was none other than Robert E. Lee.

"John Brown's body lies a-moldering in the grave... And the truth goes marching on!" The raid on Harpers Ferry as a symbolic act galvanized this national conflict, and sparked the gap of Brown's "holy mountains", igniting the fires of the Civil War. As a result, slavery was ended in Virginia, and throughout the South, and the sin of slavery was purged with the nation's blood. All were fulfillments of Brown's vision. The question remains, would the raid have had a similar effect if it were in any place other than Harpers Ferry? The power of place, in this instance, was greater than all the combined efforts of Brown, Douglas, and the Abolitionists of the time. Entering the supra-consciousness of Washington DC and the States of the North and South through Brown's holy mountains and the Potomac River, this act of sacrifice changed the world. Mister Brown, with the sword of Frederick and Washington held high, transformed liberty and unity into a practice, which hitherto was an unpracticed ideal of the Constitution.

Looking in the 'Old Testament eyes' of the Abraham seated in the Lincoln Memorial in Washington DC, one sees the spirit of John Brown shining through.

To what degree there was a conspiracy and a Masonic Agenda, and to what degree they controlled or influenced the national evolution of power is unclear. One wonders about any secret society as powerful as this one at the forefront of national design, power, and revolution. Yes, there was an influence, their mark is on the landscape. Washington DC reflects their design considerations, and symbols, which was not unusual given the time and people involved.

As the conspiracy of the Secret Six suggests, Boston was the seed point of the Revolutionary and Civil Wars, a hotbed for Masonic agendas. Taken in the context of our central geomatrix, these six men connecting with Boston's hexagon dynamic awoke the central Arkhom Gaia Matrix geometry, and projected this power to the spiritual divide between North and South in the raid on Harpers Ferry. Or was it simply that the Harpers Ferry Armory held a strategic position in relation to Washington and the South, and was thus the only likely site for a raid that would drive the point of freedom home? Whatever their understanding was, Brown, his followers, and supporters were engaging powerful geomantic dynamics.

The Tale of Three Cities is a tale of evolving development over three centuries. How could a consistent agenda remain in place over that space and time, and lock into a Gaia Matrix which was, with the help of modern cartography, only discovered in 1993? The three cities were placed as they are because of strategic considerations of trade, navigation, and defense by the French, Dutch, and English. In fact, all three cities were planned for efficiency given the geographical limits of the sites. Albany needed the most direct route from its port to the Erie Canal, hence Central Avenue. Manhattan Island lays at such an angle to point the entire city in the direction of the zero point of the continent. When filling bays or laying out roads a straight line is the most efficient when trying to get from point to point.

Laying out the District of Columbia, were Washington planners preparing for the day when John Brown would come to Harpers Ferry, and the great armies of North and South meet in at the crossroads of Gettysburg? Was the Organization of American States sited at the center of DC to set the agenda for control over the Americas, or was it placed there to be symbolic of the spiritual unity of North and South?

To many of you it would be very comforting if this terra-forming of culture could be attributed to a human agenda. But it points to an agenda that is timeless, with unlimited power which plays the Masons, history, culture and landscape in a conspiracy beyond human capability. This questions the *nature of free-will* itself when all the myriad decisions, plans, and human acts expressively organize according to a precise terra-form of hitherto unknown origin.

Does this prove the existence of God's Grace? Does it show a species supra-consciousness? Is it the work of a Gaian Mind, a sentient biology of which we are all a part? It is up to you the reader to pick your *ambrosia*. So, unless the Masons' fess up to the contrary, it is safe to say that we are all exercising our free-will with the illusion of power, when in fact we are integrated with a *will* quite extraordinary, omnipresent, omnipotent, and all pervading.

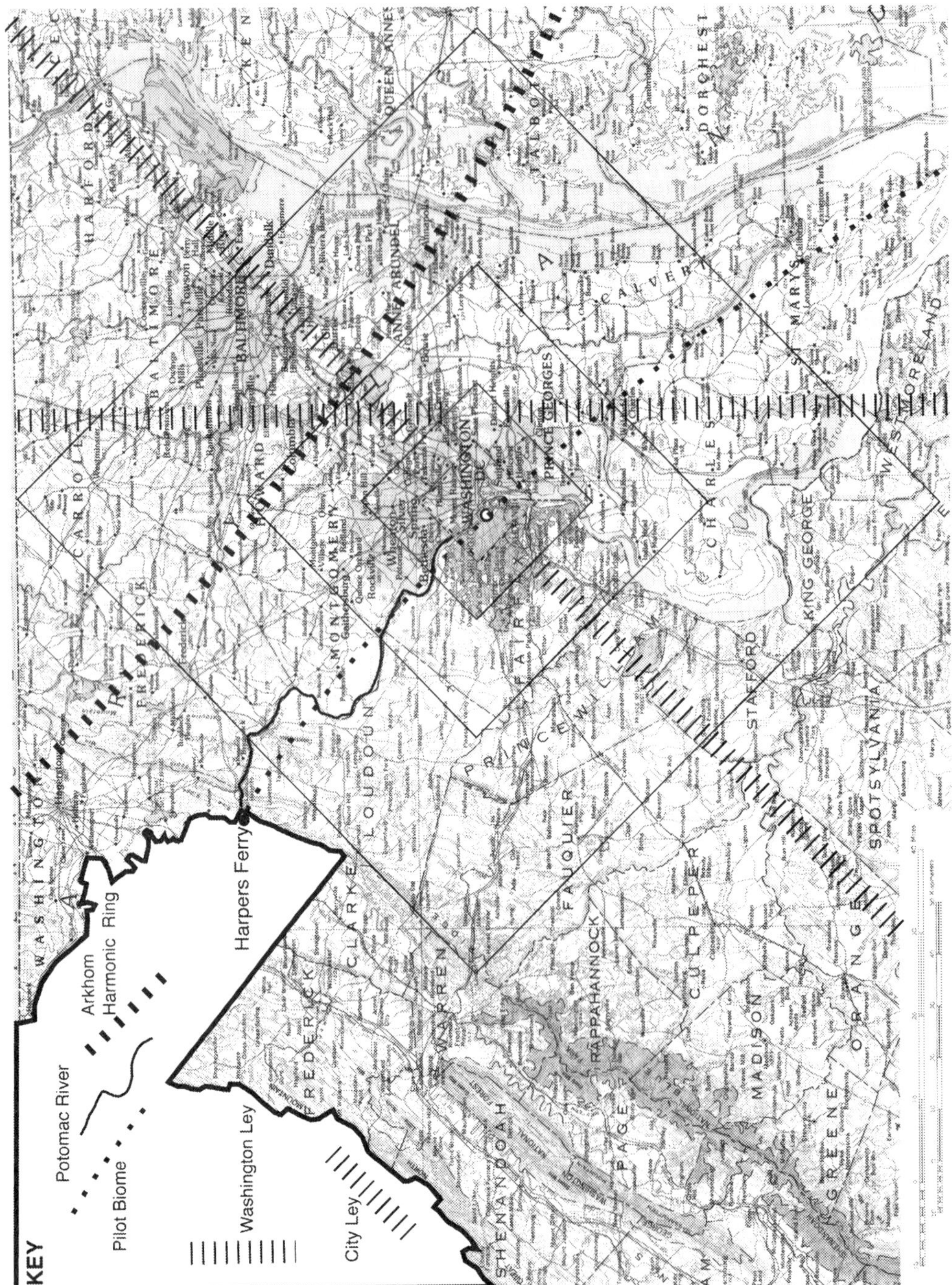

17.14 Washington DC Region

The harmonic expansion of the District of Columbia Square is illustrated in relation to the Southern Biome, Arkhom (1st harmonic), the City Ley, and the Washington Ley. The Harmonic locks DC into the Mason-Dixon Line, and the Appalachian Mountains. The passage of the Potomac River marks the middle of the harmonic's northwest side.

18: The Western Wheels

In the east we witnessed the Gaia Matrix grow from three mountains to a core geometry. We have seen how three fractal expressions grew out of the Gaia Matrix, which match three democratic forms of government. The Three Biomes developed from the next harmonic expansion of the core matrix, Arkhom. All have an interrelated complexity which boggles the mind. Moving westward, the Gaia Matrix expands in harmonic dimension and landscape expression, and a degree of independent power comes on board, distinct unto itself. Within this fourth-level harmonic are the independent countries and cultures of the Caribbean, Central America, the American West, Western Canada, Iceland, Greenland and the newly established self-governing territory of the Inuit Peoples, Nunavut. Opposite one another in this tectonic ring are Iceland and the Yucatan. Iceland, home to two of the oldest cultures in the western hemisphere, has the world's oldest parliament, dating back to the 10th century, while the Yucatan was fertile ground for some of the oldest autocratic societies in the Americas.

Within the borders of the United States, between the Mississippi ring and the West Coast ring, we find the sovereign nations of Native peoples. The following discussion will be limited to the cultures and landscape of this area, since it is the only area geomantically documented to date.

The Great Western Wheel

The discovery by Dorothy Leon of a centric geometry in the American western landscape precipitated our own large-scale study of the effects of land on human society. Called the *Circle with 19 Points* by Leon, this geometry covers a vast area from Canada to Mexico and from the West Coast to the Great Plains. According to Leon, the *Earth Star* is made up of a circular series of nineteen evenly spaced and sized equilateral triangles, which create a circle around the central pole of Grand Teton Mountain. Each of the nineteen triangles is drawn from three major land features that self-organize in this consistently dimensioned triangular pattern.

A signature of the centric geometry discovered by Leon is its preponderance of magnetic anomalies integral to the form. One could call the Earth Star magnetic in nature, a kind of large-scale magneto for the gaian engine. The most salient feature of this, for our purposes, is the circular template of the Earth Star, centered on Grand Teton.

Grand Teton, meaning "Big Breast", was named by the French trappers who, along with the Native peoples and mountain men, recognized it as the center of the North American west. Yearly rendezvous were held there by the French voyageurs. The steep pinnacles of the Tetons are a typical central feature of western geomorphological structures. Evenly spaced around the 1,200-mile-wide circle, Earth Star's nineteen primary points are as follows, from the north point clockwise:

18.1 Grand Tetons Wheel

Dorothy Leon identified this wheel with nineteen triangles on its circumference. Each triangle marks three geographic features of note. Punctuated by geomagnetic anomalies, this geometry nests between the West Coast and Mississippi harmonics of the Gaia Matrix. This form, centered on the Grand Teton mountains, reflects the Yucatan and Nunavut wheels of similar size.

1) Sullivan Lake and Red Deer River, Alberta
2) North Saskatchewan River, Saskatchewan
3) Qu'appele River, Saskatchewan
4) Souris River, Manitoba
5) James River, North Dakota
6) Missouri River, South Dakota
7) Platte River, Nebraska
8) Arkansas River, Kansas
9) Cimarron River, Oklahoma/Kansas
10) Mount Taylor, New Mexico
11) Mount Humphrey and Sedona, Arizona
12) Colorado River (Lake Mead and Lake Mohave), Nevada
13) Mount Whitney, California
14) Lake Tahoe, California
15) Mount Shasta, California
16) Three Sisters, Oregon
17) Mount Rainier, Washington
18) Okanagan Lake, British Columbia
19) Lake Louise and Mount Temple, Alberta

Readily identified by the arc of the Cascades and the Sierra Nevada Mountains, this circle mimics the curve of the west coast. This Great Wheel (or Earth Star) is pertinent to our discussion because it ties into the western boundary of the North American tectonic plate, along the outer harmonic of the Gaia Matrix. Linked with the core geometry centered in the hills of Massachusetts, this western boundary creates a unified field in which the Great Wheel is nested. A mechanistic model of this would be to a fly wheel and its belt, the breadth of the tectonic plate. The New England region represents the spindle around which American culture evolved, and the west increases the culture's dynamic power with its abundance of natural resources, mystical landscape, and technology.

The Great Wheel is a relatively new research subject for us, but there is no doubt that its geomorphology and related social/ historic markers are just as complex as the clustered biome of the east. Dorothy Leon has done an extensive numerological study of the form and an exhaustive documentation of its mountains, faults, and magnetic features. As Leon has stated, it is just a beginning. With technologically enabled mapping techniques, a more precise study of the structure's geography is now possible. For the moment, however, it (as indeed do all of the geometries of scale) holds more questions than answers.

Four Corners and 150 million years ago

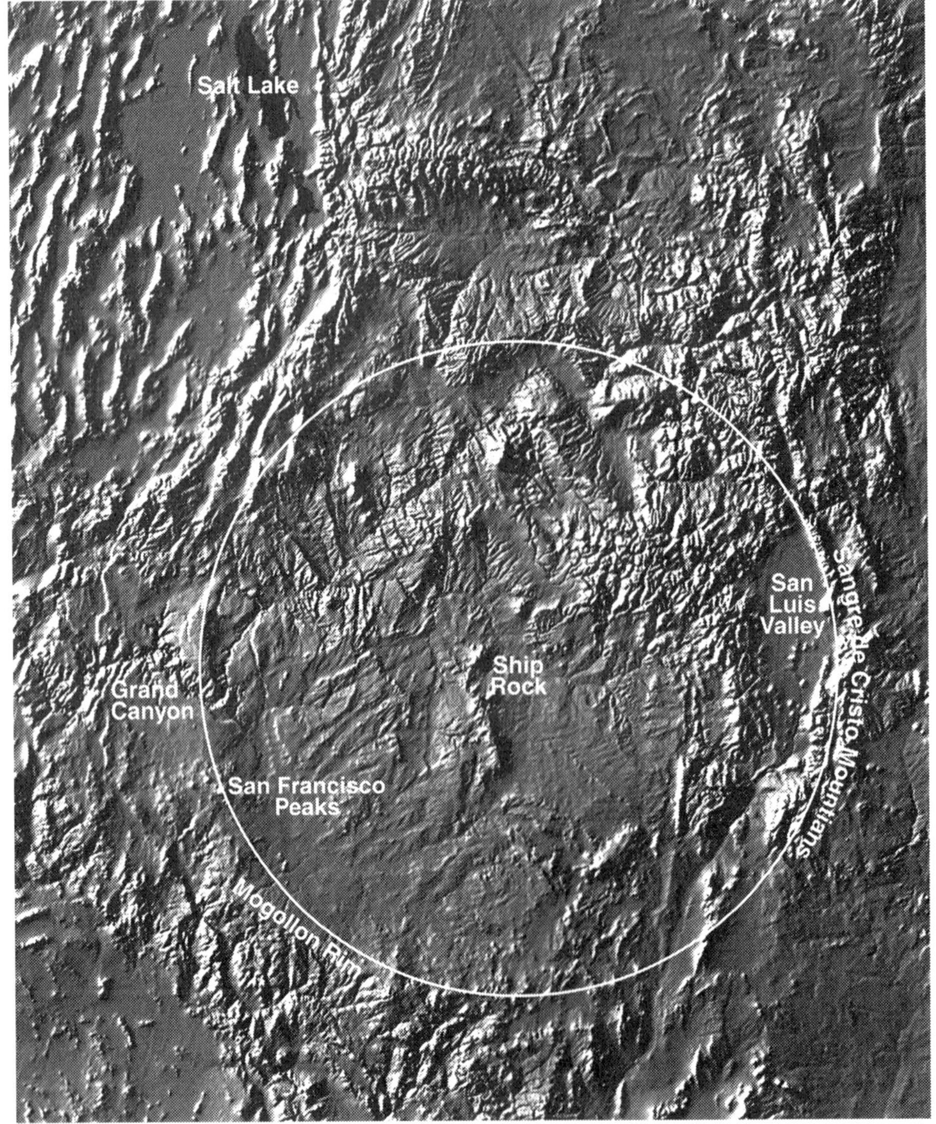

18.2 Four Corners

The geomorphic circular shape of the Four Corners region shows clearly in this Digital Elevation Model of the southwestern United States.

Another preliminary geometric find in the American West is the Four Corner Medicine Wheel. The circle can be seen in most satellite images and Digital Elevation Models of southwestern North America. Centered on the pinnacle of Ship Rock, in Shiprock NM, just southeast of the point where the states of Colorado/ New Mexico/ Arizona / Utah meet, this spin field holds the spirit of what was manifest politically by these four states. Geographically part of the Great Basin, this geomorphic circle is bounded by the High Rocky Mountains to the North, the Sangre de Cristo Mountains to the East, the Mogollon Rim to the South, and the San Francisco Mountains, Grand Canyon, and Colorado River to the West.

You will note that just as the Great Wheel connects to the circular edge of the tectonic plate, the Four Corner Medicine Wheel connects to the southern boundary of the Great Wheel. These greater and lesser circles cross at Mt. Wheeler near Taos NM and at San Francisco Peaks near Flagstaff AZ. Both are holy mountains to the Pueblo peoples of the region. Ship Rock, the center point of the Four Corner Medicine Wheel, is thought to be a rock with wings, or Tse Bi Dahi, in Navajo creation myth. The story is that the original Navajo peoples traveled to this land on the back of this great bird now turned to stone. To the author it looks more like hands clasped in prayer -- the hands of the Great Mother piercing the sky at the center of this sacred space, a prayer of creation at the center of the world.

The Hopi, who have lived within this Medicine Wheel longer than any people, believe that the first humans emerged from the Grand Canyon. A very old and very sacred landscape, this ground has been most coveted of late for its uranium, coal, and hydroelectricity, making it, in secular terms, the power plant of America. Native peoples and many Anglo-Hispanics hold the area within this Medicine Wheel to be of even greater benefit as a spiritual power to Earth/ Human/ Cosmos consciousness and health. Anasazi, "the old ones", built their entire culture within this Wheel. From the Mesa Verde plateau, Ship Rock can be seen as the omphallus of this ancient American culture, with Mesa Verde, Chaco Canyon, and Canyon De Chelly clustered near to its spires.

The circumference of this Medicine Wheel is a contemporary iconographic tale of sacred landscape. When one thinks of the Rocky Mountains, the mountain definitive to their grandeur is Maroon Peak, better known as Maroon Bells. Positioned like a pearl on a string, the Maroon Peak is central to an arcing series of high peaks which scribe the northern edge of this Medicine Wheel. Stretching from the cliffs of Redstone, Colorado to the Taylor Reservoir, this arcing line includes Capital/ Snowmass/ Maroon/ Castle/ Crystal/ and American Flag mountains. In so many words, the Aspen ski complex. It is perhaps the most coveted mountain landscape on the continent. Aspen is known for its silver deposits and also as the playground of the rich and famous. Some of the best skiing in the world can be found there, and in this respect it is held as a sacred icon of contemporary moneyed culture. Land there is so coveted that a small home on a postage-stamp lot can easily fetch one million dollars.

Curving southeasterly the arc cuts through Taylor Reservoir, swings near Monarch Pass and continues along the west slope of the Sangre de Cristo to Blanca Peak. This stroke includes the town of Crestone/ the Baca Grande Land Grant/ and the Great Sand Dunes National Monument. Sangre de Cristo means the Blood of Christ. Like so many droplets of blood in the last light of the setting western sun, the Sangre de Cristo lives up to its name as sacred ground. On its west slope, with a dramatic view of the San Luis Valley's lensic expanse, Crestone is the site of retreat centers for Zen and Tibetan Buddhists, a Carmelite monastery, a Hindu Temple, and other spiritual organizations. It is also home to centers and schools exploring permaculture and ecology. The Manitou Foundation (an Algonquin term, Manitou meaning

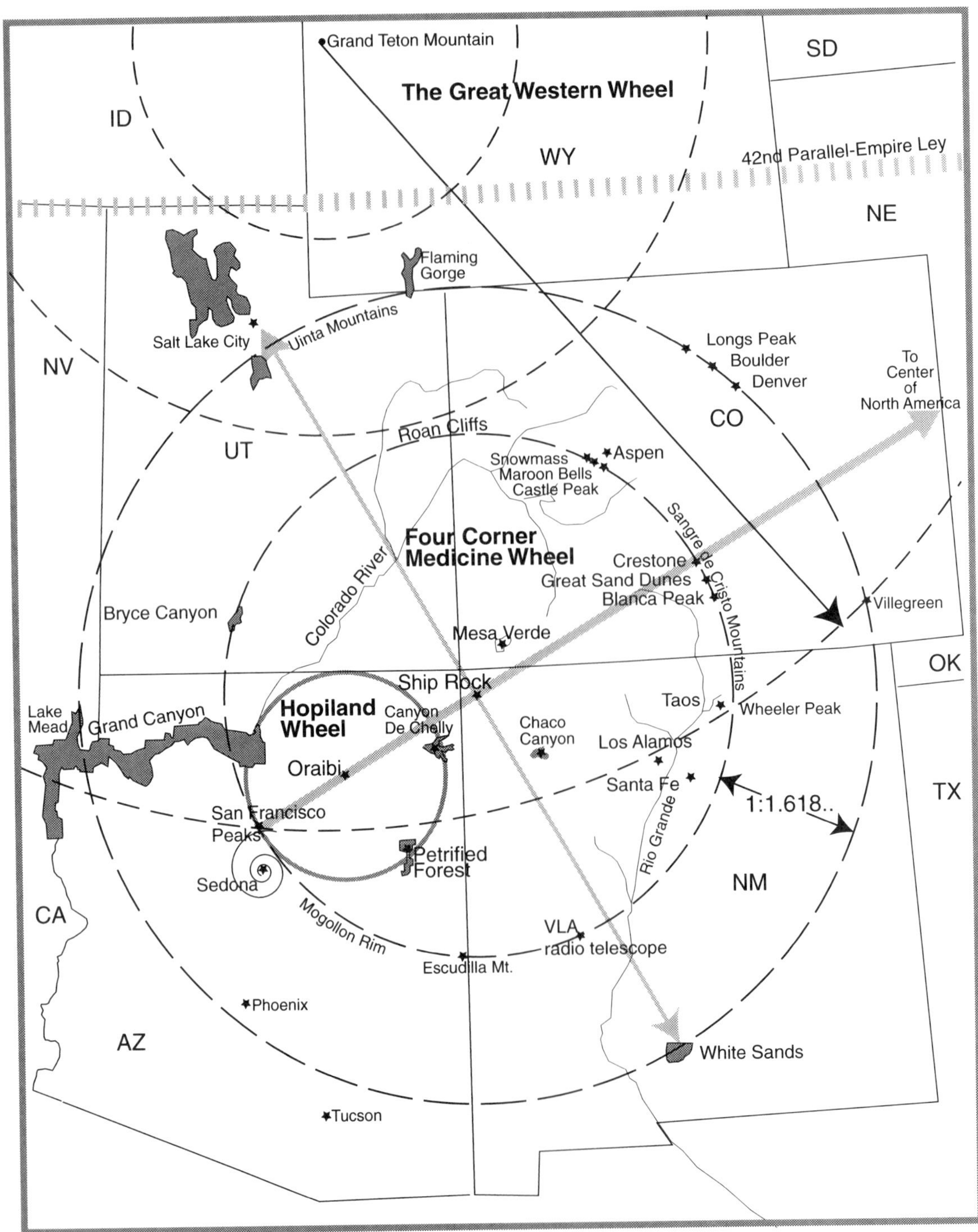

18.3 Western Wheels

This complex graphic depicts the dynamic interplay between the Great Western Wheel centered on Grand Teton, the Four Corner Wheel centered on Ship Rock, and the Hopi Wheel centered on Oraibi. All three wheels meet at San Francisco Peaks. An alignment beginning there connects the power of this field to the core geometry of Arkhom, or visa-versa.

"Great Spirit"), offers free land to religious groups to establish retreat centers within the Baca Grande development. The mountains which form the backdrop of this Holy City are reminiscent of holy mountains of the world. This varied mountain terrain, likened to the silhouettes of all the major sacred mountains of the world reflects the diversity of religious ideals. A kind of Mecca to some, the Baca Grande is a contemporary expression of the Cosmic Christ and the unity of religious ideals.

South of the Baca lies the Great Sand Dunes National Monument. As beautiful as it is mysterious in its soft, stark contrast to the jagged mountainous backdrop, this localized geologic, environmental phenomenon has baffled scientists since its discovery. Ending the arc of the Sangre de Cristo Mountains is Blanca Peak. Metaphorically, this whirling form is like a shooting star with the Sangre de Christo trailing behind like so much star dust. A killer mountain, its talus slopes have four arms that curve outward from its peak, forming a swastika-like vortex. (Throughout world cultures the swastika is connected with life-enhancing wholeness and is not to be confused with the bastardized swastika popularized by the Nazis.)

Beginning at the Colorado/ New Mexico border, the second half of the Sangre de Cristo's arcing course passes over Wheeler Peak above Taos and Turchas Peak above Santa Fe. As stated earlier, the Great Wheel, centered on Grand Teton, intersects the Medicine Wheel at Wheeler Peak. Being the convergence of two very large geomagnetic/ geomorphic/ Gaia Matrix fields, the Taos area has been the center of Pueblo culture and trade for centuries.This point is known for an auditory phenomena called the "Taos Hum". This sound has been attributed to a top secret military installation there; however, it may be a result of the interpenetration of the two wheels, a low F, not unlike the hum of whirling turbines of power plants. A similar low F was heard in the Northeast kingdom of Vermont with widespread reports coming from multiple sources.

South of Taos, Santa Fe is a land of artists. The unique light, land, and people of this region have inspired many, from the builders of the miraculous Lorretto Chapel, to Georgia O'Keefe, to the thousands who flock there with beads and bells and books on Indian lore. Once a place considered a cultural center, Santa Fe suffers the same fate as Aspen of being -- coveted and crushed by its popularity.

Winging south through Glorieta Mesa, the Galisteo Valley, and over the Manzano mountains through Ladron Peak, our next stop is the Very Large Array (VLA) astronomical radio telescope. Placed in the middle of the Plains of San Augustin, seventeen miles of rail tracks carry twenty-seven movable dish antennas. From here scientists are studying the nature of the physical universe. It has become an icon associated with the mysteries of creation, the big bang, the SETI (Search for Extra Terrestrial Intelligence) project and the makeup of clusters of galaxies. From one Medicine Wheel to another, galaxies both land-based and star-studded, share a common engine of Grace generating their form.

Passing through Apache country we enter the highlands of Arizona along the geologic structure called the Mogollon Rim. Bisecting Arizona diagonally, it separates the Sonoran Desert in the south from the Painted Desert in the north. The home of the White Mountain Apache, the Mogollan Rim's southern slopes were also settled by a branch of the Anasazi culture. Some of Arizona's most pristine wilderness lands are there. Striking a northwestern alignment, the Rim points to the San Francisco Peaks and the Grand Canyon.

Saint Francis of Assisi, for whom the San Francisco Peaks were named, is a Saint associated with God's Grace expressed through nature. The Peaks are considered the home of spirit beings, the Kachinas, by both the Hopi and Navajo peoples. Another crossing of the Great Wheel and the Four Corner Medicine Wheel, the San Francisco Peaks are the center of a dynamic flow of earth energies.

To the south of this convergence is Sedona. Known contemporarily for its "vortices", it is a kind of center for New Age thinking. The earth energies of this place are so strong that nearly anyone can feel them. Because of this natural phenomena, Sedona has become synonymous with earth energies. When two moving waters meet what happens? Vortices. In a similar way, the Sedona vortices are simply a release of energy generated by the crossing of the Great Wheel and the Four Corner Medicine Wheel well to the north. The Sedona experience is thus a case of being enraptured by effect. It just feels good to a feel-good culture.

Northward from the Peaks we cross the Grand Canyon at Sublime Point, the approximate divide of the Grand and Marble Canyons along the Colorado River. Touching on Bryce Canyon, the Wheel includes Arches and all of the national parks and recreation areas of southeastern Utah. Curving around the Roan Cliffs, the hoop completes its circle at our starting point of Redstone Castle in Redstone, Colorado.

In total, the Four Corner Medicine Wheel is a creation process ongoing for the last one hundred and fifty million years or more. Doorway to the heart of the American Southwest, it is home to some of the most profound expressions of the American spirit, both native and imported.

Hopi Land - Heartbeat of America

The Hopi people have lived on their traditional lands perhaps longer than any known culture. Their myth has it that the first Hopi people emerged from the Grand Canyon. Groups of the people wandered the four directions before returning to their mesa home. The traditional Hopi believe that what happens to the Hopi happens to the world. They wrote of this in their newsletter concerning Hopi Land:

> The Great Spirit has marked out this part of the land for the Hopi to live upon. We will not forget His spiritual knowledge and wisdom by which the Hopi are to take care of the land and feed His children while communicating with the nature forces for their health. The Hopi must plant seeds and watch them grow, he must pay attention to the signs of change in natural order. He must watch with close attention the behavior of all life on earth. Any change or odd behavior will be the sign that the natural order of the earth is getting out of balance. The Hopi believe that Hopi Land is the Spiritual Center where changes will be visible to the trained mind and eye.

One might ask what Hopi Land is. The Bureau of Indian Affairs sees it as a reservation within the Navajo reservation in northeastern Arizona. A traditional Hopi might define Hopi Land as the whole planet. Geomorphic analysis of Hopi Land places Oraibi AZ at the center of their spin field, as this was the spot where Maasaw, their world teacher, imparted the knowledge and path of Hopi spirituality to the

People. Other indicators of their boundaries are suggested in their reverence for both the Grand Canyon where they emerged into the world, and the San Francisco Peaks where the Kachinas (spirit beings) and a band of Hopi live. By striking a radius from Oraibi to the Peaks, the area of Hopi Land is defined. Tribes still migrate from Oraibi to the Peaks yearly during late July through August into September. Scribing this circle encompasses all of the present-day Hopi and Navajo lands to the New Mexico and Utah borders. You will note that this circle intersects the Great Wheel and Four Corner Medicine Wheel at the common ground of the Kachinas, San Francisco Peaks.

Assuming that the Hopi belief is true, that their actions impact the balance of the world-- By what mechanism are their actions transferred to the gaian mind? The Hopi have a 216-day ceremonial cycle performed by their women's and men's groups according to season, based on an agricultural cosmology. Many of these ceremonies take them to sacred sites like the Peaks and Grand Canyon. Through this ceremonial cycle crop growth and tribal health are insured. Rain ceremonies and planting ceremonies affect not only the tribe, but the whole Earth from this place. The Traditional Hopi take personal responsibility seriously. The Hopi have a huge lesson for us all with this sense of responsibility. Traditional practices observing natural cycles, even simply growing corn and praying to these plants contributes to a world in balance.

With every turning of the seasons, the Hopi turn their ceremonial wheel. This wheel turns the Four Corner Medicine Wheel, which turns the Great Wheel of the West. The Great Wheel turns the outer harmonic of the North American plate, which spins around its axis point in New England, the focus of North American power. The delicate harmony preserved in Hopi Land keeps the world in balance through the nature of North America's balanced form. Simple and founded on common sense, this premise, if followed to its conclusion, calls for the Hopi Way to be preserved as a national cultural treasure. When the Hopi heart stops beating, so does America's. It's that simple.

This would be a huge weight for the Hopi to bear if it weren't for their humility. We as a united people must support the great work they accomplish in the action of their direct life-ways and ceremony. We must not try, as we have for the past 300 years, to bring them into "mainstream" belief and life-style. A big issue in Hopi Land today is the strip mining of Big Mountain. A sacred site, this act in itself may be just the straw that breaks the Hopi heart. This disputed land is claimed by both Hopi and Navajo, and the Peabody coal company, who owns the mineral rights thanks to an obscure mining law from the 1800's. Peabody, a Mormon-owned company, is shooting itself in the foot with this one. The electric power plant of the region needs coal and water to slurry it there. Big Mountain is the closest deposit, so it makes sense in the morality of maximized profits for this short-term gain to take precedence over Native beliefs about a mountain. Profit now and pay for it later with the demise of our ecosystem. The interplay of land energies couldn't be more clear on this.

The Four Corner and Hopi Wheels have a ley alignment which is the path taken by the Hopi prayers to the Gaia Matrix they enliven. This alignment is arguably the most important to the spiritual and physical health of North America. One might consider it to be the powercord delivering the juice from the Magneto Great Wheel to the drive matrix or engine of North America.This alignment is called the Kachina Ley in honor of those spirit beings whose home is the San Francisco Peaks. From this portal of power, the ley makes an arc across the continent to what appears to be Shelburne Falls MA, give or take a hundred miles. It starts from the San Francisco Peaks / heads northwesterly through the Hopi town of Oraibi at the center of the Hopi Wheel / to Ship Rock at the center of the Four Corner Medicine Wheel. From there it passes through Crestone, that city of light in the Sangre de Cristo Mountains and / across the continent to the Arkhom Gaia Matrix.

Located at a right angle perpendicular to the Kachina Ley, in alignment with Ship Rock, is Salt Lake City. Given Salt Lake's place in this scheme of things, a look at the Mormons may shed some light on the subject.

18.4 Joseph Smith Obelisk

This memorial in Sharon VT honors the birthplace of Joseph Smith, the founder of the Church of Jesus Christ of Latter-Day Saints. He lived for ten years at this point on the alignment between Mounts Ascutney and Mansfield, on the initializing triangle of the Gaia Matrix. The bright reflection at the tip of the obelisk was captured the day before our visit by a Mormon Sister and speaks of the light of Joseph's revelation which later spanned the continent.

The Mormons

The Mormon Church got its start from the revelation of Joseph Smith and a visitation on the Hill Comorah from the Angel Morni, who gave Smith the Golden Tablets which are the basis of the Mormon Bible. This revelation was that Jesus came to America after his resurrection, and taught the indigenous people the "Way". It would thereby be preserved for a latter time when people had lost its true teaching after centuries of translations. (Apologies are extended to all Mormons for this short description. The Book of Mormon is available free to all through the Mormon Church if this strikes a chord.)

Joseph Smith was born in Sharon VT in the center of one of the highest concentrations of Early Sites in New England. In the White River valley, where Sharon is located, there are many megalithic calendar sites of note. From an early age Smith was exposed to these enigmatic structures and their associated vibratory signature, which no doubt unlocked some racial memories during his formative early life. At a young age Smith and his family moved to western New York State, after three years of failed crops in the rocky soils of Vermont. Establishing themselves in Palmyra NY in the middle of what once was Iroquois country, the young Smith was again exposed to remnants of an archaic culture with its oral tradition of a great teacher known as the Peacemaker. Perhaps his sensitivity to these ancient cultures and his exposure to them were factors contributing to his revelations. From this town of Palmyra, Smith and followers embarked on the adventure which made a desert bloom.

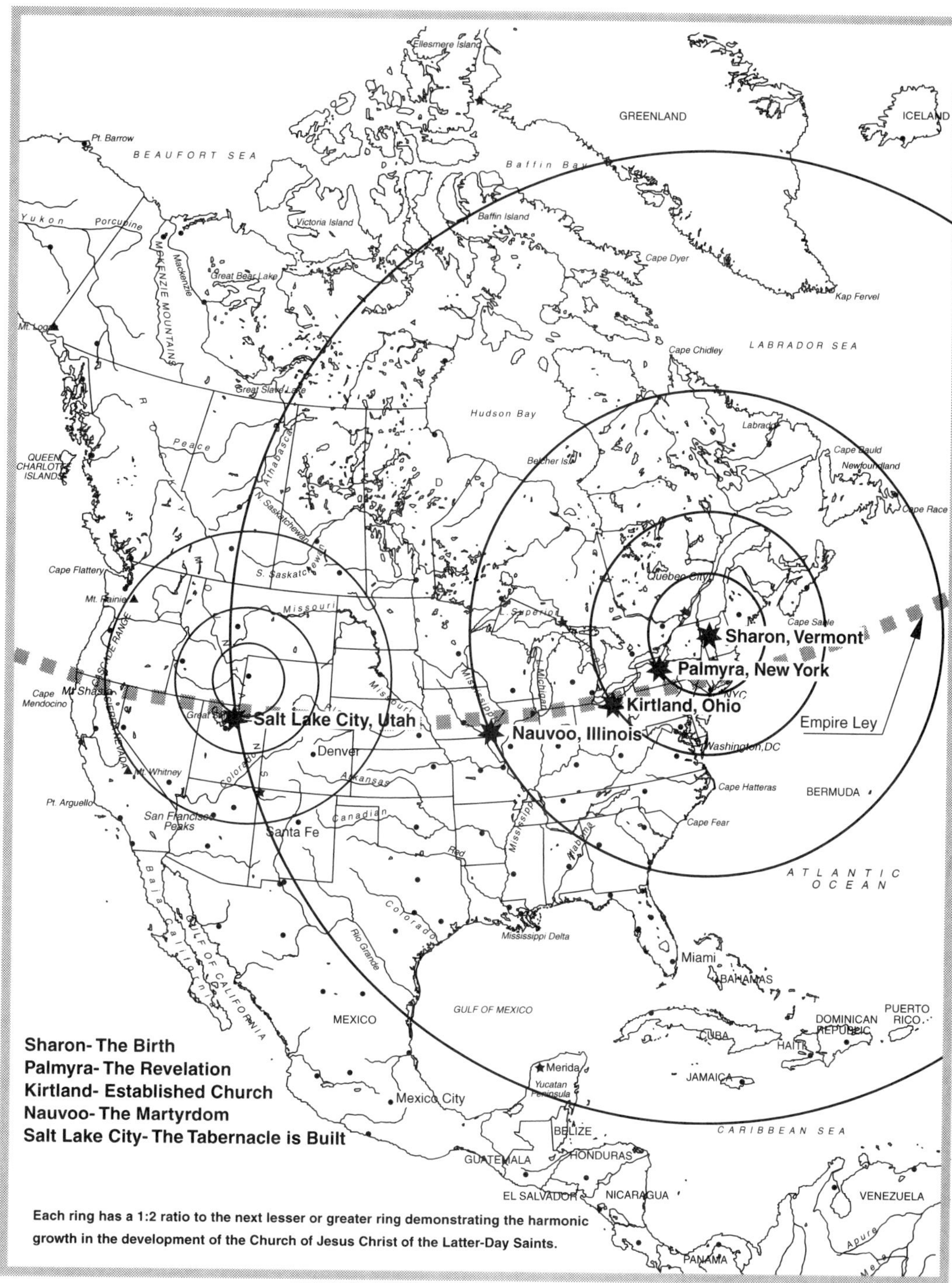

18.5 The Harmonic Expansion of Mormonism

This map traces the development of Mormonism. Their pilgrims' progress west followed a harmonic progression similar to, yet different from the rest of the Gaia Matrix. This gave the faith its connective power but set the group apart from the emerging social collective.

Western New York, you will remember, is within the first-level harmonic of the Gaia Matrix. With Smith's birthplace-- Sharon VT on the alignment from Mount Mansfield to Mount Ascutney, and Palmyra located next to NewARK NY, numerous correlations can be drawn the Gaia Matrix. To honor Smith's birthplace an obelisk was placed there, further strengthening the line and the power of that neck of the woods. This obelisk was hewn from a single piece of flawless *Barre Vermont Granite(see 18.4)*. From the place of this obelisk the message of Mormonism has spread across the land.

The trek of the Mormons originated out of the formative mountain triangle of the Gaia Matrix. The harmonic growth of Mormonism expands in a 1: 2 ratio. Sharon to Palmyra (1) Sharon to Kirtland, Ohio (2) Sharon to Nauvoo, Illinois (4) Sharon to Salt Lake City (8). The regularity of this expansion is illustrated in the accompanying graphic. Whatever the divine purpose the Mormons bring to the world, the space, place, and grace of their revelation and expansion proves their intimate or intuitive relationship with the American landscape and the Great Spirit which presides over its destiny. Yet another proof that seed thoughts originating in the Gaia Matrix grow to become part of the fabric of North American culture.

The fact that the Mormon harmonic originated near the center of the Gaia Matrix, yet apart from its core, accounts for the lack of tolerance for their ways by the culture at large. The Mormon pulse was similar enough to the matrix to support its generation, yet so different a take on the Matrix that the lack of understanding and persecution of the Mormons was inevitable. Settling in the Salt Lake Valley within the independent harmonic field of the West allowed them to create a country and state of mind unto themselves.

Another important figure in the success of Mormonism was Brigham Young. A genius in social architecture and invention, it was the leadership of Young which made the deserts of Utah into a garden (his original irrigation systems design) and home (no nails used) for these much despised faithful. Mister Young was born in Whitingham VT on the *Inner Life* harmonic of Arkhom. These men, powered by this engine of Grace and Providence, driven westward by religious persecution, landed in the Great Land of Zion, the Great Salt Lake Basin. This westward trek was a passage along the Empire Ley of the 42nd parallel, and *King* Brigham did just that -- built himself an empire, 42 wives and all.

18.6 The Angel Moroni on Hill Cumorah, Palmyra

At this site, the Angel Moroni led Joseph Smith to the Golden Tablets containing the tenets of Mormonism. This revelation set the pulse for this truly American religion.

Positioned along the 42nd parallel in a saline solution perpendicular to the Kachina Ley, and within the central harmonic of the Great Magnetic Wheel of the West, Salt Lake and the Mormon Tabernacle are in a place of *kingship* with the land. As we know from history a good *King* preserves the resources for continuity. Certain lands were set aside for hunting, certain for domestic crops, certain for homes, and certain lands for the Temples. In this case "the Temple" includes Hopi Land. If this book gets into the hands of the current Prophet of the Mormon

Church we ask that the work of a good *king* be done, and stop the desecration of your sacred precinct of Big Mountain by the Peabody Coal Company! Harvesting this mountain for its coal is comparable to harvesting the gravel from the glacial drumlin Hill Cumorah, the most sacred site of the Church of Jesus Christ of Latter-Day Saints.

Metro West

A secondary feature which appears to be present within the structure of the western spin fields is the ring of western metropolises. These cities are on a ring which is a phi harmonic greater than the Four Corner Wheel. That is, if one increases the radius of the Four Corner Wheel by 1.618, this phi harmonic is drawn. Centered on Ship Rock, the ring includes Longs Peak/ Boulder/ Denver, as well as the/ arc of the Uinta Mountains/ Flaming Gorge/ White Sands NM. Also scattered around this wheel's circumference, at an equal distance from the line, are Phoenix/ Tucson/ Las Vegas/ Salt Lake City.

These preliminary findings are meant to be an introduction to the possible existence of equally complex geometries throughout North America and the world which are equal to the central Gaia Matrix. In introducing this work, the *what about* questions are inevitable. To answer them would be a prodigious endeavor indeed, requiring more time, research, and authorship than is possible in this book. Offered as models, we hope these studies will afford a greater understanding of the interconnected nature of our world. The Traditional Hopi is clear about his place and grace. One can only imagine the results of conscious, peaceful, prayerful cocreation on a scale the size of the Four Corners Medicine Wheel, or the Earth Star, or the entire planet. The Hopi have survived this long in some of the harshest conditions imaginable *for some reason*. May the teachings of Maasaw be practiced always in peace, in cocreation with Great Spirit.

There is a tendency to possess in the Western mind. In the Native view of the world, respect must be given places that are only God's to possess. That is why the Indians of North Carolina and Maine and New Mexico pay homage to their sacred peaks but leave them in peace. The knowledge of Ship Rock being the center of the Four Corner Medicine Wheel will no doubt attract Bahannas who want to possess it by climbing it, meditating on it, doing magic, or praying on it. This would be sacrilege to the spot and an insult to the Navajo keepers of this holy site. Respect it, honor it from a distance. As you have seen, the greatest action comes at the edge of the storm, not the peaceful center. The Navajo have "No Trespassing" signs all around Ship Rock and they mean it. It is only through mutual respect that humanity evolves. Take a vision/ spirit journey and hold these poles of creation in your heart as a center from which to grow.

Lakota Medicine Wheel

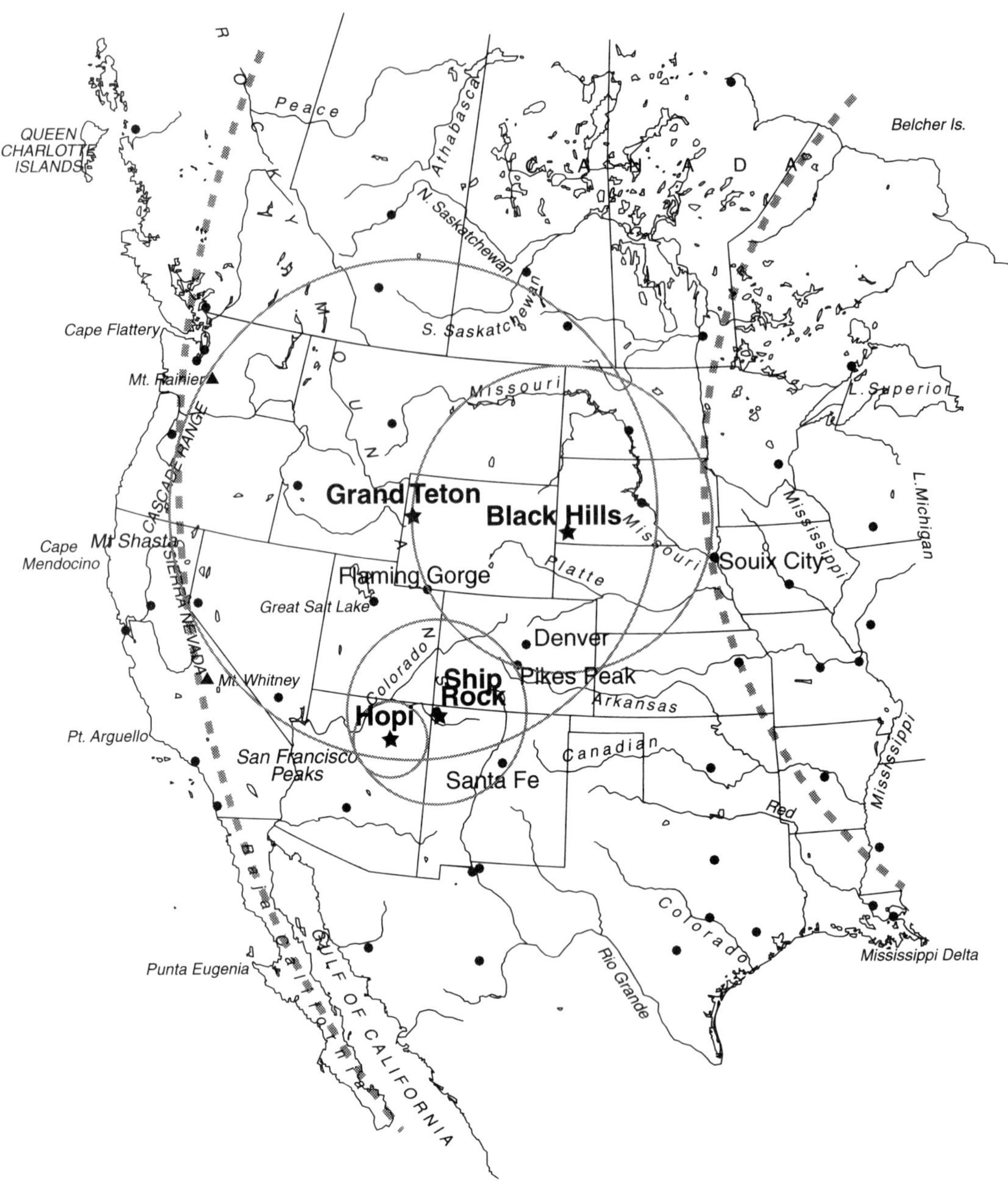

18.7 Lakota Medicine Wheel

The Lakota Medicine Wheel is shown centered on the Black Hills. Please note-- due to map projection inaccuracies-- the Ship Rock Wheel is shown as connecting with the Black Hills Wheel, when in fact the two rings *only* nearly touch in *middle-park* Colorado. The illustration positions the Lakota as the Indian group to take the heat-- in the west, of 'European' expansionism.

Drawn as this book went to press the Lakota wheel is yet another wheel of the west which points to the importance of sovereign native stewardship of these portals of Grace. Centered on Harney Peak, the high point of the Black Hills of South Dakota, this geometry appears to have twelve points. The points delineating its circumference are the Great Wheel's center point Grand Teton/ Leadville/ Pikes Peak/ Sioux City/ and the Canadian Border. This circle includes many tribal lands but predominately those of the Seven Bands of the Teton Sioux, the Lakota Peoples. Sacred mountains for the Lakota and us all, the Black Hills are the gold-filled grounding rods of the Western Wheels. Integral with the Lakota ceremonial cycles, the preservation of both the Black Hills and the Lakota culture are on par with the Hopi as keepers of sacred peaks. Part of the whole, the Lakota Medicine Wheel links the Grand Tetons centerpoint to the harmonic rings defining the continent.

The Kogi of South America, the only tribe to escape the 500 years of western homogenization, speak of the importance of gold as a material that connects the worlds. The gold-filled Black Hills are the golden connection which maintains the vital pulse of the North American spirituality. Thus destruction of these mountains and loss of their keepers would effect the social, spiritual, and environmental health of us all.

The Black Hills are threatened by development and mining. The Lakota Peoples are experiencing a cultural and physical genocide at the hands of the greedy who covet their natural resources. It is through God's grace alone that these people remain to bring their eyes to the vision of the world family. The keepers of this great land for fifty thousand years, the Indian's place and vital contribution must be honored as a priceless cultural resource for the whole earth. The vitality and health of the High Plains and the Gaia Matrix depends on the elevation of the Native Culture to its deserved position as the earthkeepers of Turtle Island, this place that brings balance to the world.

When we as a Western culture honor the mysteries of the Indigenous peoples the cancer in the spirit of America will begin to heal. The King and the Land are one. What was done and continues to be done to the Native peoples must stop. The karma we carry because of this continuing ethnic cleansing of the indigenous people is unconscionable, impacting all of our spiritual lives. Western spiritual evolution is dependent on Native spiritual evolution.

A good start down this road of reconciliation and renewal would be the freeing of the political prisoner, Leonard Peltier. After all, he was only protecting these sacred mountains, his family, tribe, nation, and the white man from himself at Wounded Knee, the wound of the Grail King.

18.7 The Gaia Matrix

19: Conclusion

This Gaia Matrix has grown from a triangle of three mountains to a interconnected biology. We have shown how it helped create three North American democracies and keyed the development of the United States from birth through harmonic expansion to global power. We have presented evidence that geometries, alignments, places of power, and subtle energies have contributed to the success of social programs promoted by The Peacemaker, the Masons, Feminists, Abolitionists, and Mormons.

The nature of the power behind this design remains a question. People will no doubt attribute it to God, devil, humanity, or Gaia, depending upon their predispositions. It is not for me, a singular mortal, to do more than bring this dynamic to light. In any case, the Gaia Matrix reveals that we and the Earth are part of one co-creative evolution. With this knowledge available to all in a free society like the United States, government could take on an organic quality. Having this knowledge we are now separate from the mother who birthed us. We can objectify ourselves as a species, much like the experience of seeing the Earth -- our blue green dot-- from space for the first time. It also shows that we are a biology whose peace is dependent upon the peace of all.

This knowledge might be considered a new freedom for you to ponder, a third freedom. The first was political and religious freedom (American), the second a freedom from physical enslavement, accomplished in our Revolutionary and Civil Wars. This third freedom might be described as a freedom of the soul. A freedom won not through conflict and blood, but through right action, compassion, and love. Freed from the slumber and tyranny of our species, we are revealed as interconnected parts of a whole system instead of the arbitrary, transcendent, individually motivated competitive, and radically separated souls we thought we were. The people and the land are one. This is a thought heard around the world. It announces an evolutionary victory for all the remaining planetary species embodied by Gaia.

Just as John Brown and Sojourner Truth heralded the abolition of slavery through their selfless devotion, so too will the third freedom be accomplished by the inspired actions of each one of us. Every person's voice contributes to the harmony of the greater "song". This era of the empowered individual enhanced by the Internet's global impact, allows us all to be Brown and Truth. Jodi Williams is a contemporary example of how one determined person can change the world. She used the internet to coordinate a global movement to ban land mines. Her efforts resulted in an international treaty signed by most of the worlds' nations-- with the glaring exception of the United States.

One might conclude that computers minimize the need to be connected to the Earth. The success of William's campaign shows the opposite: her home in Putney VT lies on the Chakra Ley at the edge of the Inner Life harmonics of the core Arkhom geometry. In this way, key places in the Gaia Matrix hold greater potential for inserting gaian values into group consciousness.

Knowledge promotes freedom, with freedom comes responsibility, and with responsibility hopefully right action. Perspective may be gained if, for a moment, we accepted the idea that we are reborn to this planet. If you assume that your present deeds affect seven generations to come, then any act of consequence, large or small, will affect the quality of your own next life. Leaving environmental cleanup to the following generations is leaving it for yourself to deal with. Forgoing the short-term profit in favor of your next 10,000 lives makes eminent sense. This freedom walks the talk of an immortal soul. Even if this one lifetime is followed by a place of milk and honey, it will be linked to the unity of all creation, to the heaven or hell propagated in this present life.

The living landscape geometries of the Gaia Matrix have presided over the great human events in the life of the continent, including the conflict between North and South, and those between French, English, and Iroquois overlords. They have keyed the dynamic expansion of a market economy, broadened religious and world views, and promulgated the homogenization of a culture born from the center of the Gaia Matrix. Asserting control over the Matrix, the founding merchant-Masons solidified their control through geomantic artifacts such as obelisks, city design, and battlements.

Focused for the most part on the lower half of the geometry, the cities of the megalopolis have held power for three centuries. The Cycles of Destiny reflected in the core Arkhom geometry orient us to the evolution of our culture. Turning north to wisdom for the next cycle of destiny, a new pulse is released in the land. The impulse went from Boston toward westward expansion, then to the New York / Philadelphia / Baltimore / Washington corridor. The Gaian engine of culture once again spins northward. We can already see expressions of this turning at the grass-roots level: people reflecting holistic gaian values in their everyday lives and communities, organizations, as businesses bring forth cutting-edge, environmentally sound technologies with the help of governments like that of Vermont encouraging "green" values and practices.

The doubling of Arkhom's central heptagon (7 points) yields the harmonic ring on which we find the three portals of democracy. For the past 300 years, the Philadelphia field has dominated the evolution of our political/ economic power structures. But just as the Iroquois Confederacy portal in Seneca Falls yielded its influence to Philadelphia at the completion of its historic ascendancy, so too will the Philadelphia period give way as the gaian Cycle of Destiny points north. Where the Seneca Falls portal propagated a matriarchy and Philadelphia a patriarchy, the next cycle, taking clues from Montreal's sense of place, will be a sacred marriage of the two. The cycle holds the potential for the sharing of power in a holistic model, as opposed to the polarized control of the past.

Turning north to the cogenerative power of the three mountains, the alignment of Mount Ascutney and Mount Mansfield focuses on the island portal of Montreal. The islands comprising metropolitan Montreal portray two figures with place names associated with the divine masculine and feminine. Contained within a Vesica Piscis, they point to the unity of spirit and matter, and male and female, as the essence of the next cycle of power to manifest itself culturally on the continent. A divine marriage of Earth and Sky. This shift of portals, of course, has yet to happen, but there are indications of this shift of power and focus. A subtle energy, it will be an outgrowth of the hand of Grace. Not knowing the time relationship of this shift, it will inevitability be accomplished as indicated by the progression of the previous cycles of destiny.

This treatise contains considerable criticism of American culture. "Love It or Leave It" might be the response of some. Should one love and accept America's angst, moral malaise, violence, and destructive business practices, or should one leave it? At this change of millennium, we are being asked to reinvest the social good of the world family. The 600-year-old message of the Peacemaker still rings true, as does Maasaw's. We have been given the code for life, yet many US corporations use the code to create genetic monsters out of the life-giving grains of the Great Mother. Isn't it time to take a good, hard, objective look at our culture?

The axis of the Gaia Matrix has been shown as a balance point of a yin / yang form that spans the North American tectonic plate. Having this balance and a sense of place unique to the world, North America holds within its soul the potential to bring them to the whole planet. North America holds the potential to bring balance to the whole planet. America's existing global reach illustrates this unrealized promise.

Inequitable allocation of global resources leads to insecurity, poverty, and war. Yugoslavia, with limited native wealth, coveted Kosovo's farmland and mineral resources, mobilizing ethnic hatred for an economic agenda. The United States, with its enormous concentration of resources, has consistently used military and covert action to extend American control over other global raw materials, labor markets, and economic systems. The limited resources of the planet need to be equitably managed to provide for the countries without native wealth. There is a popular misconception that if the American people were placed anywhere on the world, the same wealth would result. But the United States' wealth is directly attributable to the concentration, found nowhere else, of resources with year-round growing seasons. Such plentiful resources! But they are self-righteously squandered while many countries go begging or go to war. As an objectification of the nature of the American culture, this book's intention is not to offend, but is offered as an opportunity to "know thyself"!

By holding a mirror to American culture as it exists now, we underscore the need for our country to fulfill its geomantic destiny: to lead the global human family to balance through equitable management of the world's natural resources, creating peace and plenty for everyone.

Mobile megaliths one and all, we are a sacred species because of our very geometry. As we stand, we connect heaven and earth. We instinctually build sacred space as an inherited biological predilection. The larger the population, the larger the sacred space. A natural course of events suggests that eventually, if we don't kill each other first, a sacred Earth will be the only place large enough to house ten billion people in prayer.

Completing the Universal Ark is a process of emergence and evolution. Potential exists to accelerate this movement toward wholeness. One extreme would turn the Northeast into a Palo Solari model of a mega-environmentally-sustainable city. The other extreme would turn it into a temple of light, existent only in the hearts of the spiritually inclined. To date, built with sundry and seemingly unrelated acts of free-will, the Universal Ark continues to be built as a cocreation of humanity, Gaia, and the Creator-- a project of spirit.

Many parts of world were visited by apparitions of the Black Madonna and similar feminine spirits, which in a Christian world, are 'apparitions' and 'spirits' attributed to Mother Mary. This visitation of the Mother has been going on since time immemorial. In Greek and Aramaic, the original language of Christianity, the Holy Spirit or Ghost was spoken of in a 'feminine' context. One would then surmise that the original Trinity was made up of the father, son, and mother energies. It follows that the feminine manifesting spirit of the creative-God has appeared as the Mother Mary, the Black Madonna, White Buffalo Calf Women, and Lilith, and is in residence as Mother Gaia. Showing herself in concordance with the contemporary mind, we are visited by Gaia. Our Earth is God, as is all Creation. Let's have a little respect here.

A vessel of an emergent consciousness, this naturally occurring social architecture is kept afloat with both clear intention and humility. The Gaia Matrix reveals itself at this time in human evolution so that we may fulfill our promise as cocreative beings. The Hopi exemplify this with a living prayer cycle that includes 216 ceremonial days a year tied to patterns of planting, growth, and internalization. Through prayerful interaction with everyday life, they reinforcing the health of the land and community and keep the world in balance. It is an acknowledged truth that, when the Hopi stop planting their corn, the world falls out of balance.

We are not all Hopi, so it would be inappropriate for everyone to live in this manner. What we suggest is that, if our culture walked, drove, played, worked, produced, and made love and decisions in a framework of spiritual intention in sync with the cycles of nature, all would be well in the garden again. Every act, every individual and corporate act, made in a conscious, spirited, prayerful manner, impacts the vitality of the common unity.

Much remains to be discovered. Together we can renew the Ark, the Gaia Matrix, and truly make it our home. All we need is to have a little respect here, not another religion. Our Earth is God, as is all Creation. A pole of evolutionary power, this spirit of the Earth also needs our pioneering efforts to cocreate a world of peace, unity, equality, abundance, and true freedom. The geometrics of destiny points the way.

19.1 Creator with Compass

Space for you... These pages were intentionally left blank for you.

You are the foremost contributor.

It is only through the eyes of the many that we can truly see the world. The expression of this relationship is as diverse as each of you. May this information serve you as an expression of hope, love, and being... in the end making us all more respectful, appreciative, involved -- evolved examples of our species-- hue / man.

20: Your Ark

21: Celestial Ark

The Arkhom geometric model is one of many grids one can map on the Earth. In fact there are so many grids that if one were to map them all there would be nothing but graphite. One primary planetary grid pattern is the Becker and Hagens UVG, the bone of the planet, its crystalline form. Spun over this lattice work is the web of the Arkhom grid. A biospheric web, like muscles and organs, Arkhom in this case is the stuff between the lines. Line and point, the two match at five different vectors, in the Arkhom geometry. One of the traditional forms used to depict an Ark is a basket. This next evolution is brought to you by Bethe Hagens and her Celestial Ark.

The Celestial Basket was first presented in the summer of 1999 in Tenerife, Canary Islands at the Oxford VI International Archaeoastronomy Conference. It will be published in the forthcoming Conference Proceedings and is published herein with the permission of the author (c. Bethe Hagens).

Celestial Basket

by Bethe Hagens, Ph.D

For some twenty years now, I have worked from the perspectives of art, geometry, and anthropology to understand how human beings "see". I visualize an eclectic, integrated ancient geometric art / science in which certain principles of shape and connection applied equally well to body, mind, and soul— earth, animals, and sky. I have intentionally filled this presentation with questions, and I am painfully aware of how broadly I am casting the net. The geometry I call the ***Celestial Basket*** is, at the very least, a teaching tool and data-storage mnemonic. I am presenting it in the spirit of Mnemosyne, the Greek goddess of Memory and daughter of Gaia, from whose name we get the word "geometry".

Some of my earliest research involved figures from Upper Paleolithic Europe known in the vernacular as "Venus figurines." Marija Gimbutas pioneered the scholarly attempt to label them as representations of the Divine feminine, "goddesses." I noticed the startling similarity of the earliest of these figures (dating from 21,000 to 12,000 BCE) to the midbrains of animals, particularly reptiles and birds. It became clear to me that ancient humans were superb anatomists and were fascinated by ambiguity, especially in their artwork. (Hagens 1991)

Concurrently, I studied two of Plato's texts that I now believe have the potential to make a major contribution to archaeoastronomy. The first book, *Timaeus* (Desmond Lee translation, 1965), outlines virtually every principle of R. Buckminster Fuller's spherical geometry. (Becker and Hagens, unpub. ms. 1991) I was extremely fortunate to work with William S. Becker, a colleague of Fuller, who taught me to "see". By very ancient tradition, it is held that certain enlightened individuals naturally see geometric structure. Others, like myself, must be initiated. I have seriously wondered if Plato was unable to "see". He did not put drawings in his texts and had a difficult time trying to describe what he had been shown. (This may be a problem of translation, and I will need in the future to work with original texts.) In any case *Timaeus* identifies a primordial, vibrating, invisible female geometric shape (*the* ***Nurse of Becoming***) as an essence that all matter, "above and below", imperfectly approximates. Plato begins the text of the second book, *Critias*, with a "call on the gods, adding the goddess Memory [Mnemosyne] in particular... For my whole narrative depends largely on her." The geometric mnemonic is lost on most readers--as are the connections between astronomy, cultural history, and the precession of earth's axial pole. The text is widely regarded as an insignificant account of the rise and fall of a fictional utopia called Atlantis.

Humans enjoy the experience of geometry, consciously or not, for they have forever constructed artifacts, landscapes, temples, shrines, and so forth to reflect integrated, highly complex geometric principles. (Becker and Hagens 1993) As human *beings*, we share a deep identity with the "perfect" three-dimensional geometric shapes Plato identifies in his texts (tetrahedron, cube, octahedron, icosahedron, and dodecahedron). These figures are the shapes of the connections between the atoms and molecules of our bodies. We can't actually "see" these connections, but we make assumptions about them based upon structural building principles that apply at other scales of reality. We somewhat unconsciously project these perfect geometries "above and below" and see them as "reality" because they are so aesthetically satisfying and resonant with who we are as intelligent creatures.

Plato's divine Mother, the *Nurse of Becoming*, is an etheric shape made up of 120 identical right triangles. There is only one figure this can be: the spherical hexakis icosahedron. It can be visualized in two ways, however: first, as 120 right triangles joined together symmetrically to create a sphere; and second, as a sphere of 15 identical interlaced hoops, each of which bisects the sphere. Elsewhere (Hagens 1992) I have shown how this figure encompasses all of the perfect solids as well as two important rhomb-based figures identified by Kepler (but known and constructed by the Etruscans). The Nurse of Becoming appears to be the energetic matrix from which (to name just a few) "quasicrystals", viruses, pollen, and microorganisms all grow. Or at least we can handily project this matrix onto what we are able to observe! In the same paper, I show the remarkable and apparently very ancient consistency of esoteric color and element sym-

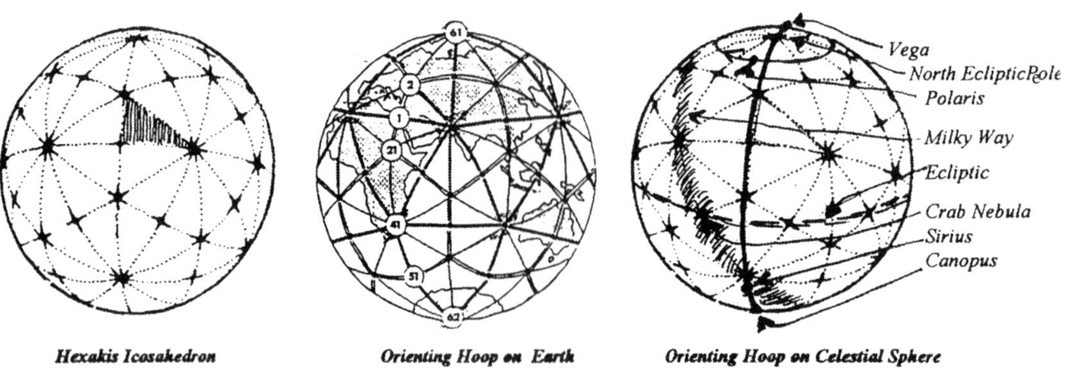

21.1 Celestial Basket

bolism (e.g. earth, air, fire, water, ether) attached to the perfect geometric shapes in cultures around the world. In a Sioux legend about the creation of Mother Earth, the Creator calls "the 15 hoops" to the plane in which Earth is to revolve around the sun. A 16th hoop is its orbit, the ecliptic. An identical geometry of the divine feminine was known on both sides of the Atlantic but was visualized differently.

Pythagoras supposedly taught that geometry (geo = of earth; metr = measure, mother, fate) involved only a single operation: bisecting an angle. (A line is a 180 degree angle.) I have constructed all of the Platonic geometries on the ground with a stick and a piece of vine. I have carved them from soap using the proportions of my hands. I believe Pythagoras! For the initiate, complex geometry is easy. The once controversial idea that ancients engaged in sophisticated earth geometries (e.g., Stecchini 1971), is now almost routinely being stretched to encompass planet -scale geometric alignments of sites (e.g., Hancock and Faiia, 1998).

The scholarly consideration of geometric mapping and siting to take advantage of "earth energies" is a related tradition that extends back at least to the Middle Ages in Western culture, and almost infinitely far in others (Becker and Hagens 1993). Valery Makarov, a Russian engineer, and his colleagues at the USSR Academy of Sciences, made some of the earliest contemporary studies of such a geometric "planetary grid". They proposed a "meaningful" alignment of spherical Platonic geometries in the earth, such that the vertices and edges of the figures marked resource deposits, atmospheric and ocean currents, migrations, archaeological sites, and an array of other phenomena. Becker and I were able to extend Makarov's work by showing the underlying pattern of the hexakisicosahedron. We also identified an "orienting" hoop that connected the north and south geographic poles through the great pyramid at Giza. This was the key insight that led me to "see" the same geometry in the sky. I visited Makarov in Moscow in 1994 to show him my model of the celestial sphere, and he told me that he and his colleagues had suspected that it must exist. Here is what I have found.

A great deal of "natural" geometry can easily be seen in the sky once it is pointed out. The sun and moon, for example, are each approximately 1/2 degree in diameter as seen against the sky, and are possibly a source for the 360 degree circle. One moon, one sun per day: 360 suns and moons make an "ideal" year. I happened to notice on my celestial sphere that Regulus and the Pleiades lie almost on the ecliptic, 90 degrees apart. Midway between them, a meridian can be drawn between Canopus and Sirius (the two brightest stars in the sky) and extended around the celestial sphere through the north and south ecliptic poles. It will run perpendicular to the ecliptic and pass through Vega (the fifth brightest star). I know these stars from their importance in world mythology, but do not even pretend to know astronomy. I simply made the assumption that this must be the orienting hoop. It was a simple task to add the rest of the Celestial Basket. Two things were immediately apparent: (1) one of the fifteen hoops marks the plane of the Milky Way; and (2) the geometry divides the ecliptic into 20 equal segments.

In previous work with the Aztec sun calendar, I have become convinced that part of its genius is that it can be read on multiple levels and is an example of intentional ambiguity. The sex of the central figure is considered ambiguous to this day. On one level, the calendar can be interpreted as a zodiac of 20 houses-

-which could imply a connection to the Platonic geometry. An even stronger relationship is suggested in the zodiac ceiling from the Dendera temple in Egypt. The Dendera zodiac, which is based upon the Pleiades and Regulus as geometric marking points, appears at first to highlight eight segments of 45 degrees; but the upper arms of the figures clearly mark out 20 identical segments of 18 degrees. (A ring of diamonds or "rhombs" of the Celestial Basket creates the 20 segments of the ecliptic--and an ancient derivation of the word *rhomb* is "upper arm".) I used this zodiac as a framework to align three geometries of precession (see ***Solstice Zodiac*** illustration). Drawing heavily upon *Hamlet's Mill* (Santillana and von Dechend 1977), I set the hoop of the Celestial Basket between the Dog and Monkey on the Aztec zodiac; the fish-tongue hanging from the mouth of the central sun figure marks this meridian. On the Dendera zodiac, a fish-shaped marker which symbolizes the precessing pole is positioned at this same location. I superimposed the 12 -equal-segment Greek zodiac and discovered that it aligns with Aztec houses at Taurus, Leo, Scorpio, and Aquarius: signs traditionally highlighted in prophetic books such as the Bible and identified as "fixed signs" by astrologers.

But why would ancients create geometric zodiacs based upon the Celestial Basket? I am pursuing this question by asking three others: (1) Is the summer solstice significant in prophetic zodiacal systems? (2) Is ***Critias*** an allegory and/or cultural history of the consequences of precession? and (3) Do ancient icons use intentionally ambiguous sexual symbolism to represent the dynamics of precession and zodiacal geometry?

The First Question: Significance of the Summer Solstice It occurred to me, working with my celestial sphere, that the position of the summer solstice might be important to prophetic zodiacal systems. At midday on the summer solstice, an arc perpendicular to the ecliptic rising up 66.6 degrees from the sun will target the position of the north celestial pole. As will be explained immediately below, the ecliptic zodiac is a magnification of the essential cosmology played out in polar constellations as the pole proceeds to trace its circular path over the course of 25,920 years. The solstice sun is an easy gauge of the exact precessional time as well as an indicator of any wobbles or inconsistencies in the system.

I immediately noticed the odd coincidence that in 1000 CE, the summer solstice sun fell exactly on the orienting hoop just above Canopus and Sirius. Each of the 20 segments of the ecliptic represents 1296 years in the 25,920 year cycle of precession; I rounded that number to 1300 and assigned a summer solstice date to each geometric divider on the ecliptic. For example, in **12,000 BCE,** half a precession cycle back from **1000 CE,** the summer solstice sun coincided with the orienting meridian below Vega. Dr. Joseph Jochmans has proposed that 11,542 BC is the date Herodotus assigned to the beginning of the Egyptian historic/ mythical calendar. This is very close to 12,000 BCE. My research suggests that 25,920 was a reasonably universal "number of precession," but I feel certain that specific dates and details of the zodiacal calendar were as much a source of debate for astronomers then as now. The Celestial Basket is perhaps best viewed as a window of opportunity. For perhaps the last 25,000 years, it has served as a universal scientific observational framework. But geometry is constant only as an ideal, and it is incredibly illusive given the shifting nature of material phenomena; the pole is always wobbling, and the stars move. In time, the Celestial Basket in the sky will simply disappear.

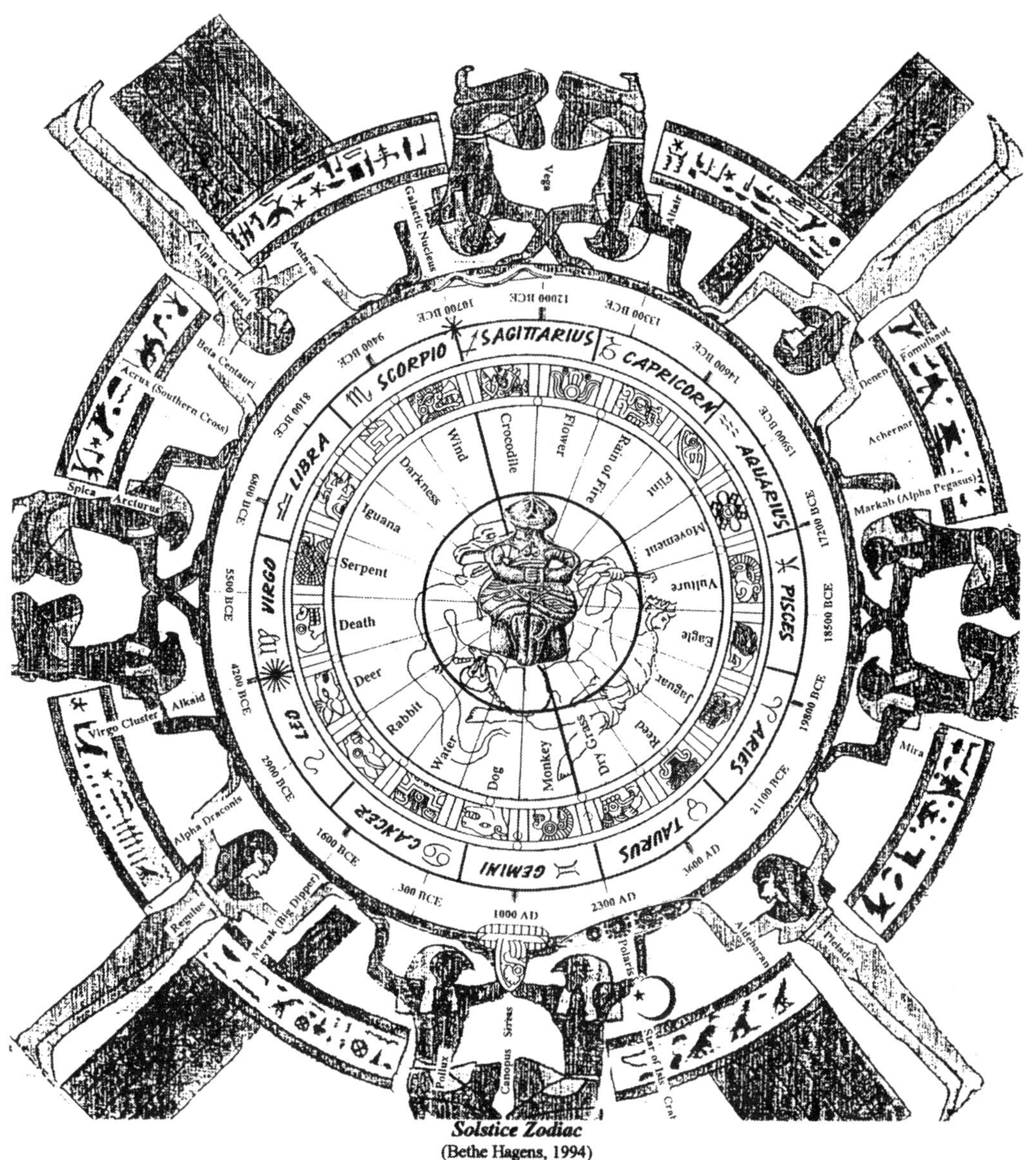

The concentric rings of this zodiac represent the ecliptic. The dates mark the position of the summer solstice in the northern hemisphere, the winter solstice in the southern hemisphere. The Aztec (partly combined with Mayan) and Greek zodiacs are superimposed on the framework of the Dendera zodiac (outer ring). At the center are the constellations surrounding the north ecliptic pole and a Neolithic precession icon, the "Pregnant Goddess" (c. 4500 BCE). The zodiac is read as if looking down on the celestial sphere. Star names indicate alignments with the meridians of the Celestial Basket geometry.

21.2 Solstice Zodiac

One way to gauge use of the Celestial Basket as an observational and predictive system is to look for patterns that emerge if and when solstice dates align with significant events. (Each **bold faced** date is one geometrically determined by the Celestial Basket.) For example, in **6800 BCE,** rice cultivation begins in

Southeast Asia and Catal Huyuk assumes a position of prominence for 1300 years until **5500 BCE**, the date assigned in the Jewish Genesis for the origin of the world (5508 BCE). In **4200 BCE**, Chinese civilization begins in the Yellow River Basin; Indo-European language speakers begin to migrate from the Caucasus; Eskimos and Aleuts speaking off-shoots of Nostratic migrate to North America. **2900 BCE**, marks the beginning of Indus Valley civilization as well as the dynasties in Egypt, the Sumerians begin using North Caucasian words; and a major period of astronomically-oriented megalithic construction begins in Britain. **1600 BCE** brings the end of both the Indus Valley civilization and the Egyptian Middle Kingdom. The Rig Veda is written and King Minos begins his legendary rule at Crete; Thera explodes. **300 BCE** marks the beginning of the Ganges civilization in India, the "classic" Maya in MesoAmerica, the Ptolemaic Dynasty in Egypt, and the high point of the Zhou Dynasty civilization in China. Olmec civilization comes to an end; the Great Jewish Synagogue completes the Canon of the Old Testament and falls from power. Did a system of prophecy drive migration patterns? Does such a system lie behind mythologies of the "moveable feast", where fortune shifts and some places either lose their power in time or are destroyed by natural catastrophes? This would certainly explain the worldwide panic and boom in the construction of observatories around the year **1000 CE**. There was no telling what might happen.

The Second Question: Geometric Stages of Fate in Critias. In Critias a heavenly king (Poseidon) marries a human woman (Cleito). Their ten sons marry and each is given a kingdom (10 kingdoms, 20 royal family members). They live attuned to their father until, over time, they unwittingly fall away from their divine sustenance (the milk of the gods), go to war, and are destroyed by a variety of catastrophes that they should have seem coming. "The survivors of this destruction were an unlettered mountain race who had just heard the names of their rulers but knew little of their achievements...for many generations they and their children were short of bare necessities, and their minds and thoughts were occupied with providing them, to the neglect of earlier history and tradition...This is how the names but not the achievements of these early generations came to be preserved."

Critias is strikingly similar to mythologies associated with the ring of constellations around the north ecliptic pole. A clear correspondence exists between this ring (which is traced by the north axial pole over the course of precession) and the ring of constellations around the ecliptic known as the zodiac. The drama of precessing "ages" in zodiacal constellations also plays out in the polar constellations, and the summer solstice sun indirectly marks our place in the drama. For example, at the present time, an arc of 66.6 degrees extended perpendicular to the ecliptic from the summer solstice sun will fall on Polaris, our current pole star in Ursa Minor. At the ecliptic, for the next few hundred years, the summer solstice sun will shine at the tip of Orion's club. The Celestial Basket reveals how truly exceptional this solar position (at the tip of Orion's club) really is: it marks the intersection of the Milky Way, the ecliptic, and the Crab Nebula. Most ancient zodiacs (e.g. Aztec, Mayan, and Hindu) mark this zodiacal date as the end of a major cycle in time. At this same time, the north axial pole is maximally oriented *away* from the center of the galaxy; Polaris (the dog's tail or *cynosure*) is the "call to attention". (Allen, 1963) As precession continues, the pole will pass up through the chakras of the body of Cepheus, "an inconspicuous constellation, but evidently highly regarded in early times as the father of the Royal Family." (Allen 1963) Cepheus' head is surrounded and illuminated by the Milky Way: he is wise, "cephalic." Over the next several thousand years, the pole will move into his upper chakras, out of his body, through the wings of Cygnus, and finally into Lyra (the harp of Hermes the trickster). For several thousand years the pole will be very nearly parallel to the Milky Way. Marija Gimbutas identified this time in the previous precession cycle, from **21,000 BCE** until **12,000 BCE**, as the period during which the "Venus figurines" (bird-reptile-brain icons) were made. At approximately **12,000 BCE**, the pole moved into Draco which according to Allen, is most commonly portrayed as a combination bird/reptile, the "tempter of Eve in the Garden." While Draco wraps entirely around the ecliptic pole, the path of the celestial pole traces much of its body for nearly half a precession cycle. By **10,700 BCE**, the pole reached the head of Draco. At that time, greenhouse gases began to build up; the North Atlantic Deep Water Current suddenly turned on, and soon after the northern ice sheets began to melt. A major meteor struck the north Atlantic. Plato's date for the demise of Atlantis is **9400 BCE** when the pole reached Draco's jaws: the Gulf Stream suddenly stopped and the first wave of Na-Dene speakers migrated from Asia into Alaska and Canada. From **9400 BCE** until **8100 BCE**, the neolithic agricultural revolution began and spread through Turkey. This latter date marks the end of the Pleistocene and beginning of the Holocene, our current biological era which now stands threatened.

The Third Question: Intentionally Ambiguous Sexual Symbolism of Precession I picture the celestial pole as a vector floating peacefully in the Milky Way during a Golden Age that extends from **21,000 BCE** until **12,000 BCE**--the period during which the Venus figurines/brain representations were made. An extremely curious property of these "buxom" Venus figures is that, if turned upside down and sideways, the image clearly reads as a rather emaciated male with an enormous erection. They may even symbolize a balance of mind/body, male/female energies authors such as Gimbutas have proposed for the cultures of this time. I imagine a shift in consciousness on Earth brought about by the "polarization" of precession--an increase in the angle of orientation of the pole vector with respect to the plane of the Milky Way. If the Venuses are representations of brain stems of birds and reptiles, there is a strong temptation to relate them to Draco. Perhaps the "Eve" mythology ultimately stems from a one-sided perception of these icons.

The mid-5th millennium "Pregnant Goddess" from east-central Europe sketched at the center of the *Solstice Zodiac* above may relate directly to Plato's royal couple in *Critias*, the earthly queen Cleito (root of *clitoris*) and divine king Poseidon (root of *potent* and *seed*). This mid-5th millennium Neolithic clay figure from Bulgaria has rhombs encircling her waist and a prominent pubic triangle marked with a double spiral that could suggest the gyroscopic motion of precession. She can be seen as an elephant and is in this way reminiscent of Ganesh, the Hindu divinity of transition and change. Alternately, she can be seen as a hippo and calls to mind Taweret, a much-loved Egyptian goddess who protects women in childbirth and appears in the position of the north ecliptic pole on the Dendera zodiac. While very consistently described in the literature as female (Gimbutas 1989), her head and neck--if not her entire backside--are an unambiguous representation of male genitalia. Her legs join together at a representation of a bull. She is clearly intentionally ambiguous. Viewed from above, she is a zodiac and almost certainly a representation of the transitional energy of precession. Her body is a perfect circle, her head offset 18 degrees (1/20 of the circle) from the line of her legs. This 18 degree angle is characteristic of many similar figures from this period.

Why would the ancients create geometric zodiacs? Possibly for the same reason I have recreated them. The ancient Egyptian word for geometry of the Celestial Basket was *MR*; the same sound also meant love, death, and the energy of cultivation. Geometry is a phenomenal tool for personal growth. In Greek, a very similar sound, *Moire*, means Fate. Geometry is an elusive and captivating mystery. The divine Christian feminine is *Mary*. I feel an extremely sacred and comforting Presence when I engage in this work.

*"**The Paradise paper**" was given as an invited keynote lecture in 1992 to the 24th Annual "Meeting in Finland", an international congress sponsored by the Association of Finnish Adult Education Organizations. It was first published in the Conference Proceedings and presented again at the 1994 Annual Meeting of the American Anthropological Association. It is reprinted here with the permission of the author (c. Bethe Hagens).*

Dreaming the Lost Geometry of Prophecy:

The Legend of Paradise and Precession

by Bethe Hagens, Ph.D.

There is a secret stone, hidden in a deep well,
worthless and rejected, concealed in dung or filth.
It is a thing which is found everywhere,
which is a stone and no stone,
contemptible and precious,
hidden, concealed, and yet known to everyone.

So many metaphors are encapsulated in legends of this secret alchemical stone, the Philosopher's Stone, that it is almost impossible to know where to begin. Buried within the self, within the everyday world, within life itself, is a common essence-- a *shape*, a creative vessel in which the elements of creation are mixed and transformed. This "stone which is no stone" is intangible--a metaphor as deep as Breath, as profound as Love, and as intelligent as Light. It is an ideal form, one that can be grasped by the intellect but never actually seen. Eternal and unchanging, it is the sacred container of ever-changing cosmic processes-- the *Rock of Ages*. It is an image that sheds light on form, gives the illusion of predictability or "memory" to events that might otherwise seem random.

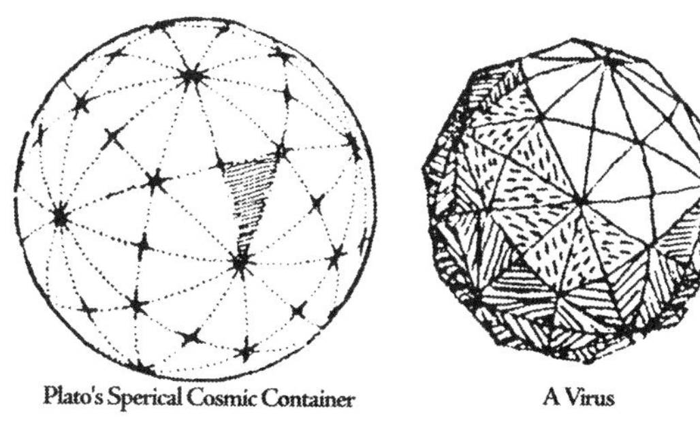

21.3 Plato's Earth (left), Virus (right).

Plato used a kind of Philosopher's Stone to organize his teachings about the origins of life. He called it the ideal body of the cosmos, a perfect composite sphere of 120 rounded triangles that "contained" five dynamic creative elements: Fire, Earth, Air, Water, and Aether (Life Energy). Great spiritual leaders among the Indian tribes of North America had remarkably similar visions. The Sioux universe, for example, was also spherical and contained the same five creative elements. In the Beginning, they said, the universe was composed of numberless hoops, each a kind of skeleton with no substance. All was orbits within orbits within orbits. Primordial Earth was made up of sixteen sacred hoops, to which the Creator called the various powers and manifestations of material reality. Fifteen of these hoops interlocked to create a sphere of 120 triangles identical to Plato's. The sixteenth was Earth's orbit around the sun -- the ecliptic.

Most, if not all, of the world's cosmologies accord to the same five dynamic elements primary roles in the transformation of the material cosmos -- the *environment.* "Fire" is purification. "Earth" a principle of materialization, "Air" a cosmic cycle of breath, "Water" flow, and "Aether" a refinement. In the Platonic cosmos, each element was symbolized by one of five perfectly symmetrical geometric shapes (the so-called Platonic solids). These same shapes were well-known and modeled by many earlier cultures, though *geometry* (the art/science of Earth measuring) is usually attributed to the Greeks.

These perfect geometric shapes are all "contained" in the Platonic Philosopher's Stone. Each one can be enclosed by the 15-hoop, 120-triangle sphere in such a way that its corners fall *only* on corners of the triangles. In this way, the Stone organizes; it is hidden, found everywhere. It is the masterplan of natural structure.

The perfect shapes can be seen at virtually every scale imaginable, from galactic walls to crystals, pollen grains and plankton. The microscopic protein shell of many common viruses (shown above) is actually a structural *nesting* of two of the shapes-- the icosahedron (Water) and the dodecahedron (Life Energy). It can be thought of as the crystalline materialization of the perfectly spherical Philosopher's Stone. Even Plato's elemental symbolism applies to the virus. Viruses are now being identified as primary agents of the evolutionary process (Life Energy) that can proceed only within the fluids of a host cell (Water). The words *virus and environment* stem from an identical linguistic root.

Plato arranged the elements in order of increasing geometric complexity, from the most *basic* (the tetrahedron) to the most complex and difficult to construct (the dodecahedron). Scientists today use an identical geometric hierarchy to explain principles of molecular and cellular growth and bonding. The most basic molecule, for example, is modeled as if it consisted of four atoms (energy bundles) spaced equidistantly from each other at the corners of a tetrahedron (Plato's first element, Fire). The same model is used

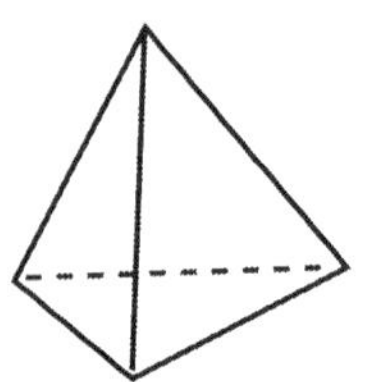
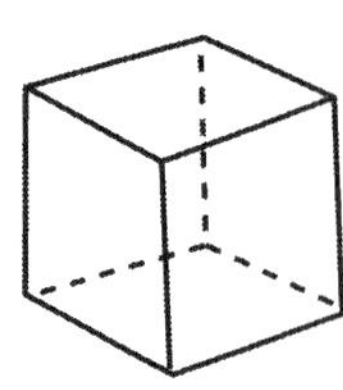
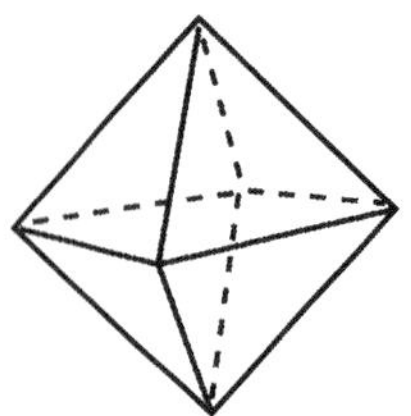
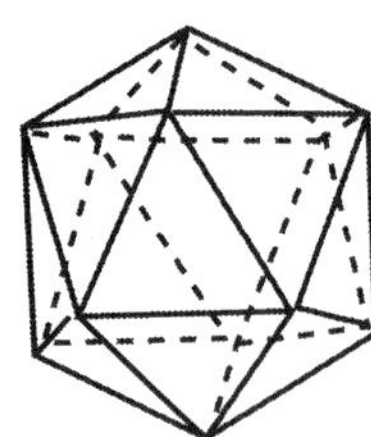
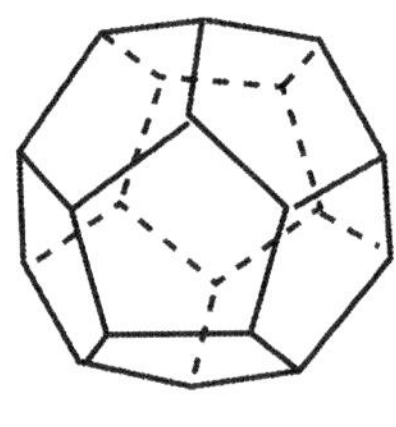

21.4 Five Platonic Solids

to describe the miraculous growth of a fertilized egg cell. The initial division of the egg into interconnected halves of a sphere is followed immediately by a second division that creates a blastomere, a tetrahedral cluster of four cells.

The Periodic Table of the Elements is organized around these same five geometric shapes. Elements with the same molecular base shape (gold, copper and silver are all cubic, for example) have many broadly analogous physical properties. Chemical bonding of molecules with different base shapes is possible because of their unique structural transformability and ability to "link" at various corners of the 120-triangle perfect cosmic container, the phantom-like spherical Philosopher's Stone.

At a macroscopic level, Earth itself is now being modeled as a kind of galactic—scale molecule, a composite body gravitationally bonded or "fused" together out of numerous "planetesimals" that once orbited the sun. Scientists believe that the intense heat of this primal fusion (*plasma* or Fire) drove the lighter elements (*solids* or Earth) upwards to form the crust of the planet. Over time, *gases* (Air) and *liquids* (Water) bubbled up through cracks in the crust. These were the preconditions of biological transformation and *evolution* (Life). The order of elemental transformation is identical to Plato's.

The ancient Chinese cosmos of Fire, Earth, Metal/Air, Water and Wood was diagrammed as a pentagonal Chart of Elements. Each dynamic element in this system was the equivalent of a color, a function of an organ in the human body, and a position (rather than a shape) in the universal scheme of creation and destruction. The *Creative Order* (symbolized by the pentagon) led to increasing material complexity. The *Destructive Order* (symbolized by the pentangle) led to progressively more subtle states of matter. No direct evidence survives to indicate whether or not ancient Chinese philosophers also used geometric shapes to represent the five elements in the Chart, but it seems almost certain that they did. The most ancient Chinese wisdom is now long lost to book burnings. In any case, Plato also attached colors to his shapes-- and Greek and Chinese color symbolism is identical. The Creative Order in the Chinese chart reflects the order of increasing geometric complexity.

There is also a faint trace of the Platonic shapes in Buddhist *stupas* (or *sotobas*), traditional grave stones that are still used throughout India, China, and Japan. These markers are stylized miniature replicas of the great architectural dome stupas that contain purported physical remains of the Buddha and that symbolized the eternal return of matter to the real world of spirit. The base of the *stupa* is a cube that represents Earth, the stable foundation upon which all is built. Stacked upon it are a sphere (of Water), a triangular shape (representing Fire, symbol of elements in transformation), a crescent (symbolizing Air, the inverted vault of the sky and the wind), and finally a tapered sphere (Aether dissipating into perfect space). The elements of the *stupa* are always stacked in this order, one identical to the Destructive Order of the Chinese cosmos.

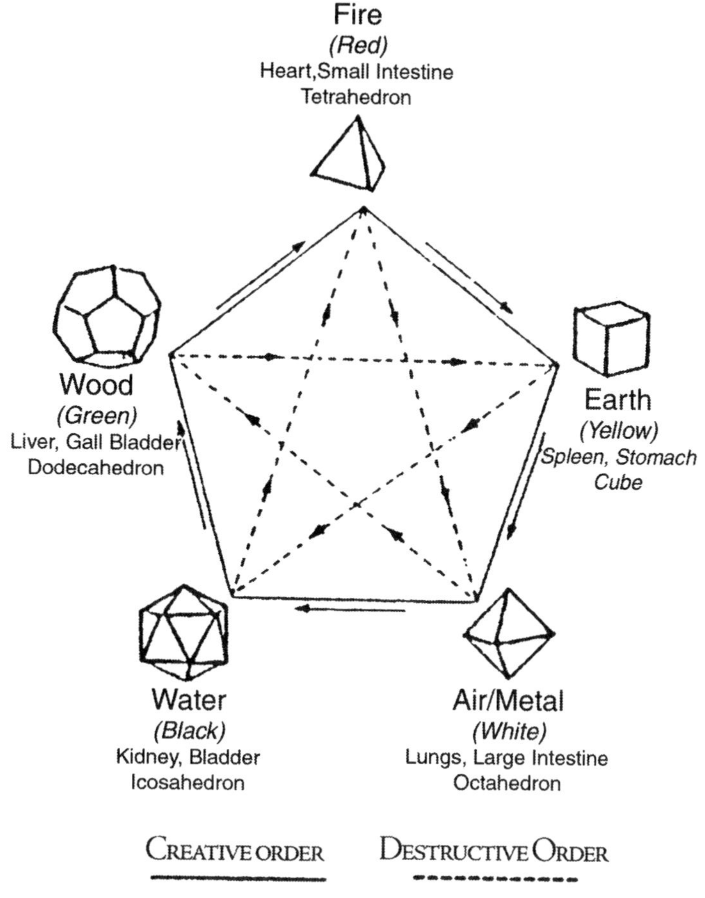

21.5 Chinese Elements

In the Americas, cosmic diagrams were often laid out as medicine wheels-- large circles of sacred stones that represented the transformative, healing powers of the elements and their geographical orientation in the universal scheme of creation. Like Stonehenge and other ancient megalithic astronomical observatories, these much smaller scale stone constructions functioned as calendar clocks. Every medicine wheel was intentionally designed to honor and to maintain the regenerative energies of a position in the cosmos unique in time, space, and transformative significance. Each was built "in harmony" with the sacred, hidden, ideal order. In addition, the stones were road signs that could be "read" by the rising and setting positions of the sun, moon, planets, and stars as they traversed their hoop-like paths around the Earth.

Position in time and space, in the context of endless cyclic flux, seems to have far outweighed any importance that might have been attached by American Indian cultures to the "order" of the elements. The medicine wheel merged element, season, direction, color, and life form. It served as a plan for ceremonial lodges and a compositional framework for sacred art. It was a totality, an ideal of life fully and properly lived. The responsibility and privilege of being human was, over the course of a lifetime, to embrace and know each of its elements, thereby "closing the hoop" and completing an individual sacred

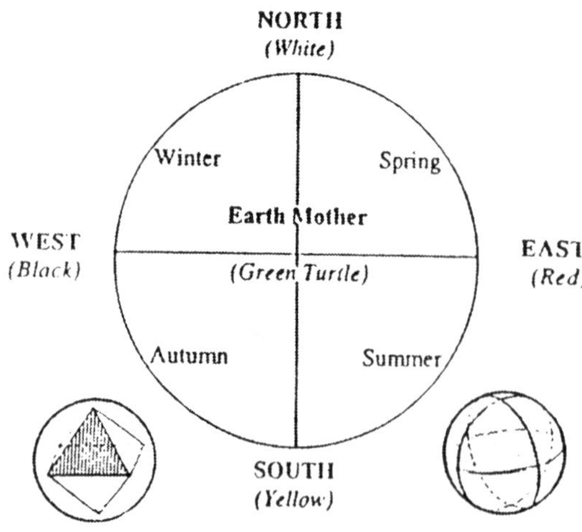

21.6 Sioux Sacred Hoop

circle. The Sioux holy man and visionary Black Elk used colors identical to those of the Chinese and Greeks to symbolize these elements.

According to legend, the Philosopher's Stone is "concealed in dung", and this aspect of its mysteries is most clearly illuminated in ancient Afro-Egyptian cosmology. Their Stone is the image of a dung-ball rolled across the heavens each day by the sacred scarab, *scarabaeus sacer*, a winged beetle. The scarab symbolized a universal power of self-regeneration. It drove the Sun along its path. Earth contained and transformed this power.

It is very difficult to estimate just how far back in time scarab symbology really extends. A number of carved artifacts from Paleolithic Europe that have been identified as regenerative goddess figures are also extremely accurate models of beetles emerging from pupae. In fact, the fit between ancient cosmologies and contemporary biology is so remarkable on many fronts that the future almost certainly holds a partnership between these two currently unrelated academic fields.

The scarab was the emblem of a culture that placed great value upon the life-sustaining transformative processes *and* products of bodies. The postures and proportions of the bodies of animals, plants and humans were uniquely transformable, one into the other. In a very real sense, bodies were temples -- compatible shapes "cut out" or "faceted" in time. Egyptian artwork built upon similarities of posture and proportion to combine human, animal, mineral, vegetable and celestial shapes in much the same way that chemists today diagram molecular connections. Species were merged, one into another, along regular geometric pathways-- the angles of elbow, ankle, knee, or joint; the tilt of a head on a stem or spinal column.

Equally respected were the residues of all these bodies. Human by-products (especially feces, spittle, and phlegm) were the foods and creative substances of the gods. The mythology of *Gaia*, the Greek goddess of Earth whose name is now used to label the scientific hypothesis about the unitary nature of Earth as a sun-powered living system, is probably a derivative of this tradition. In many cultures, the sounds *ga-ya* or ge meant "Earth" and implied a divine transformative capacity. In Egypt, this power was *Geb*, the divine nature of Earth. In Semitic (the language family of Arabs and Jews), it was *galel* and *galel*-- both of which meant "to roll dungballs". The terrible *Wheel* rolling in the air in the Old Testament Book of Ezekiel is composed of *wheels* that "turned not". In the original Hebrew text, the *Wheel* itself was a rolling dungball-- a living solar system.

Clearly, it takes some rethinking to imagine Gaia or our Solar System as a dungball, and yet this is the essence of the most ancient wisdom. Earth and Sun are uniquely compatible spherical partners that contain and shape the life of the cosmos. There is much more than poetic beauty in this cosmology of Earth. It metaphorically encapsulates the bio-geo-chemical processes of Fire, Earth, Air, Water, and Life that maintain planetary ecological balance (oxidation, reduction, gasification, liquefaction, evaporation, distillation, bacterial bloom, viral encounter...).

Since at least the time of the ancient Egyptians, however, the Western conception of the cosmos has become increasingly antiseptic. Plato was educated in Egyptian traditions, yet his perfect cosmic body was much more austere: "Neither was the rounded spherical shape in need of any organ by which to take food into itself and discharge it later after digestion... for it was designed to supply its own nourishment from its own decay." He imagined Earth as a game ball, a spherical dodecahedron-- a soccerball. "Earth looks from above, if you could see it," Plato once wrote, "like one of those twelve- patch leather balls."

Within the last twenty years, close on the heels of our first view of Earth from space, Plato's model has again been embraced as a research tool by small circles of scientists and seekers in countries all over the world. The 120-triangle, 15-hoop sphere is being visualized as a Map-- a contemporary cosmic design that can be used to bring harmony and order to global patterns of clouds, ocean currents, mountain ranges, river systems, coastlines, and other terrestrial energy formations. These exercises in geometric geography have led to another discovery, vast in its implications. The very same cosmic design "links" sites of human activity recognized today as having had overarching importance in the ancient world-- Egypt's pyramids, Easter Island, Mohenjo Daro, Macchu Picchu, the Southwest United States "Four Corners" region, mythic Shambhala, the Upper Amazon Basin, Angkor, Chichen Itza, Persepolis, Great Zimbabwe, Benin, and Timbuktu among many others. So many sites fall on or very near the intersections of the Map that it appears not only possible, but even *probable*, that an ancient global culture actually used the Map as a planning tool-- perhaps even as a system of coordinates, not unlike latitude and longitude.

Seen from the perspective of this Map/ Philosopher's Stone, Earth appears to have a natural cleavage-- a primary division not unlike the fertilized egg, the brain, or the countless other dihedrals in nature. This mystical division of hemispheres can be thought of as the *orienting ring*. As seen from the AfroEurAsian hemisphere, it marks a conventional dividing line between East and West identified by the historian C. Northcote Parkinson. More than 125 years ago, Charles Piazzi Smyth (Astronomer Royal of Scotland) established that it passed over more of Earth's land surface than any other line of longitude that could be drawn. Perhaps more significant are the "corners" of the Stone that fall along this ring. Corner #1 is a global focal point that dramatically illustrates how the crystalline shape seems to "tune" human consciousness. It is a highly- charged symbol of the power of the pharaohs, the rise and fall of civilizations, the ancient and continuing conflict between Arabs and Jews, the triumphs of technology, the tragedies of human stupidity and greed, the wealth of the Nile, and the mysteries of life and death. It engages the

Plato's Earth

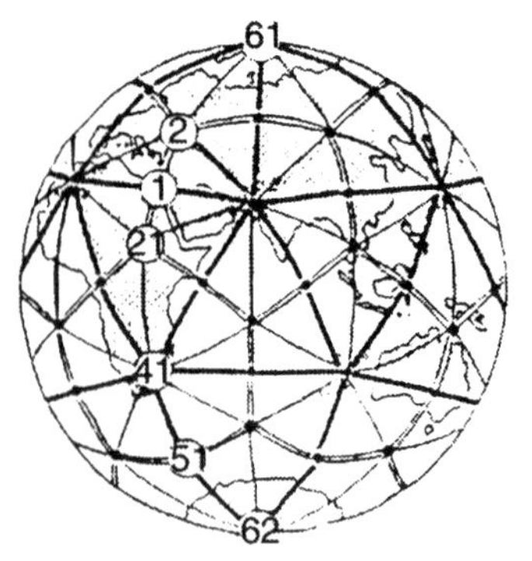

The 15-Hoop, 120-Triangle Earth Map with Orienting Ring

21.7 "Map" of Earth

entire spectrum of human moods and capacities in ways that are passionately logical and emotional at the same time. In ancient times, the corner marked Behdet-- a geodetic point in a spherical world mapping system that has been described in great detail by the prominent historian of measurement, Livio Catullo Stecchini. Jerusalem, Alexandria (seat of the great library), and the Great Pyramid complex at Giza are nearby.

Kiev (corner #2), the most beloved of all (formerly western Soviet) cities, is an ancient pilgrimage site that also marks the site of the most disastrous nuclear accident in world history, Chernobyl. Corner #21, near Khartoum, lies at the heart of the ancient kingdom of Kush. In 1992, this was the center of a devastating locust plague, one the United Nations believes will exceed any in recorded history. To the south, near corner #41, is Great Zimbabwe, the most impressive megalithic structure in all Africa. This corner seems always to have symbolized the divergence of biological types and the hope of peace. In the early 1900s, Raymond Dart made his landmark discoveries of hominid fossils here. The struggle against apartheid is, perhaps, its legacy. Corner #51 marks a natural whale refuge. Corners #61 and #62, the axial poles of Earth, symbolize orientation in space with respect to the sun. The concept of an "ozone hole" was first applied to the sky over the south pole. Finally, Corner #7 (not shown) falls at the site of the Valdez-Exxon oil spill.

Contemporary research based on the Map has been uniquely cross-disciplinary and cross-cultural because the *research design*, the Map itself, is an inherently sacred symbol-- a Philosopher's Stone. Its meaning and implications are buried deep within every culture's mythology, religion, and science. The real enthusiasm is not so much over what the Map *is*, what is precisely "on" or "off" the rings and corners, as where it may lead. Potentially, it is a base from which an equitable global conversation about the future can grow-- a context within which different historical understandings and beliefs about the nature of the environment can enhance, rather than compete with, one another. We may never know how, or even if, the Map was actually used in the past. (Maps such as the Piri Reis chart of the Atlantic and the 14th century diCanestris "diamond" map of the Mediterranean suggest its use in ancient cartography.) We can, however, make the operating research assumption that humans share a basic, highly sophisticated geometric intelligence that has taken them in different directions-- all metaphorically compatible.

The Map is unquestionably a **sacred geometry**. The proportions of the different figures it "contains" are encoded in the architecture of important structures as seemingly diverse as Gothic cathedrals, Solomon's Temple, Stonehenge, Maori *Whare Wananga* ("sacred colleges"), and Buddhist shrines. The various car-

21.8

Celestial Maps

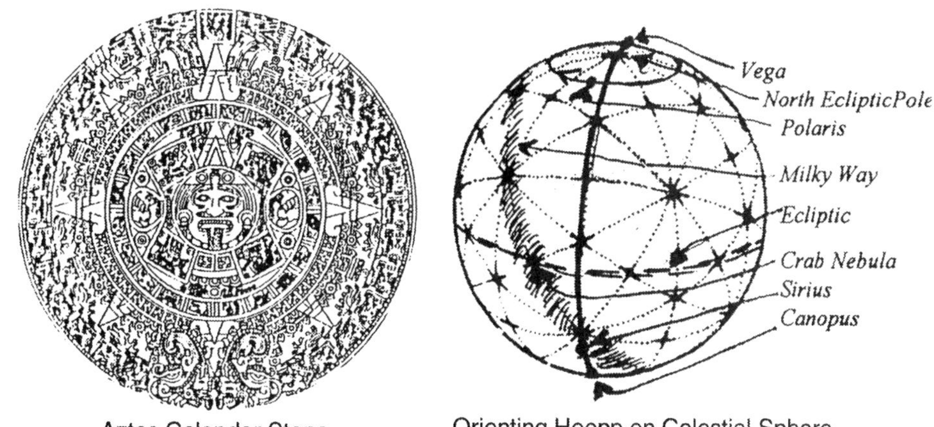

Aztec Calendar Stone Orienting Hoopp on Celestial Sphere

penter's rules and stonemason's measures used to build these edifices also reflect the sacred geometry. Insome parts of the world, even the distances between settlements in a region were fixed by these same geometric proportions. In places as widespread as China, Turkey, Scotland, and Australia distances and lengths were equivalent to precise musical sound frequencies. The Map could be sung! In the world of the Pythagoreans, all of this was the Music of the Spheres. Today the sides of the triangles of the Map, in miles, are 1440, 2160, and 2592 miles respectively. The distances are equivalent to a diminished 7th chord-- D, A, C.

Geometry and the Philosopher's Stone are implicit even in the Christian Lord's Prayer. The Greek word *epi*, which is used twice as the preposition in the phrase "Thy will be done, *on* Earth as it is *in* Heaven," implies an all-encompassing power superimposed in time, place, order, direction, distribution, and authority. This is very nearly the character of the Map as an ideal structure. Johannes Kepler seems to have been struggling to recover an ancient cosmology that places Earth *inside* a celestial Philosopher's Stone. He spent much of his life modeling nests of heavenly crystals and speculating about their impact upon the Earth. In fact, a Map *with* a *celestial orienting ring* can be drawn on the celestial sphere in such a way that discoveries of modern astronomy and cartography are in remarkable alignment with ancient beliefs about the stars and the divine figures they represented. The ecliptic is the equator of this sky globe. The orienting ring runs perpendicular to it through the north and south ecliptic poles, Sirius, Canopus, and Vega. In this way, the geometry of the Map is fixed in space. Remarkably, the Milky Way falls exactly along another of the 15 rings.

The concept of the spherical geometry container is lost to Western science, however, though it was still alive in Mesoamerica in the 1200s when the Aztec Calendar Stone was constructed. Its inner ring of twenty segments is a very accurate geometric representation of the *ecliptic*. Each segment of this zodiac symbolizes a period of 1300 years time in the precession of Earth's axial pole -- marked by the observed position of the sun against the background stars at daybreak on the summer solstice. The tongue on the stone hangs down to mark the celestial orienting ring, which falls between Canis Major and Orion (in

Aztec, the age of the Dog and the Monkey). The meanings attributed to these constellations are virtually universal. Orion is probably Hanuman, Prometheus, the thunderous spirit of the bullroarer, Osiris, and the Accursed Hunter. The Present position of the summer solstice sun marks the prophesied time of upheaval and transition. It is our time that has been predicted, awaited, hoped for, and feared. Human survival is uncertain.

This brings me to the very difficult questions I've been asked. Have there been developmental phases in the relationship between humans and our planet? Was there a more perfect harmony prior to industrialization of human society? And most importantly, why did we denounce Paradise?

Part of the ecstasy and terror of being human is that we are capable of even asking such questions. It seems obvious that over time, every people in every part of the world have established different ways of knowing nature. I am not convinced, however, that the harmonies of these ways of knowing can be placed on a hierarchical scale. Harmony exists in the soul of the one who listens. It can be expressed as a geometric abstraction, such as the Philosopher's Stone, but comparison is more difficult. Humans have continually yearned for more perfect harmony -- and have in this way "denounced Paradise" (technically, *denounce* means "to announce the end and proclaim the beginning"). Humans are curious beings. We are "in harmony" in stages, in periods separated by episodes of *punctuated evolution* in which a tonal "progression" (rather than hierarchy) can be distinguished. Why should Paradise be any different?

I was surprised to find, in preparing my remarks, that the linguistic roots of the word "Paradise" actually mean "circular Earthen wall". I have begun to wonder if Paradise is the wheel or zodiacal "wall" of the ecliptic as seen from Earth and upon which the precessional path of the sun at the summer solstice has been marked in virtually all the ancient calendars? Is it the cycle or spiral of the evolving life of Earth? I believe that it is. Concepts such as the zodiacal ages, the wheel of karma, and even the coming of the New Jerusalem are remnants of a way of thinking about Paradise that industrialized society has abandoned as both superstitious and dangerous. We have not typically thought of ourselves as *precessional beings*, as evolving spirits who inhabit the "memory" of the geometric universe. It has been too claustrophobic and fatalistic an image for industrial culture.

The key to understanding our position in time, in Paradise, may grow from our work in molecular biophysics. Just in the past few years, scientists have discovered several "new" kinds of microscopic crystals (known as quasicrystals) and molecular carbon cages that can act as energy storage batteries (fullerenes) not previously known to exist. Both substances exhibit the crystalline geometry of the Platonic Philosopher's Stone.

Models of a spherical envelope encompassing the solar system are becoming increasingly common, and it will not be long (I would predict) before the various galactic impacts upon this celestial sphere will be able to be mapped with the very same Philosopher's Stone model. These impacts will be likened to the impacts of solar and lunar influences upon the crust of the Earth and its core (which is already being modeled as if it were a crystal). Were it possible to rise above this "solar sphere", an interesting energy impact would immediately be revealed. A straight line could be drawn from the center of the galaxy, through the Milky Way, out through the Sun, and on to the tip of Orion's club (which falls at a "corner" of the celestial Philosopher's Stone). At no other place in the celestial sphere are there so many bright stars clustered together as around Orion. Over the 26,000 year course of precession, Earth's polar axis tilts toward and away from the galactic center. We have entered a period in time (the Monkey on the Aztec calendar) when Earth's north pole is maximally tilted *away from* the galactic center. We have been moving into this segment of time ever since about 1000 AD when the summer solstice sunrise came into alignment with the celestial orienting ring. During this same period, Earth's south pole has been tilted maximally *toward* the galactic center. I believe these (for Lack of an existing term) "galactic solstices" mark the extremes in the Earth's "energetic alignment", when our axial pole is maximally tilted toward or away from the Sun. The question I want to consider is an ancient one: what impact, if any, does this polar orientation have upon the quality of human life on Earth?

There are remarkable coincidences between "historic events", the precession of summer solstices along the ecliptic, the celestial positions where rings of the Philosopher's Stone cross the ecliptic, and periods symbolized on the Aztec calendar stone (which are usually interpreted as "Days"). The Day of the Dog, for example, extends from 300 BC (the time of Alexander the Great) until 1000 AD (the Millennium). I suspect that the wave of fear that arose at this Millennium built upon a vestigial knowledge of the Celestial Map lost in superstition many hundreds if not several thousand of years earlier in Europe. The period in which we believe the Egyptian dynasties began (about 2900 - 3000 BC) marked the end of the Aztec Day of the Deer and the beginning of the Day of the Rabbit. The hordes that Marija Gimbutas and Riane Eisler believe plundered the matriarchal cultures of Old Europe began their invasions in 4200 BC at the beginning of the Aztec Day of Death and the end of the Day of the Serpent.

These events may represent *mythologies* of the lost celestial Philosopher's Stone, or they may represent sequential, developmental stages of consciousness and potential within human culture that are geometrically punctual-- and punctuated. Perhaps they can be predicted.

We have, in Plato, a warning about a period that occurred almost opposite our own on the precessional clock-- at a time when Earth's north axial pole was most tilted *toward the galactic center*. It was known as the destruction of Atlantis. This is not the time to discuss the numerous controversies that surround this story, but I mention it because the clear message in Plato's *Critias* is that human actions exacerbated the catastrophe. Today, geologists are beginning to scientifically study this period for entirely different reasons. They are now able to measure a point in time about 10,600 BC when the North Atlantic Deep Water (NADW) current "suddenly" turned on. This current flows south from Greenland and around the tip of Africa and plays a critical role in today's climate, keeping the environment of Western Europe relatively mild. The NADW forms when dense, salty water from the south cools near Greenland, and grows heavy enough to sink to the ocean bottom. It was extremely weak or even non-functional during the last Ice Age, but seems to have abruptly started up again at 10,600 BC -- precisely the end of the Aztec Day of the Crocodile and the beginning of the beginning of the Day of Wind. Concentrations of greenhouse gases increased at this same time. Scientists have documented the accumulation, but they do not know whether or not it caused the climate warming. Several hundred years (just a few degrees of precession) later, there is evidence that northern polar ice sheets began a rapid melt and the sea levels began to rise. The chain of activity that led to these events is unknown.

By using this example, I *do not* mean to excuse industrial society its excesses. Perhaps we, like Plato's Atlanteans, have become greedy and jealous and have initiated a process that will end our species and many others. Our current Day in the calendar, as mentioned above, is that of the Monkey-- of Orion, the hunter condemned to endless chase. It will culminate about 2300 AD with the beginning of the Day of Dry Herbs-- which perhaps presages global water shortages we are almost certain to face at that time. In many interpretations of mythology, Orion the Hunter has been equated with the accursed hunter. He symbolizes (to quote J.E. Cirlot) "the falling away from the center-- or the tendency to do so-- towards the endlessly turning periphery of the wheel of phenomena... to the sterile urge of the pursuit of worldly things." Could there be a more accurate astronomical metaphor of our times? The key word, however, is *tendency*--a tendency to abandon the spiritual. Is this the galactic potential, the "intelligent cosmic energy" in which we live that was geometrically predicted thousands of years ago and that we have forgotten?

Questions such as these are ancient. The best answers are mythological, and many of them have been delivered by tricksters and sacred clowns. Among the Oneida Indians of the Iroquois Confederacy, for example, a story is told about Shagadjowe' Gowa, a being who lived "in the beginning". Alone and without companions, he simply presumed he had created all the forms of nature. This angered the Great Maker, who punished him for his pride by smashing him up against a cliff. His broken jaw and nose are symbolized in the distorted "false face" masks the Oneida wear in their ceremonies, and which preserve the memory of his primal error. The masks are also reminders that Great Maker spared Shagodjowe' Gowa's life because he agreed to work among humans, imparting to them his knowledge of how shape could be used as a protection against enemies to their health and happiness.

In the beginning, in one West African origin myth, the creator and chief of gods was Nyankupon. All the sacred stories sang his praises. Anansi, the spider, was extremely jealous that the stories were not about him. He had a very high opinion of himself. Nyankupon told Anansi that if he could capture and bring him a beehive, a boa, and a tiger, that the stories would henceforth sing his praises. By subtly manipulating *containers* (shapes), Anansi was successful, and the chief of gods was amazed at his cleverness. Nyankupon ordered that all tales, old and new, would from that day forward mention only Anansi. He left Earth and returned to his home beyond the sky.

Both Shagodjowe' Gowa and Anansi the Spider are typical "geometry spirits" who clearly communicate that geometry is not God. In turn, science has proven conclusively that material creations only approach geometric perfection. Earth is not quite a perfect sphere. Most viruses are *nearly* icosahedral. Nevertheless, material reality can be extremely well understood by imagining it as if it were geometrically perfect-- as "that which always is, but never becomes".

How can we begin to separate excessive human greed, pride, individualism, and stupidity from our collective material memory-- the "Paradise of Precession" that has spiralled through the eons as a progressive harmony in our brains? This is the ground upon which science and religion meet, the ultimate mystery, the "ancient future". What if a perfect geometric Map does somehow contain this ***life of the universe*** and the processes of physical and cultural evolution? What does this mean? Where can such a theory lead? Can cycles of consciousness be anticipated? Can we regain an ability to think and plan in terms of hundreds and thousands of years impact? I believe that we must, at the very least, begin to seriously ask these questions.

What if, in the beginning, geometry was an original blessing of the Creator, a natural system of knowledge that all humans, at all times, could (did, and do) use to chart the course of Earth life on its journey around the edge of the great shining Sea we know today as the disk of the Milky Way galaxy. If we just imagine this to be so, the entire world of time is no longer chaotic. It is transformed into a sacred laboratory with semi-predictable boundary conditions. Today its legacy lies unrecognized in museums, sacred texts and temples, archaeological sites, and even in the truths we hold to be self evident. This stockpile of global creativity and diversity is the ancient future that the Philosopher's Stone/ Map can illuminate and integrate for the humans who survive the Day.

Allen, Robert H., *Star Names: Their Lore and Meaning*, 1963. ISBN 0-486-21079-0

Becker, William and Bethe Hagens, "Ancient Futures and the Geometry of Life," 1991, unpublished ms.

Becker, William and Bethe Hagens, "The Rings of Gaia," in James Swan, ed., *The Power of Place: Sacred Ground in Natural and Human Environments*, 1993. ISBN 0-8356-0670-8

Gimbutas, Marija, *The Language of the Goddess*, 1989. ISBN 0-06-250356-1

Hagens, Bethe, "Venuses, Turtles, and Other Hand-Held Cosmic Models," in Myrdene Anderson and Floyd Merrill, eds., *On Semiotic Modeling*, 1991. ISBN 3-11-012314-2

Hagens, Bethe, "Paradise and Precession: A Geometric Legend," in *Environment - A Challenge for Adult Education: Proceedings of the 24th Meeting in Finland Seminar 1992*, Helsinki, 1992.

Hancock, Graham and Santha Faiia, *Heaven's Mirror: Quest for the Lost Civilization*, 1998. ISBN 0-517-70811-6

Lee, Desmond (trans.), *Plato: Timaeus and Critias*, 1965. ISBN 0-14-044261-8

Santillana, Giorgio de and Hertha von Dechend, *Hamlet's Mill: An Essay Investigating the Origins of Human Knowledge and its Transmission through Myth*, 1977. ISBN 0-87923-215-3

Stecchini, Livio Catullo, "Appendix," in Peter Tompkins, *Secrets of the Great Pyramid*, 1971. ISBN 06-014327-4

A gift of the future, it remains to be seen if Arkhom is ahead of its time. When looking at the big picture there is no time. The common denominator of this group is that we are all futurist idealists. With a few 'ist' for good measure. Reverend Buelher's contribution is towards elucidation of the meaning, historic (pre-- post) use, and potential of the Arkhom geometry. Showing us Arkhom as an engine of esoteric power, Bill alludes to Arkhom's potential and power to shift consciousness. From the Oritronic (present mind set) to the Metatronic (future heart set) to occur when 40% of humanity become Lighted souls, LP40. From here on in your on your own.

22: Metaphysical Ark

Arkhom: A Gift from the Future

by William Stuart Buehler

Foreword

This story will be strange even for seasoned mystics. Strange as it is there still exists the Reshel patterns in the land and temples as testimony to its reality at least in the minds of ancients and more recently the Knights Templar and early Masons. Since I am not a Mason, perhaps I may be permitted a certain freedom in discussing what must have once been their innermost secrets. However this is the time that the secrets are shouted from the rooftops and their general knowledge *is needed* for the evolution of the Race and whole continuum. The details of operating time gates however would still be guarded or available from spiritual source based on a need to know. This is as much for the protection of the users as for the organizations using the gates. Inept time implosions can virtually destroy light bodies and chakras. However correct usage with highest intent under inner planes supervision is safe and "timely."

Open to me the GATES OF RIGHTEOUSNESS;
I will go into them and I will praise the Lord; this GATE OF THE LORD into which the Righteous shall enter.
I will praise thee; for thou hast heard me and art become my salvation.
The STONE which the builders eliminated has become the HEAD-STONE of the CORNER.
This is from the Lord; it is marvelous in our eyes.
Psalms 118: 19-23

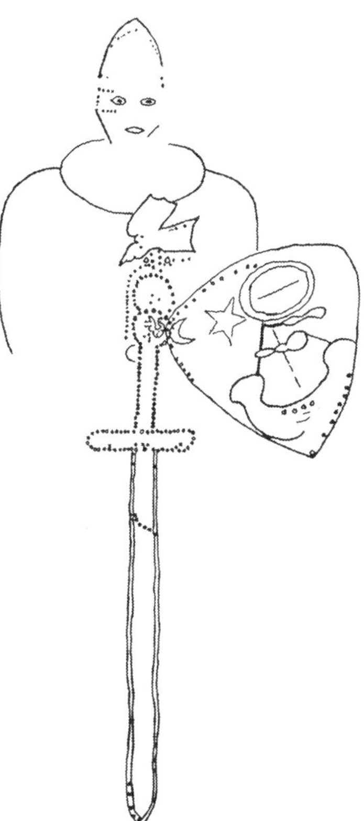

22.1 Westford Knight
Westford, MA Petroglyph made with punch on horizontal stone outcrop. Circa 1398 CE, probably by Sinclair Expedition.

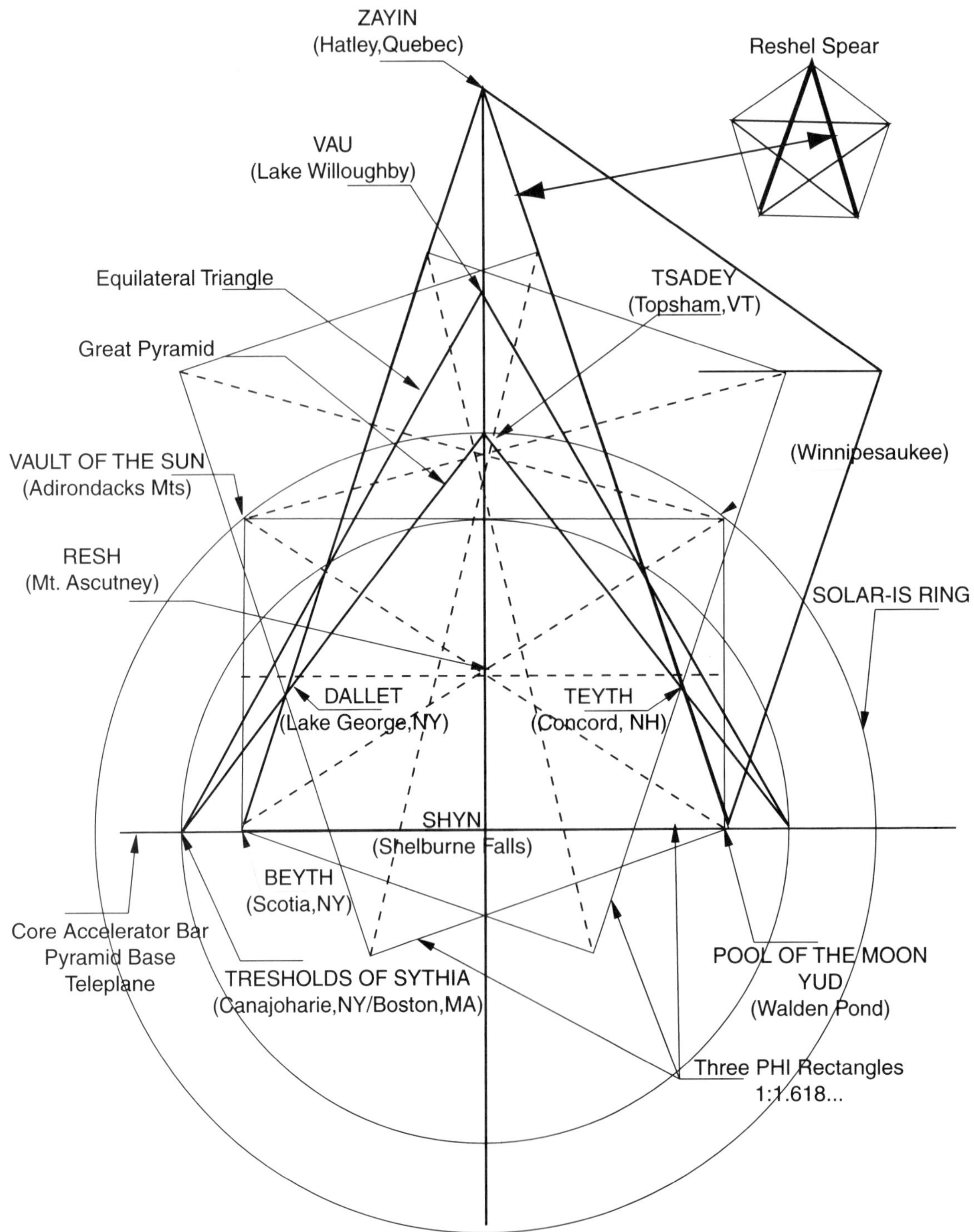

22.2 Resh--"The Chief Headstone".

Preface

The above passage refers to an ancient grid which contains two sets of Time Gates ostensibly noted in the Psalm. The gates are in the geometry of a golden ratio rhombus and use the "L" shape or "corner" as the short version of the rhombus. The grid is called the RESHEL, Hebrew for the "Chief Head Stone of God" and the controlling pole of the grid is called the RESH (Chief Head Stone). Thus it was shown us by the inner planes illuminary, Thoth Hermes[1] or "Thoth Raismes of Aphra" as he wishes to be called. The grid was provided to our light groups to facilitate restoring the presence of the "fallen Female Pillar" and to assist the groups in more efficient time gateing. We used the grid as a group configuration but since that time I have found that the Reshel is found in major temples and in the Earth Grids. ARKHOM is one such.

The "L" format is more than only a notable gateway system within the Reshel, it is an energetic and consciousness matrix resonant with one of 24 Breastplates of Metatron. Metatron is the highest archangel whose level of consciousness and state of being is used to describe the quality of the new time continuum into which we are presently evolving. We are now moving rapidly from a continuum of fallen or "Oritronic" light into a full-light spectrum of the same level from which we fell. This higher, Metatronic level is called the RANNA TIME WAVE. There are therefore three time continua...all existing concurrently in an "all-time, no-time" mode... which have always occupied most of our spiritual organizations in their work of keeping all three glued together and their evolution moving forward.

Yeshua, the Messiah, has been likened to the Chief Head Stone[2]; it is emphasized that use of the Gates and Reshel Grid must be in resonance with the Christ and the Righteous...with Metatron. *Anything written here concerning the use of the grids should NOT suggest that they can be used by any group or individual without very clear Christic intent and clear communication with inner dimensional agencies, Hierarchical or angelic, at the Metatronic/Christic level.* These gates must NOT be confused with any project or process used by the Montauk Project.

I had studied Reshel Earth Grids, as well as group application, for a number of years when my friend Dan Winter enthusiastically told me of a grid that covered the whole East Coast and I'd better right away touch base with its discoverer Peter Champoux (in team with Susan). When Peter sent the diagram of *ARKHOM* I found that the Reshel grid fit over it with amazing exactness. This was exciting for me since this was the first such grid found by another person not having any conscious awareness of

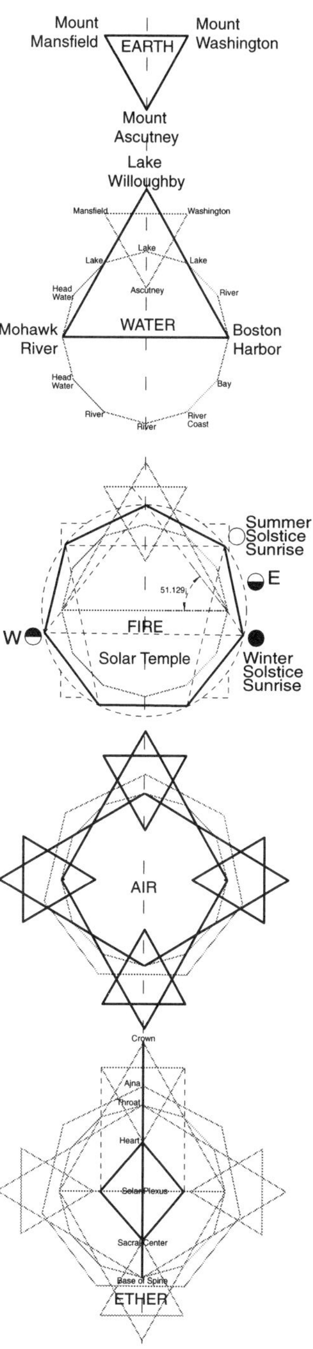

22.3 Arkhom Geometry

the complex Reshel format. Although we had discovered a correlation with the Rennes le Chateau grid[3], the ARKHOM discovery is much more detailed and advanced in complexity.

The Gift

So far the story is not strange but now it begins. Quite a few synchronistic events then rapidly began to bring things together. I had recently begun to work on the Reshel geometry of the famous Clan Sinclair ROSSLYN Chapel south of Edinburgh and that also led to learning of the WESTFORD KNIGHT[4] in the Boston suburb of Westford. I found that the Reshel fit Rosslyn Chapel perfectly both in its horizontal plan and its vertical elevation. I also found the same to be true for Chartres. Both use the L-Gate in the same manner and both were designed as remarkable "time temples."

I saw that the Westford Knight also carried Reshel codes punched into stone. I also knew that the Knight's design was a grid schematic and not simply a funerary marking for a knight buried beneath the stone. Understanding the carved Knight's coding and placement is critical to understanding Arkhom in the 1398 CE "upgrade." The Knight's position, function in ARKHOM is as its major code insertion as far as the 1398 Expedition was concerned. It is located in the EASTERN pole on the Arkhom E-W generating axis of the grid. The eastern pole contains "intent" or the inseminating codes and purpose of the grid. The codes in Bostons' energy sites supplement the Knights' codes and will provide upgrading formats. The SHIELD or "ARMS" always contains vital programs whether a shield of an aboriginal native or knight. The shield is carried in front of the carrier, supplementing the codes carried on that person's vestments. The persons' chakras are the basis of the vestment-shield combined matrix and will be physically matched. The primary device on the shield is the Arkhom grid; thus I see Arkhom as a main interface and empowering mechanism. This is commented on below.

These are the Knights' vital carved codes with summarized interpretations:

•SHIELD: Two concentric rings and heavy axis line: This is a critical reference lock over which I placed the two key rings of the Arkhom's Reshel grid and aligned the shield glyph's axis with the Arkhom's axis. This gave me a huge intercontinental grid. It locked onto a "Templa Mar" site Thoth had our groups install on the Mogollon Rim a few years prior so I assumed that the grid was correctly placed and sized.

•SHIELD: A crescent and 5-pointed star: This is the basic symbol for the Reshel grid. Ironically it is also related to the establishment of the power and presence of the Goddess or as Thoth put it, "for the re-erection of the fallen Female Pillar". This symbol confirmed that the Reshel grid was the key system.

•SHIELD: Single masted ship seen as a crescent with the Arkhom-rings above it... the two viewed as a Reshel crescent and star, Arkhom being the star. The Ship's main mast appears to identify Block Island which is the main power controller of a three-island "resh" or control system. Montauk Point is the time gate controller (reason for the Grey incursion in that area via human "Montauk Project") while Newport Island is the knowledge-wisdom controller. The 1398 Expedition built a tower in Newport which still exists. The main mast or "main power line" aligns with the Knight's eye which is also the main resh pole in the huge "Bakhira Grid" that covers North and South America. This vital pole is at Madison, Wisconsin.

•SWORD: The sword is a "two mouthed", double pommel type typical to the period. The sword's main symbolism is found in Hebrews 4:11-13 which also says that the Sword or Logo of God is alive and active. A knight's sword is broken at his death. Both are resurrected eventually. The Sword has a break in it at a 51 degree angle. This break is also at the golden ratio point (1.618) between the sword's point and the base of the pommel. The 51 degree line tells us that the Great Pyramid is located there and that the sword's axis is a reality frame or "teleplane" creating some sort of cosmic containment field based on life rhythms (Pyramid sockets). The golden ratio dynamic is a life supporting and definition system. Thus, to bring the sword back to "life" and wholeness the Pyramid and golden ratio must be activated. These two

22.4 Bakhira Grid

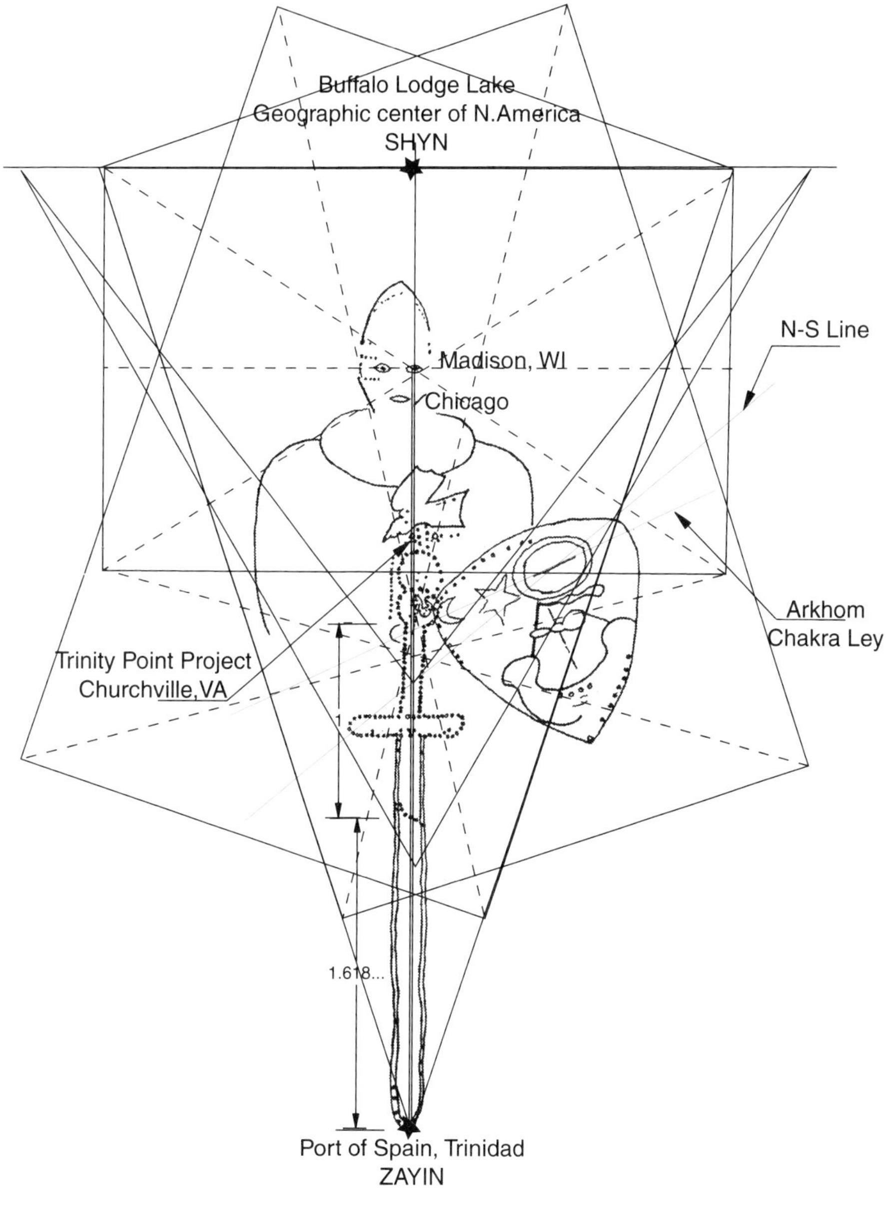

systems more than any other together form the generating or "Glory" pole for the Reshel Grid. This pole is effectively the best Grail Core geometry, using the Bethlehem Triangle of 26.3 degrees that I have found yet. It is the core matrix of the Metatronic Arieopax (Reshel upgrade).

•SWORD: The upper limit of the dual pommel. The main axis of the sword makes a 3.5 degree offset from the quillon (cross piece) to the tip of the pommel. At the top of the pommel is a great bird carrying a serpent...corresponds with the bird-serpent staff archetype. This archetype is Moses' Serpent Staff that healed the tribes; Yeshu the Messiah correlates with the same staff related to second Birth (John 3:14-15) and it is also the Serpent Staff of Aesculapius, the Caduceus of Thoth-Hermes, the Feathered Serpent. Mastery of this redemption dynamic opens all 13th rays and aspects.

Thoth agreed with the design as shown and added that it also contains something Thoth called an EDEN STAR with a vibration of "18." The offset axis links into a site named TRINITY POINT which was discovered by Mr. Philip Khnopp. The site has three mounts arranged in a 51 degree Great Pyramid geometry. There is also a great bird seen in the hills' contours, the bird "carrying" the river as a serpent correspondent. In considering the Eden Star, "18" in Hebrew is the word "chay" which means "regenerating life." "Eden" in Hebrew (there are two spellings) means "strength, controlling foundation, sockets." Thus we have a very complex archetype directly corresponding with the Sword's regeneration. Trinity Point is that place where the whole transcontinental Bakhira Grid axial energy from its offshore center comes ashore.

Both the Sword and Trinity Point site have the Great Pyramid dynamic appearing. Note that the translation for "Eden" relates to "controlling foundation, sockets." A little known aspect about the Pyramids' sockets is that they are carved into the bedrock at various sizes and depths$_5$. Bernard Pietsch found that the differences would chart the Circadian Cycle. (This is a daily cycle that plants and animals revert to when denied sunlight.) I also noted that the numbers roughly relate to the four human biorhythms. Thoth later commented on the sockets' values, or the observed rhythm as being cosmic. He also remarked on the Capstone's number: 50. I believe that the Pyramid and the golden ratio describe a vital life support system that is universal and that any reality frame or continuum must contain this format. I think that the Hebrews 4:11-13 reference mentioned above, to the two-mouthed sword best describes this coding of the Knight's sword.

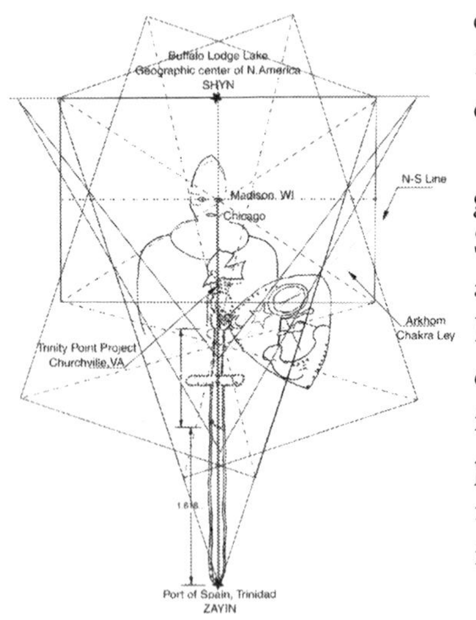

• KNIGHT'S LEFT EYE: The Knight's left eye is on the main grid axis. The is the operative "resh" pole. "Resh" means "Chief Head Stone" in Hebrew. This eye or resh pole and the sword's point give us a lock on the Reshel's positioning by placing the "resh" pole in the Reshel on the eye and the "zayin" pole on the sword's point. The left eye in the Hebrew alphabet is found in the protosiniatic glyph used for the letter Resh, #200. This was drawn as a head showing its left profile (right brain). The use of the "eye" as a Hebrew archetype also relates to the letter Ayin, #70 which was drawn as a vesica with a dot in the center. Ayin means "eye, fountain or well" and is one of the divine letters along with Aleph, #1/1000. As it turns out the eye's position is Madison, Wisconsin, which has a large lake and University.

When the vast Reshel format, called the BAKHIRA GRID by Thoth, is spun in its circular "spinner" dynamic the eye swings over the former position of the HOLY ISLE OF RUTA in the Faraday Seamount area on the Atlantic Ridge north of the Azores and even with Paris. This alignment is probably the most important of them all and is a basic positional check.

SUMMARY OF THE SINCLAIR KNIGHT'S CODING: It may perhaps be strange for the reader to imagine that a vast intercontinental land area could be influenced or "coded" by alchemy contained in and around a stone the size of a kitchen table yet that seems to be the case. The coding is within a larger mechanism, located in its coding section (East). The power modem is Nova Scotia linked through the three resh or control islands: Long Island at Montauk Point, Block Island and Newport Island. The Eastern "knowledge" or coding pole is modulated by Newport Island and the Expedition Tower placed there.

The codes are boosted and actualized by the E-W GENERATING AXIS which includes the base line or EVENT HORIZON of the Great Pyramid dynamic. This contains the sockets and defines the "teleplane" or continuum. The capstone of the Pyramid generates the golden ratio spirals which create the whole form. The ARKHOM grid then can be thought of as an interface system that in turn codes the intercontinental BAKHIRA Grid which is also a resonant Reshel system. It should also be remembered that all of Europe has the same grid system and is the GAIA right forebrain which expresses as the right brain North and South American identical system. The small stone outside of Boston at Westford resonantly links into this very powerful system both in its energy form and the cosmic nature of the codes. In this context the ARKHOM E-W axis is much like a large antenna picking up the GAIA transmissions being relayed from the Sun and divine agencies.

Part of the Reshels' codes (and therefore ARKHOMs') contain the BETHLEHEM TRIANGLE which uses the "2618 Numeric" or 2.618 as the golden ratio (phi squared) and also the 26 degrees, 18 minutes of the Bethlehem Angle. This is another vital function of the Great Pyramid which is built into its two main ascending passageways. The angle is also found between the Pyramid to Bethlehem line and the Gizeh latitude line. The energetic includes the dynamics of "Absolution, Resolution, Evolution" as the Bird-Serpent Staff of the Greek god of healing: Aesculapius. Yeshu the Messiah also likened Himself to this Staff where it correlates with Moses' Staff in John 3:14-15. This dynamic relates to healing and to regeneration of Life and is a Grail action. The Bethlehem Triangle appears as two: the female Shekinah and the male Christos systems. The two triangles are base-to-base in the usual grid geometry and is found in Great Britain stretching between Edinburgh and Glastonbury.

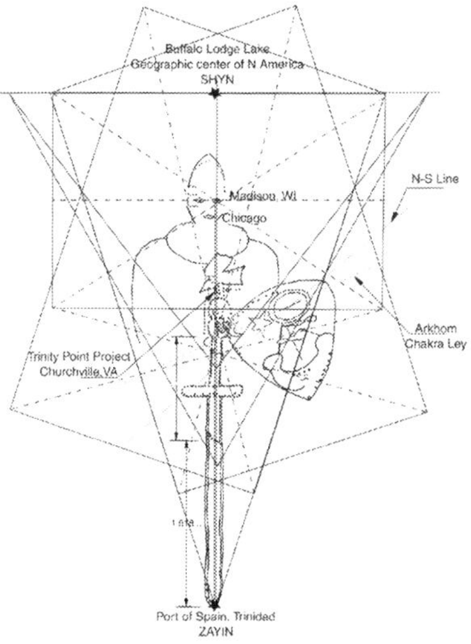

The Clan Sinclair controlled the main Reshel poles in the Thurso, Edinburgh areas and effectively translated this main Grail core geometry to the Americas via the Knight's coding and other energy sites on the East Coast of North America. These grids in Europe and the Americas were put in place by the priests of the Holy Isle of Ruta anticipating THIS PHASE OF OUR EVOLUTION!

Any study of the Bethlehem Angle should include the Hathor Temple at Dendera and its astrological ceiling. The Angle appears between the Serpent-Bird axis through Rigel in Orion (Osiris) and the Tem-

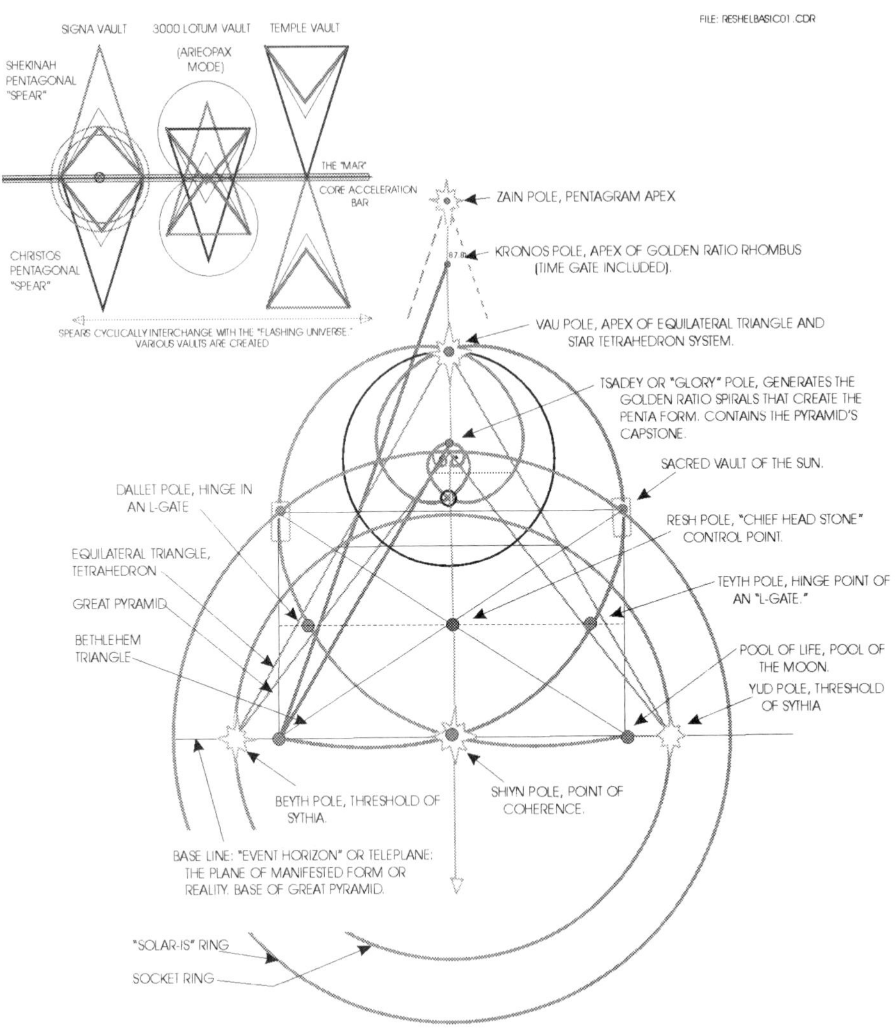

RESHEL/ARIEOPAX (TECHAD) GRID SYSTEM

SHOWING THE SHEKINAH (FEMALE) HALF. THE SYSTEM INCLUDES THE DYNAMICS FOR THE GREAT PYRAMID, STAR TETRAHEDRON, TIME OR "L" GATES, PENTAGON, BETHLEHEM ANGLE/TRIANGLE, 6 MODES OF THE ARIEOPAX, LAYOOESH PILLAR.

22.5 Metatron's Breastplate

ple axis through Gemini's female partner. The Temple axis should include Sirius even though it is a few degrees off the axis. This separation is what is called a "Selah Axis" or a spinning spoke of divine Silence or Life which empowers all systems.

The Reshel

(CHIEF HEAD STONE OF GOD)
A SUMMARY

BACKGROUND: Ten years ago our groups in the Midwest, about 80 persons in half a dozen synergically unified groups, were going through "time glitches" due to our collective increasing energy. This is common in group work. Time instability is due to increasing energy breaking down temporal mental forms, so the continuum is not as well defined in the local vortex. People begin to bilocate, things disappear and return (sometimes) and other minor annoyances occur. Part of our synergic technique was to use sacred geometric configurations in the groups' processes. Due to our energy and consciousness level Thoth Raismes offered his assistance by providing us with the "Reshel" grid format. He labeled the 9 poles using Hebrew letters; the gradually refined view of the system appears in Figure.

Thoth gave us the system for three main reasons: (1) to give us the kind of Metatronic system that would assist us in the next phase of our growth and smooth out the time anomalies, and (2) reinsert into the Racial Mind the major system for reestablishing the "Fallen Female Pillar", that is to rebuild the seriously damaged female Presence and Authority, as well as (3) provide the main LP40 (Transition) mechanism: the "Techad" or "Arieopax" as the 3rd Breastplate of Metatron. We didn't know all this in the beginning nor did we know the great history or massive application of the Reshel system.

GENERAL TECHNOLOGY: The Reshel, also called the Eye of ISIS and Eye of Ra is a pentagon or 5point star. The Reshel's pentagonal "Spear" or triangle in Figure shows one half of the system, the Shekinah or female half. This is characteristically an ascending system that "weds" with the other male or Christos half. We know that the Templars and their Masons knew something of this Templa Mar format since we see evidence in the layout of Chartres and Rosslyn as well as many earth grids. The Templa Mar or "Temples of the Emerald Mar" are "time" temples, that is they have the Reshel capability in their design and function. This includes major Earth Grids found, for example, in Rennes le Chateau, Edinburgh, Bornholm Island, all the BarSheeba grids in Europe and Great Britain, the Arkhom Grid in America. The "ASCENSION GRID" related to the continua transition or LP40 has four levels: (1) the highest is the METATRONIC Grid seen as a complex MStra or Metatronic molecule within a double octahedron form, (2) the ASCENSION Grid seen as (presently) 7 chakra sites around the planet capable of carrying the transition Metatronic charge and function, (3) the TEMPLA MAR system, and (4) the RESHEL system for grounding and processing.

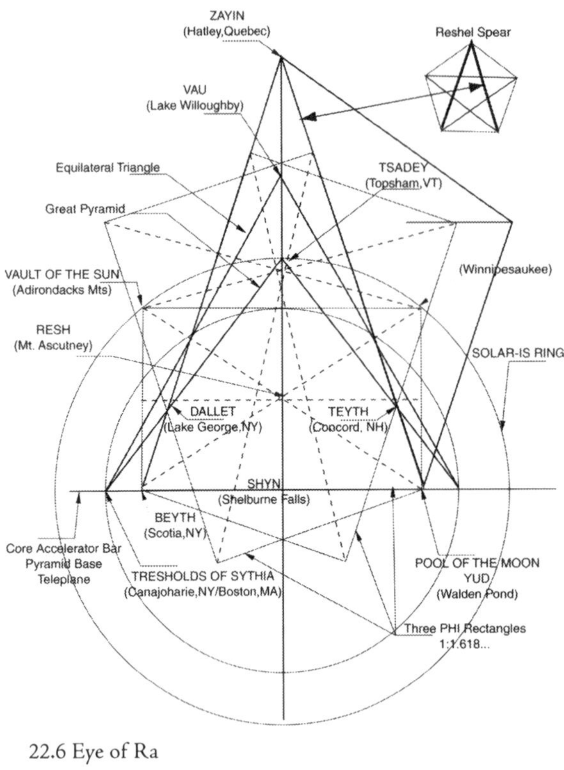

22.6 Eye of Ra

RESHEL SUBSYSTEMS: The Reshel uses a number of complementary systems. The geometric patterns shown in the Figures are "consciousness schematics", that is, they may be installed in temples, earth grids or groups to create resonant harmonics with universal dynamics. These dynamics are more related to thought forms than physical forms. They are the same thing in the Ranna continua where "what you think happens" but in this half light realm the same principle may apply but here the patterns are more "facilitators" for encouraging things to happen. Much depends on intention combined with physical resonant patterns.

(1) The Great Pyramid creates the basic form or "teleplane" as its base. Its sockets contain codes for duplicating the Circadean Rhythm which is our local system's expression of a much larger cosmic life supporting rhythm.

(2) The Pyramid's apex or "TSADDY Pole" also called the "GLORY Pole", synthesizes the above cosmic codes and organizes a basic seed core expressed as a pentahedron using the "Bethlehem Angle" of 26°, 18'. The base of this pentahedron generates golden ratio spirals that create the rest of the system, terminating in two "Pools of Life" or "Pools of the Moon" located in the base "Event Horizon" for the Reshel.

(3) The EVENT HORIZON contains the main spiritual reference ULTA Point. It is the time continum or reality frame for whatever is being created. The Event Horizon has two planes that resonate with the two bases of the two Reshel Spears that are in constant movement. The SHIYN Pole in each Spear downloads the Ulta Points' codes regulating the whole event.

(4) The spirals converge above the Pyramid to create the VAU Pole or apex of a tetrahedron system. The two tetras create different forms of the "star tetrahedron" also called a number of things including the DWELLER OF DIVINE FIRE where the Lords rule. This locates the Thrones of the Elohim and their physical representatives (ultra terrestrials, Hierarchy, devachan). This star tetra is also the first of several forms used in creating the LAYOOESH PILLAR which connects the Oritronic and Metatronic realms. It is the "Pillar in the Temple of God" or "Key of David"

(5) The Eye of Ra is a system for interlinking "ley" lines in all time continua, thus the time gate function is important. The "L-gate" often seen in grids is a short version of the more complete Eye of Ra. The Eye of Ra is a rhombus both 1.618 and 2.618 values. In the Reshel it has its minor axis in the Event Horizon and its main dual rhombus' poles in the Pyramid apex or Tsadey pole (1.618 point) and the KRONOS Pole (2.618 point) above the Vau pole in each Spear. There is also another sub system of L-gates or Eyes of Ra in each Spear. The 90° bend of each L is found in the DALLET and TEYTH poles on each side of

the RESH pole. Each Spear has a double L format controlled by the Resh or "Chief Head Stone" (in Hebrew). This system is called in Ps 118:1923, the "Gates of Righteousness" in verse 19 and the main system is called the "Gate of Yahway (Lord)" in verse 20. The "head stone of the corner" is the Resh controlling the "L" function. The Christ has been called the Chief Head or Corner Stone that can not be ignored.

(6) The ZAYIN (Zion) Pole is the apex of the pentagonal Spear, synthesizing all poles related to the Pentagonal format. The Shiyn, Dallet, Teyth and Tsadey form the "4" dynamic, the beyt, Yud (Pyramid sockets on the Event Horizon) and Vau poles are the "Haepathia" dynamic related to the tetrahedron and form the "3" dynamic. Together these poles create the "7" and the Zayin pole is the 8th aspect. The Resh is the 9th or ENNEAD pole controlling all actions.

(7) The Resh pole is the apex of a Bethlehem Angle pentahedron whose base is in the Event Horizon and is the same as that of the Great Pyramid. Thus the Pyramid has two apices of considerable power: the Capstone at the 51.8 degrees slope angle and the Resh at the 26.3 degrees slope. There is another point in the Pyramid called the MIDDIN CHAMBER in the middle of the Pyramid's cube. The slope angle for that is 44.497 degrees (the added bit to make 45 degrees is a Selah spoke, or divine spinning energy "beam"). This chamber does not appear in the Reshel grid but is a part of its advanced application.

(8) The SOLARIS Ring is a ring or sphere generated by spinning the Glory or Tsadey pole. It is the primary Sun or divine generation pole for life and life support systems, hence the association with the golden ratio spirals which are a major life support system. Where the SolarIS Ring cuts the golden ratio spirals we have a "Sacred Vault of the Sun." These are located in direct alignments with the Pools of the Moon/Life.

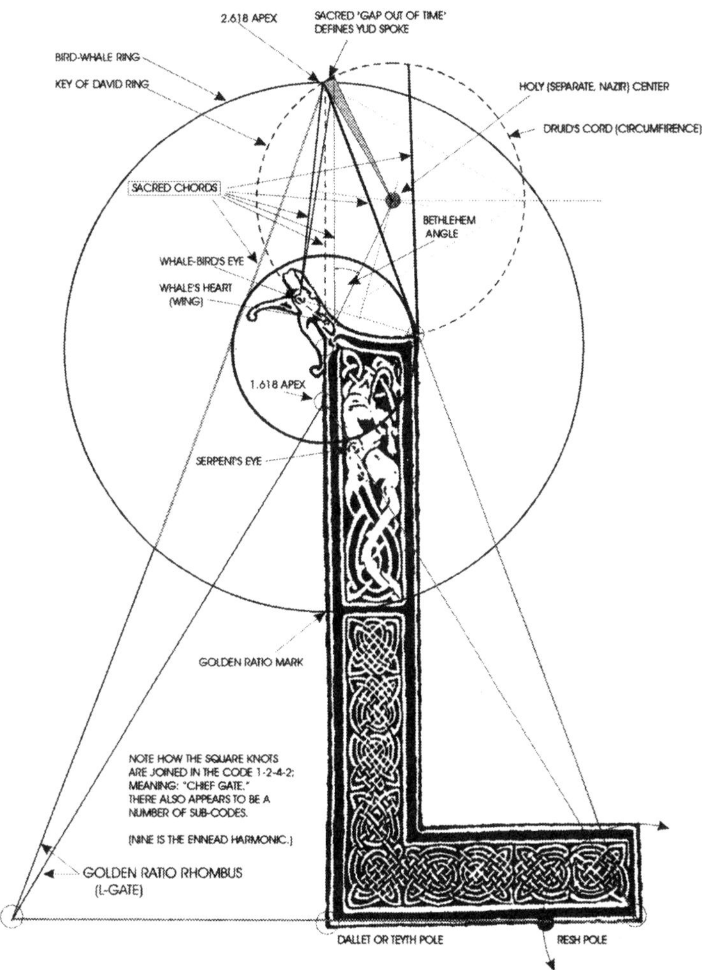

22.7 L-Gate

When the two Spears' resh poles merge in the center, remember that the Spears are constantly cycling, the Pools of the Moon of one Spear merges with the Vaults of the Sun of the other Spear...in effect creating an eclipse. This opens a major Gate, called the LION GATE. In Reshel terms the two double gate or Eye of Ra systems come together on the Event Horizon creating one system of two gates or L's. The main central gate or pillar system then forms when the Spears proceed to next merge shiyn poles. The two outer pillars (L's) are the archetypical two temple pillars best known as the Boaz and Yahchen Pillars in Solomon's Temple. These are also called the Pillars of the Abode; they stabilize the central pillar or Layooesh.

There are many variations of energy patterns open to the cycling Spears. An infinite number of systems can be created within the Spinner field.

RESHEL SYMBOLS: The main symbol is the Crescent Moon with 5point star above it most often seen as Islam's logo. It was once found as the logo for Proctor and Gamble until the Christian Coalition forced them to change it. The Templars used it with an additional two stars. It is the protosiniatic Hebrew letter glyph for Aleph, the bull, chief friend, etc.... It was drawn as a Taurus sign with circle and crescent. The Jews once related to God as the "Unseen Rider over the Bull." That is, the Glory pole or "Tsadey" over the crescent. The Reshel system is a primary format in the Hebrew alphabet, obvious when studying the original pictures used as letters. The woman standing on the Moon's crescent is another. Another symbol is the decapitated head or skull, much used by the Templars. The "double resh" then shows up as the head or bird with two faces or two heads, the split stone or mountain, or split head.

WHY TIME GATES? And what is "this phase of our evolution" all about?

When our light groups, still in training, were boosting their frequencies and stability the matrices defining our time continuum were beginning to become hazy and we were experiencing time glitches. This is an indication of inefficient processing and it could become dangerous if the wrong moves were done out of ignorance or without proper communication with Metatronic inner planes mentors. This had occurred once in earlier years when a group tripped out of this continuum and their room disappeared for several minutes, the members experiencing vertigo attacks from the inner ear problems associated with inept time transport. (Their mentors had permitted it to occur as an object lesson.) Thoth provided our groups with the Reshel format as noted above but he also set up educational experiences demonstrating our ignorance of what was going on in the realm of time traveling. If we were going into serious light work we needed to know who the players are and what issues are driving the action. We dramatically learned about the MONTAUK PROJECT and its abominations. We learned about the Kumir ("Grays", non en souled ETS), Lucifer and his fallen angels, who the bad guys are and why as well as the good guys[6].

The summarized story was noted in the Preface and is this. Our time continuum is a fallen, half light ("Oritronic") spectrum with racial consciousness also at the fallen level. We dropped out of the RANNA TIME WAVE which is in the full light, Metatronic, spectrum. (Metatron is the highest archangel; the quality of consciousness and being of the Ranna Wave is best described as "Metatronic.") The Fall was keyed by the time implosion in the Lucifer Star Gate induced by a suborder of the Melchezedek Order whose ideas were larger than their intelligence. This mother of time implosions keyed into the ("future") Crucifixion and then into a number of other harmonic implosions including those of the Montauk Project. In effect we have been working in three continua: the First, that we dropped out of, the Second, fallen one, and the Third which is our future formed by the best wisdom of both the First and Second. Our *PRESENT EVOLUTIONARY MOVEMENT* is the return to the Metatronic Ranna Wave albeit at its lower frequency range.

The bad guys have been trying to break up this evolutionary jump since the beginning of the Fall. Their usual pattern has been to scare humans into believing there will be a comet strike the planet, and/or a terrible plague. "BUT never fear! Help has arrived with our higher ET technology we can save you and give you great technical gifts (which by the way make really great weapons!)...sign up here!" Their strategy is also to guide relatively aware persons and groups into positions of "locking in" in the higher Oritronic range with the idea that they've "made it" and there is no need for more ascension. The old ways are resurrected and the "Oritronic Ceiling" begins to solidify in the Racial Mind further influencing all concerned. The good guys are called the SOLARIANS and are known as the "Shepherds" or "Eagles of Starr." They have a number of programs which work throughout the three time continua in creating avatars, messianic programs and actions providing us with a level playing field (still honoring Free Will). The Solarians are humans, that is ensouled beings inhabiting the stellar worlds and suns. There are angelic orders that also specialize in assisting the Solarians.

The Solarians work out of the main Central Sun of the future called MAZURIEL which will be located in the area of Denebola in Leo. Mazuriel has always been there but did not fall with the rest. In all intra continua work however Mazuriel is a viable and necessary primary factor. To keep their programs glued together with good communications the Solarians have established notable temples throughout the three continua called "Temples of the Emerald Mar" or "Templa Mar", relating to "Temples of Time." Chartres, Rosslyn, and other well known temples are such. We find in them specific geometries related to the RESHEL format. In many ways ARKHOM as a whole is such a temple however it is more a "harmonic" in view of its size that facilitates the overall consciousness and stability of minor time gates in its area.

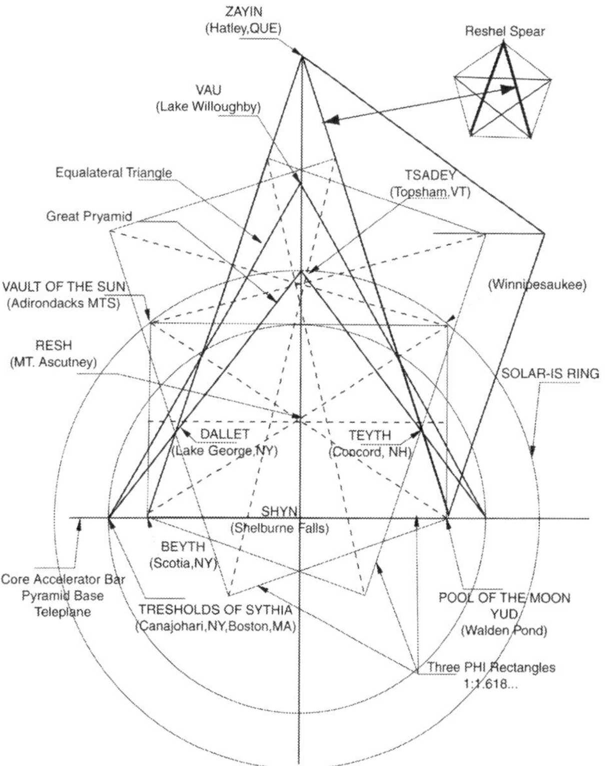

Systems that parallel the Reshel are those others of the 24 Metatronic Breastplates. So far the Reshel has been the most inclusive that I've found. We know of three at the time of writing. The priests of Ruta put the Reshel grids in place before Atlantis finally went down. These grids have always been a jump ahead of the collective Racial Mind in their areas and always have provided a strong Metatronic vector, thus making spiritual organizations more effective even when still operating in the Oritronic range.

These grids are designed to be fully activated in the Metatronic, in the lower manageable ranges, at this time when we are rapidly shifting continua. There is presently much written about the stellar races and cosmic history. Most of this is water under the dam and is more in the way than is helpful. Except that information that is bringing forward the refined wisdom needed in the Third Continuum. The Nephilim (fallen angels) via the Grays, other stellar human agencies, as well as our own confused humans have seriously damaged Arkhom via their Montauk Point contamination and control. This influence and damage will be progressively cleaned up by Solarian programs. Its left for us to do our best to continue in the ascension vector. Not to be lulled into complacency or ego arrested ideas that we have no more inner work to do either in ourselves or in helping our mates in this time-ship...the ARK-HOM.

Conclusion

In summary, there is a Solarian organization on an island base in a distant future sea, the EMERALD MAR; that island is presently known as Masada in Israel. It is called Korbola in that future time. The Solarian Korbolans have many notable programs that span back through the three continua which are designed to work with the Hierarchy, angelic orders and Ultra-Terrestrials in facilitating the redemption and evolution of this fallen continuum and the unification of the three. This present phase of the Transition from the second to the third continuum is critical. One of the systems put in place by the ancient Atlan priests of the Holy Isle of Ruta, as a part of the Solarian effort are the specialized "Reshel" grids which have a strong Metatronic vector and are in fact intended to be fully Metatronic when working at their full potential... thus are designed for now and for the future. The grids may be employed as group formats, temple geometries or the same covering large areas of the Earth. They do not control people but they are important in enhancing and facilitating spiritual programs.

That Grid now called ARKHOM is one such system. A major one. Having been "rebooted" by the Sinclair Expedition in 1398 CE, resonating with the same systems in Europe, it would have been of assistance in influencing the creation of the Iroquois Confederation and then follow-on the European North American colonial establishment. This expanded the Confederations' program which is reflected in the American Bill of Rights, Constitution. Arkhom's grid influence would have inserted a Metatronic vector into the mixed culture frames of New England that provided a thread of spiritual continuity from ancient times into the present ascension phase. This vector would also effectively facilitate ways of group thought and action that would carry over into the new continum immediately before us as well as easing our transition from here to there.

Footnotes

1 Much of my information is based on Thoth's commentaries given via Reverends Maia and Simeon Nartoomid of the Church of the Johannie Grove of the Machenaim in Crestone, CO 91131. I have done extensive interpretation of the basic information and it should --not-- be assumed that Thoth or the Church agrees with my ideas appearing above. If the reader wishes direct access to the basic information it is available in the Churches' *TEMPLE DOORS* periodical.

2 I Peter 2: 4-8.

3 *Genisis;* by David Wood, Baton Press, Tunbridge Wells, Kent, England; 1895 Rennes le Chateau in southern France is an ancient major time gate area using the Reshel grid system. This was known to the Templars and more recently by the two priests in that area, Fr's Sauniere and Boudet in the early part of the 20th century.

4 *The Sword and the Grail,* by Andrew Sinclair, Crown Publishers Inc., NY, 1992. This excellent book shows the outline of a knight punched into stone. The stone was engraved by those of the Henry Sinclair expedition of 1398 CE to Nova Scotia and the US East Coast. The expedition also built the NEWPORT TOWER which still exists at Newport RI.

5 *Voices in Stone;* by Benard I Pietsch, self published, Rohnert Park CA, 1973.

6 For more information, very readable, order the *KOALA* pamphlet from the Church of the Johannine Grove of the Machenaim in Crestone CO. The E Mail address is johgrove@fone,net or call 719 256 4057. This is the best explanation I have seen that describes these grave issues at the high level it deserves.

Boston City Hall Plaza is a major Arkhom site. The eastern point of the Grand Trine and the Circle of Twelve, it marks the dawn portal of the Base Ley. It generates seed thought and action. The American Revolution and the era of telephone communication began there, and Boston area universities lead the world in innovation and invention.

As our collective being responds to the Cycles of Destiny, individuals and groups combine age-old wisdom with cutting edge technology to meet both human and environmental needs. Henry MacLean and the Wings Lane Collaborative envision an ecological renovation of City Hall and its Plaza to renew community spirit, while proclaiming a sustainable future in which people understand that environmental and economic security are one. Henry also describes initiatives and ideas aimed at making our cities more sustainable in general.

23: Urban Ark

Restoration of a Traditional City

Boston in the 21st Century

by Henry P. MacLean

Historical Perspectives on Boston:

Traditionally, growth comes at a time when we have pushed to the limits and there is nowhere else to go. Boston is a place where limits have traditionally been broken. In December of 1773, the Sons of Liberty – members from the Saint Andrew's Masonic Lodge including Paul Revere, Samuel Adams, and others – initiated the "Boston Tea Party", a critical step in crystallizing the movement of the colonies for freedom from England.

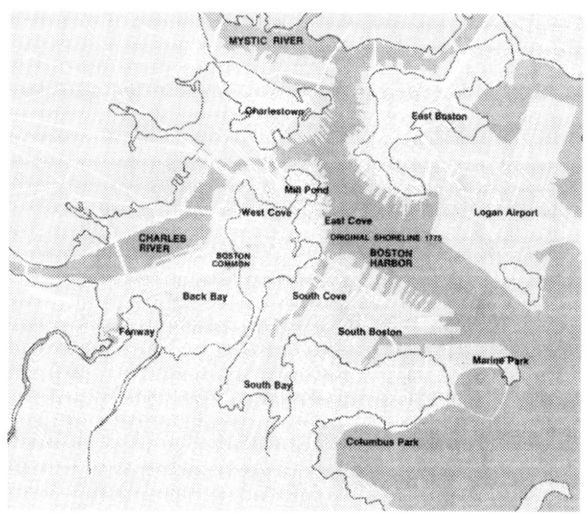

23.1 Then and Now
The infilling of the original Bays around Boston proper.

Thirty years later another form of limitation to growth was met by cutting down the drumlins and hills of the town and filling the harbor to create new land. In the next 190 years the city would fill more harbor, marsh, and river to grow four times over, from 783 acres to its present size of over 3000 acres, growing from a town of 16,000 to a metropolitan area of two and a half million people, a 156 fold increase.

[1]"At the end of the American Revolution, Boston still resembled a small English seaport of narrow streets ... that suggest a continuity of the medieval tradition." Between 1788 and 1818, [2]"Urban elegance in the terms of London, Bath, or Edinburgh came to Boston through the work of Charles Bulfinch (1763 to 1844), who literally changed the face of the town"; designing the State House, Courthouse, Faneuil Hall, four churches, three entire streets, schools, and scores of houses. In the mid 1800's the city experienced a growth of cultural institutions and annexed a number of neighboring towns where large sections of the population began moving out from the original city on new tram and electric car lines, and small towns were merged into the city in the first phases of major expansion.

Two truly inspired "Designers of American History" who left their mark on the landscape of Boston in the late 1800's were Henry Hobson Richardson and Frederick Law Olmsted. Roughly one hundred years ago H. H. Richardson brought in a new beginning in architectural development as he established his office in Brookline MA after being awarded the design of Trinity Church in Copley Square at the age of 32. Richardson fused his natural affinity for blending his buildings into the landscape with his magical use of geometry and symbolism and choice of natural rich color and material. His effect is clear today after having his Trinity Church selected as the most outstanding masterpiece by one hundred American architects, one hundred years after its construction. What people were looking for in Architecture in

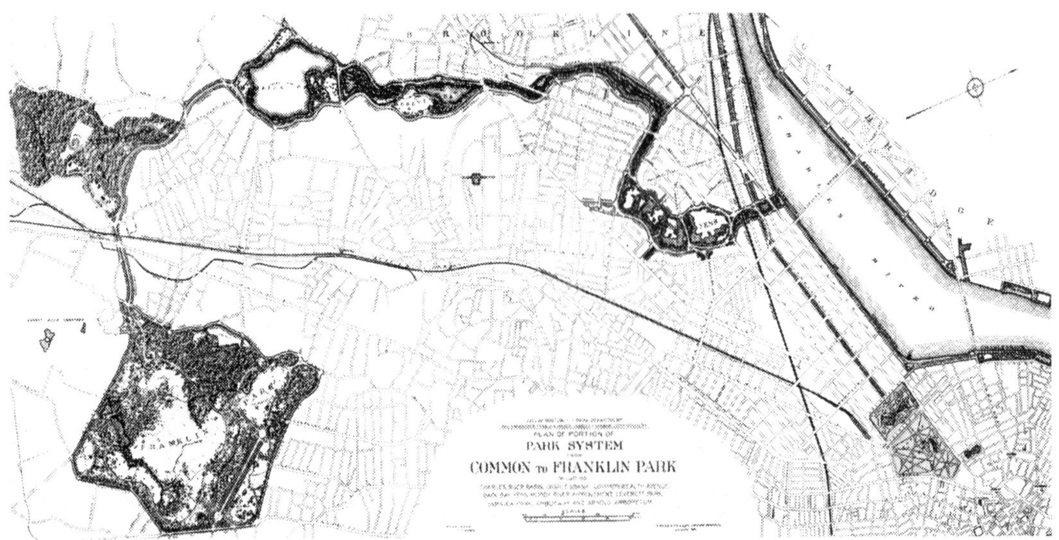

23. 2 Emerald Necklace
Darkened area shows the Boston Greenway Park system, designed by Fredrick Olmstead

1. Boston Society of Architects, Architecture in Boston, 1976, p.3
2. Boston Society of Architects, p.8

1870 is what we are looking for today –"something aesthetically sound and yet distinguished by its own life and power of development."

These same geometries have reappeared in numerous culturally and geographically distant and isolated locations throughout the history of temple building on the planet. The study of platonic solids and the nesting of the five platonic polyhedra which give rise to these geometries, outlined by Plato in his Timaeus, were used as principal design parameters in Richardson's buildings, in plan section and elevation.

Convinced to move to Boston by his good friend Henry Hobson Richardson, Olmsted's great work as Commissioner of Parks in the city was a 4000 acre park known as the Emerald Necklace.

> [3]A man's eyes cannot be as much occupied as they are in large cities by artificial things, or by natural things seen under obviously artificial conditions, without a harmful effect, first on his mental and nervous system and ultimately on his entire constitutional organization.

These words echo his great understanding, compassion, and designs which thankfully found their place in a score of large American cities. While most of this Boston park system was developed, urban renewal and highway programs of the 20th century have destroyed much of the cohesiveness of this necklace, cutting off for instance a wonderful series of parks along the Charles from the larger open spaces of the system. Slowly, sections of these missing links are being brought back.

The first half of this century saw a continuing growth of the industrial and commercial success of Boston. But the greatest changes to this and other American cities came with the end of the war. According to America's foremost historian Vincent Scully Jr. , [4]"After World War Two, the automobile came into its own, most of all in the United States, where the auto industry managed to get our trolley lines torn up and where we embarked on a joy ride that left our cities in ruins... We designed everything for it, 'to keep it happy', in the words of Duany." (planner/architect Andres Duany)

Today, this unlimited trend of cars and highways may be turning the corner. A new central artery project now proceeding in Boston (a ten billion dollar project considered to be the single largest public works project in the history of the world) will in fact include the dismantling and rerouting underground, the elevated highway that cuts the heart of downtown off from the harbor. This will open up a potential new green belt-avenue that will have a marked positive impact on the city. This is but one of many steps that gives us hope for a reformation in progress here in the"Hub".

---

3. Civilizing American Culture, *A Selection of Frederick Law Olmsted"s Writings on City Landscapes*, MIT Press, Cambridge, MA. 1971, p.243
4. Vincent Scully Jr. *Seaside and New Heaven. Towns and Town Making Principles*, Duany and Plater-Zyberk, Rizzoli, NewYork, 1992

The patterns and principles underlying the establishment and growth of this traditional New England seaport town were primarily motivated by trade, commerce, and the accrual of monetary wealth. When it became an end and not a means for the majority of our society, the real economics of nature was discarded and abused.

Looking Back and Moving Forward

> [5] At my feet lay a great city. Every quarter contained large open squares filled with trees, among which statues glistened and fountains flashed in the late afternoon sun. Public buildings of a colossal size and an architectural grandeur unparalleled in my day... Surely I had never seen this city nor any one comparable to it before. Raising my eyes at last to the horizon, I looked westward. That blue ribbon winding away to the sunset, was it not the sinuous Charles? I looked east; Boston Harbor stretched before me within its headlands...

These are the thoughts of Julian West, the protagonist of socialist and utopian novelist Edward Bellamy's *Looking Backward*, as he wakes from a deep hypnotic sleep of one hundred and thirteen years, three months, and eleven days. Surviving an unusual set of circumstances that embalmed his body in a subterranean chamber and set his systems into a state of suspended animation beginning in May 1887, Bellamy has the thirty year old West discovered by an excavation crew and nursed back to consciousness by a retired Dr. Leete in the year 2000 AD. After his gaze from the good Doctor's rooftop where he is convinced of his unbelievable situation, he responds, [6]"Only a century has passed... But many a millennium in the world's history had seen changes less extraordinary."

Bellamy embraced the vision of Whitman, Emerson, and other transcendental writers and philosophers who were all drawn to provide a space for the individual amid the rush of industrialization, immigration, and the onslaught of urbanism in the 1880s. As Dr. Leete points out to Julian, [7]"No doubt, as you imply, the cities of that period (the 1880s) were rather shabby affairs. If you had the taste to make them splendid, which I would not be so rude as to question, the general poverty resulting from your extraordinary industrial system would not have given you the means."

He goes on to describe his Boston of 2000 as a place and time where on the contrary, [8]..."there is no destination of the surplus wealth so popular as the adornment of the city which all enjoy in equal degree." Bellamy's vision of cooperation replacing competition and the idea of increasing wealth by increasing common versus individual stock inspired the likes of Ebenezer Howard and his well known Garden City proposals of the early twentieth century which integrated open space with agriculture, and took a stand against those ills of pollution, transportation, and housing shortages.

---

5. Edward Bellamy, *Looking Backward*, 2000-1887, Random House, NY, 1982, P.25
6. Bellamy, page 26
7. Bellamy, page 28
8. Bellamy, page 28

In his myopic conclusion in his introduction to the 1982 printing of *Looking Backward*, Smith College professor R. Jackson Wilson summarizes;

> [9] As Dr. Leete described in his long abstract monologues, the new Boston was a modern city, characterized by planning, integration and efficiency. But beneath Dr. Leete's abstractions, the city that Bellamy actually described, and allowed Julian West to experience, smacked more of restoration that revolution. He was still 'looking backward'.

Eighteen years later this very concept of restoration is being embraced as the only way we in the non-fictional 1990s can hope to survive and thrive into the 21st century. In his best selling new book, *The Ecology of Commerce, A Declaration of Sustainability*, green business entrepreneur Paul Hawken describes how we are a society about to shed a skin and move into a new era.

> [10] Like a sunset effect, the glories of the industrial economy may mask the fact that it is poised at a declining horizon of options and possibilities. Just as internal contradictions brought down the Marxist and socialist economies, so do a different set of social and biological forces signal our own possible demise ...The *restorative* (my italics) economy ... respects this fact. It unites ecology and commerce into one sustainable act of production and distribution that mimics and enhances natural processes.

Despite the inevitable sadness and shock that comes from looking at our real time situation here in Boston, the New England region, and America of 1999, we are thankfully now witnessing a national movement that has come of age. Perhaps in the nick of time, this movement fully embraces the notion of a restoration of nature and the ..."City as a Paradise of Culture" in the words of Richard Register, just as we have come to cherish the Garden as "the paradise of Nature." The vision has once again emerged, but alas, not to be realized for the year 2000 in Boston as Mr. Bellamy had imagined.

Current Patterns:

According to Andy Euston, FAIA Senior planner with US Department of Housing and Urban Development in Washington, [11]"Sustainability is the paradigm now and for the next millennium... How to reconcile urban-rural patterns in the industrialized world today is the core challenge of all politics, all humanitarianism, all enterprise." While cities like Boston have always had the potential of being the paradise of culture, they can also be seen as the prime concentrated source of death for thousands of species worldwide and a scourge on resources from the rural lands that surround and support them.

> [12]A hundred years ago, even fifty years ago, it did not seem urgent that we understand the relationship between business and a healthy environment, because natural resources

---

9. Bellamy, page xxxiv
10.Paul Hawkin, *The Ecology of Commerce*, Haper Collins, New York, 1993, p. 3
11.Walter, Arkin, Crenshaw, *Sustainable Cities*, Eco-Home Media, LA 1992, p. 73
12.Hawken, p. 3

seemed unlimited. But on the verge of a new millennium we know that we have decimated 97% of the ancient forests in North America; every day our farmers and ranchers draw out 20 billion more gallons of water from the ground than are replaced by rainfall; the Ogalala reservoir, an underground river beneath the great plains, larger than any body of fresh water on earth, will dry up within thirty to forty years at present rates of extraction; globally we lose 25 billion tons of fertile soil a year, the equivalent of all of the wheat fields of Australia.

Many atmospheric scientists believe that with the current level of ozone depletion, would be 15% depleted by 2005 or 2010, which could signal the systematic death of phytoplankton, the basis of the marine food chain and 30% of the oxygen producing bio-mass of the planet (from Adam Trombley, Project Earth, 1988). What we forget living here in Boston is that much of our lifestyle contributes to this process as we drive our cars, build with materials like wood that still comes from these older and distant forests, and as we import 85% of our food from out of state. The average calorie of food put on a typical Boston dinner table in 1994 was subsidized by 10 calories of energy spent to get it there. (from Wendall Berry, American writer and agriculturist)

As Sim Van der Ryn reminds us, [13]"Vast cities are short term aberrations based on fossil fuels. We can make them more efficient, in terms of land and energy use, but in many ways this simply prolongs the destruction of global natural systems, that are enslaved to the service of urban consumers." While a typical American consumes the equivalent of six gallons of oil a day, this energy of a million BTUs per capita per day could never be sustained by the planetary resources or sinks if adopted by the other 92% of the world's 5.5 billion inhabitants. We each produce a half a ton of gases a week, which includes among other things the 800 hours per person average spent just sitting in traffic each year.

According to Al Gore, we have created sinks so big that on an average, Americans produce twice our individual weight every day in household, hazardous, and industrial waste. Some 85% of the landfills for the Boston area operating in 1980 were closed in 1991. The cost of dumping a ton of trash has risen tenfold in the Boston area in that period. Recycling can be seen as a primary element in this regeneration process. And yet we are just beginning.

While the most progressive cities in the Boston metro area like Newton are recycling up to 40% of their trash, we could be recycling over 80% of our waste. To further illustrate this point, every night while half of the world's population is going to bed hungry, the traditional industrialized cities of the US including Boston are throwing away over 375,000 tons of food. (from Westy Egmont, Executive Director of the Boston Food Bank).

We are also wasting nutrients in the form of our urine and excrement by mixing them with water into our sewer systems and septic systems, continually contributing to ground water and oceanic pollution.

13.Walter, p.69

In our continued search for clean and plentiful water in Boston, we have created a string of polluted and abandoned reservoirs running out 150 miles to the west of the city.

Although the demand for water is down to 285 million gallons per day as compared to 335 million in 1987 (due to conservation and leak repairs over the 6400 miles of pipes and tunnels feeding 2.5 million people in the metro area), the cost of this deferred maintenance program is reflected in the rise in water rates which have gone up 60% in Boston in the last 10 years. With a present average age of 80 years and life-span of 100, it is estimated that 3 to 4% of the 1.4 billion net worth of the infra- structure, or twice the normal 1-2% maintenance costs, will be passed on to the consumers over the next 20 years.

After running down our drains, daily this water is mixed with another 200 million gallons of gray water and run off from the Metropolitan Area watersheds, to be piped to a waste water treatment facility in Boston Harbor. Although the immediate ramifications will allow inner harbor regeneration, the new 9 mile out fall tunnel is raising a host of new regional concerns for the safety of Massachusetts Bay. Had the State not delayed so long and then been in such a hurry to respond to the Federal mandate (to clean up what had become one of the dirtiest harbors in the world), new developments in the organic rather than chemical treatment of sewerage could have been explored, such as the implementation of Solar Aquatic Waste Water Treatment systems developed by John Todd and his research group in Falmouth Massachusetts, Oceans Arks International.

These are the pressing problems that directly affect everyone in Boston today. Unless they are dealt with soon, the quality of life in the city will inevitably worsen. Part of the problem in dealing with it all is staying clear and out of shock or denial as we begin to study the particulars of the biological, emotional, spiritual, and psychic mayhem we are dealing with, consciously or unconsciously, on a daily basis.

As we brace ourselves and move into the 21st century, these patterns nonetheless offer an opportunity to embrace our greatness. We are finally face to face with the principles our traditional growth is based on. It is not a pretty sight and we are not happy campers. We have no choice but to reconnect with nature and regenerate our relationship with this planet we have been graced to inhabit.

Working up from the Roots

For the past seven years I have been associated with an intentional community located 120 miles west of Boston in Shutesbury, called Sirius Community. I researched Sirius as one of seven case studies for a project organized by the Consortium for Regional Sustainability through the Center for Environmental Management at Tufts University, in the metro area. Funded by the Environmental Protection Agency (EPA), the focus of the study was to find the essence of what constituted a sustainable community. The work entitled *Sustainable Strategies* was published in November of 1993 and edited by the Consortium's director Elizabeth Kline.

The four characteristics that emerged in the study were the need for a vision or plan of action, a process that integrated education and economics to put that vision into play, an ecological approach to the landscape in question, and a process of insuring a quality of life that completed a balanced community. These same four essential qualities appeared whether it was a group of farmers on Cape Cod, a city of 70 thousand in Jamaica Plain, a community of 25 people living in central Massachusetts, or an individual house in suburban Boston.

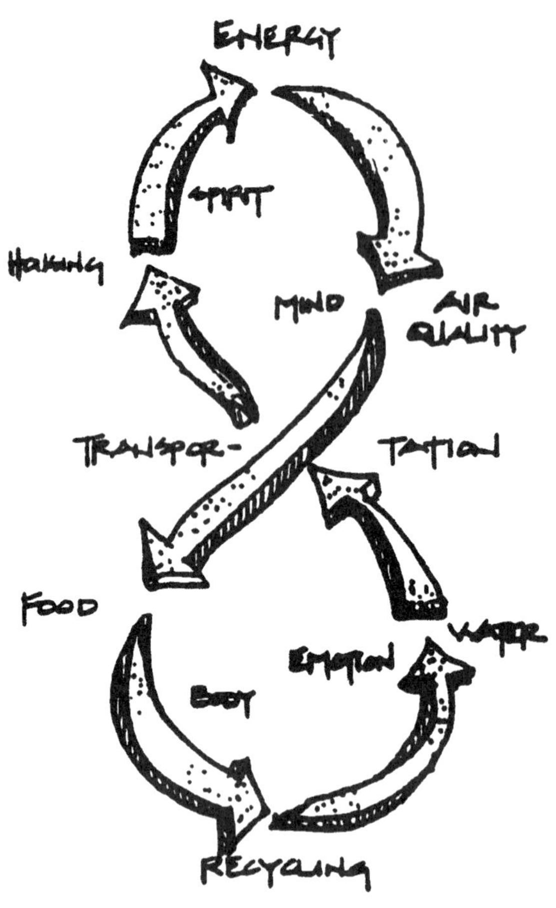

23.3 Figure Eight

The figure eight matrix that emerged covered energy, air quality, transportation/ communication, food production, water management, and housing / community issues.
Developed by Henry P. MacLean

In teaching my sustainability courses at the Boston Architectural Center of Wentworth Institute, I develop a matrix of indicators/issues that evolved from my research, to provide a form and help crystallize the inter-related and often overwhelming concerns of sustainability. The figure eight matrix covered energy, air quality, transportation / communication, food production, water management, and housing /community issues. To my surprise and delight this matrix also nested the concepts we discovered as a team at Tufts.

Another overlay of this system uses integrated needs of mind, body, emotion, and spirit. I have been rethinking the common expression left to us by our ancestors of the Bauhaus movement, "form follows function" from this new perspective. The extension then becomes form (body/earth) follows function (mind/air) which follows frequency (spirit/fire) which in its turn follows intent (heart/water). Restoring a concern for issues of the heart and spirit seem critical to our work at this time.

In the fall of 1992 Sarah and Richard Lincoln-Harrison, a couple from Marblehead (Boston north shore) organized a presentation entitled "Marblehead Beyond the Millennium". To it they brought a number of experts to represent eight categories of sustainability. At the end of a meeting, they held a brainstorming session to ask what a new ecology center in Marblehead might include. As they describe in their recent article;

> [14] Over the past few months, the idea for a community organic

14.Sarah Lincoln Harrison and Richard Harrison, *Vision Leads to Opportunity*, New England Environmental News, Winter 1994. p. 12

> farm has gathered momentum. We apparently have tapped a vein of concern among citizens who are apprehensive about the food they eat. It could also be that we have touched a longing to recover the nourishing experience of cultivating and caring for the earth.

The Marblehead Community Organic Farm Group is a diverse and talented multi-generational group of 195 households with over 600 people eating fresh organic and locally grown food over a 5 month period each year. From this group a larger organization called the Marblehead Environmental Coalition has emerged. This group links together the work of a broad range of committees engaged in a number of different projects ranging from cancer prevention to pesticide awareness. As a result the Town is now recognized as one of the Commonwealth's most environmentally active. From this notion of a simple conference, the Harrisons have taped into the root solution to the urban/ rural dilemma we are all facing. In the words of Sim Van der Ryn;

> [15]"The garden and traditional small scale agriculture represent a middle ground, a transformation of nature to human ends in a way that both the people and nature are enhanced. In our search for solutions, we can not do better than that."

While the projects in Marblehead and Shutesbury are not necessarily urban solutions, they do embody the essential ingredients operating in the center city, with perhaps a less complicated set of constraints. This allows them to set the stage and serve as models for the projects that must ultimately follow in the urban core.

One such project in the urban core gaining steady momentum is the work of Bill Taylor and his bicycle and tree planting enthusiasts known as Earthworks, located in Jamaica Plain (a south-central borough of Boston). This pro-active group is working to plant the beginnings of what they expect will eventually be orchards of fruit bearing trees all over the city. With the help of local youths, schools and community center organizations, this group is working with the hardest hit neighborhoods where gang leaders are asked to take responsibility for a young seedling in order to fully come to know what responsibility for home turf really means.

The bike routes and the edible landscapes that Earthworks is planting will ultimately become the new green-ways and corridors of the inner city. This is where intention is hardest to seed, and where our cities will be re-won. Another focus of Bill's group is to support legislation to continue the construction of bike routes in the city . It has been reported that over 50% of city trips could be made with the use of a bike instead of a car, which as Ryan Snyder tells us [16]"is the most energy-efficient form of transportation known. For 350 calories (a bowl of cereal), we can travel ten miles. An average auto uses about 18,000 calories for the same trip." Working with others, Earthworks played a strong role in recently pushing for

---

15.Walter, p. 69
16.Walter, p. 178

a redraft of the current Transportation Plan for the Boston Region, pushing to make it more responsive to the progressive Federal ISTEA measures passed in 1991.

Earthworks has also worked with groups like Fair Foods, which distributes 5000-8000 pounds of food daily and 25,000 pounds of bread a week, all of it food that would otherwise be thrown away. They are building a distribution center for this work have been located in an abandoned building donated by the city.

Seeding a Sustainable Future

Boston City Hall and Plaza, a Model for the 21st Century

23.4 Boston

City Hall andf City Hall Plaza is located in the open space in the middle of photograph.

Visualize a center where one might go with one's family to visit a museum of environmental awareness, dine at a five-star restaurant, or view an ecological display while taking in fresh air, the sights and sounds of waterfalls, and lush green gardens swirling through three nine-story open atria full of activities and light. Offices and storefronts, pedestrian corridors, balconies and other spaces are all tied together at a variety of levels, with ceremonial stairs leading up to an acre and a half of public space a hundred feet up in the air, smack in the middle of Downtown Boston.

Imagine as well a public/private collaborative paying for such a project in less than seven years, creating 100,000 square feet of new public and retail space generating hundreds of new jobs, while transforming one of the city's most well-known architectural landmarks into one of this country's most exciting architectural public spaces. Finally, picture this project as a new model for ecological architecture, as well as a center for teaching and leading the rest of the country in applying these standards in their own homes and communities into the new millennium.

Boston City Hall and its plaza were built into their current form in the early 1960's. Since that time there has been ongoing debate about the effectiveness of the original plan and in particular the barren and lifeless urban landscape presented by both the plaza and the well-known Kallmann McKinnell building. The submission of over 200 schemes in the Ideas Competition of 1994/1995 made clear that people of Boston want to see the plaza revitalized. In the words of Mayor Tom Menino this historical and geographical center of the city needs to be "preserved, ...improved, made more attractive, welcoming, accessible and usable."

This is an opportunity for the City of Boston to explore a vision for the first Green City Hall in America. With help from the Department of Property Management and Basic City Services, we have greatly accelerated our understanding of the role sustainable architecture and green building can play in City Hall and the plaza. We have found through these studies that we can pay for a sustainable building with the funds that would be otherwise spent on utilities alone. The million dollar savings per annum that we have identified would pay for a sustainable renovation in less than a generation.

We have identified specific economic, health, and ecological possibilities which could help initiate a drive to create this country's most outstanding model in cutting edge sustainable architecture and landscape architecture. This would include both the renovated City Hall and new construction proposed for the plaza.

As part of this plan, we have explored exciting architectural additions and alterations to City Hall which allow for significant pedestrian movement under, over, and through the structure. These additions and alterations to the existing building could result in reclaiming 100,000 square feet of existing and new floor area for office and commercial use. This would generate new jobs and a revenue stream from the integrated facilities. City Hall would also serve as a link between the marketplace/ waterfront and the revived plaza.

Singing to The New Center

Over the course of Colonization on the Massachusetts seaboard hundreds of towns were established. Why was it that the town of Boston should grow to become such a center? Clearly, the model of Arkhom is one way of rationalizing this fact. The growth of Boston over more than three hundred years is a story all in itself. A story to include the development of many environmental ills all too familiar in hundreds of similar cities all around this planet. Isn't it interesting that the body polotic would chose to returned to the geographical center of its original Shaumut peninsula to build City Hall and plaza, this "Hub of the Universe", after all this time and movement! How much like a living organism this is, growing so big at such a sustained and phenomenal pace while managing to stay so conscious of its center.

However conscious or unconscious it was, this memory of the Center was accompanied by a massive influx of Federal money and a brutal act of Urban Renewal that eradicated the old Boston of Scollay Square and the West End, transforming it to the barren landscape of giant concrete and glass buildings that established Government Center from 1955 to 1965. This post war boom project began a transformation that has remained unfinished to this day. Ask anyone who works in Boston City Hall, drives or walks by on a daily basis, and you might hear a refrain of sorts, that the building elicits emotional or even psychological unrest, reactions of urban malaise no matter where you might find yourself spending time. Visitors from outside the region and country are routinely left wondering how poorly they are greeted by this plaza and building and how the great City of Boston ever allowed this "experimental" centerpiece to overshadow and confuse its center as well as it does. Even the Mayor wants an office that feels and works better for him and his staff.

In the February 1969 *Architectural Record* write up praising the building as an "architecture for the people", the author Mildred Schmertz describes this new brutalist movement of architecture characterized by City Hall as an extension of a philosophy where "small elegances and refinements have no place ... since such are believed to be inappropriate to the human condition and indeed beneath us, belonging to a world which more of us, and principally the young, are learning to reject." When City lawyers in the late 60's struck down any options for a cafe and restaurant in the central space of the building as originally proposed by the architects, the small elegances were forever rejected and the building was doomed. The existential barrenness and vastness of the plaza spread through and took over City Hall itself.

In a talk given in 1959 at the 46th Paris Prize dinner three years before he and his partners won the Boston City Hall Competition, Gerhard M. Kallmann outlined his philosophy for an "Experimental Architecture that is interested no longer in simple form against a void but in contrast patterns of interrelatedness." Yet once the lawyers and bureaucrats insured that the single purpose of the building was city business, this powerful language of inter relatedness achieved by Kallmann and his partners went to work to reinforce the lack of programming and kafkaesque character of these utilitarian spaces. Without people coming to enjoy and be in awe of this architecture, the building was reduced to a maze of ideas, an idealized concept formed in countless yards of concrete and buried steel, with "City Business" as the single and only business of this new centerpiece of Boston.

In their desire for an architecture for the people, an experimental architecture, and an architecture dedicated to patterns of interrelatedness, the original architects and planners of the plaza were never given the full opportunity to see their experiment succeed. It is precisely these missed opportunities so clearly evident in the building today that form the basis for our collaborative effort to reenvision this frozen sculpture of the 60s.

Redeveloping the Open Core

The building has a hollow core of sufficient size to accommodate a regular place or center of human activity. The floor of this space, dubbed "the mound" by the original architects, is on the fourth floor level which when added up in full accounts for 40,000 s.f. of nearly vacant space sitting just one level up from the equally barren plaza below. This is a place trapped in time, a magnificent diamond in the rough, with veins of possibility and potential leaping out of every corner. Ceilings, columns, and concrete beams and girders wrap around a central patch of sky above, with receding office windows and balconies rarely visited. Two grand sets of stairs lead up to the space from the plaza and Congress Street, as well as the main ceremonial stair from inside the building itself. Access to all of them are permanently blocked to the public .

With two thousand full time residents of the building and tens of thousands of other Bostonians moving through the area on a daily basis, this place has the potential to sing with activity. It is roughly the size of Copley Plaza's central atrium which also has three or so levels of office space looking down into it's central core full of activity, with water features, plants and light flooding the space from a wonderful skylight above. Once the Mound at City Hall is enclosed from above, a whole fleet of side wall glazing set back from the pillars of the building (so as not to visibly change the exterior design) can complete the enclosure of this priceless space. By removing the hazy skylights that sit in the center of the mound and introducing another internal set of escalators down one floor, this space can be instantly reconnected to the third and main entry of the building. The dark and isolated second level that hosts lines of discouraged traffic ticket payers below would now be flooded with natural daylight and exhilarating views looking up in some areas as much as eight stories.

23.5 The Mound
Unused core of Boston City Hall is and opertunity waiting to happen.

Bridging to Quincy Market

City Hall sits at the cross point of many paths through Boston. The most prominent is clearly the walkway to the sea that places the building as an object (some would argue a blockage) between the highly successful indoor /outdoor spaces of Faneuil Hall and the transformation that awaits City Hall Plaza. So as the midpoint in this colossal trio of activity, the role of this building as a bridge seems to warrant a further look. In fact this notion of using the building as a bridge for large streams of pedestrians solves a few of the issues faced by the most recent proposal for the long debated bridge across Congress Street.

23.6 Boston City Hall circa 1999.

By relocating the handicap lift component of the pedestrian bridge to the southeast corner of the building, a new elevator and its expanded lobby could receive a ramp off the new bridge, inviting pedestrians from the Plaza and the tail end of Washington Street directly into the building. The renovation would be completed inside by providing a full circle pathway around the ceremonial stair leading up to the mound. (This would connect this new lobby to the new escalators and the main entry lobby and elevators. It would ultimately reconnect Faneuil Hall to City Hall Plaza.) It would also be happening at the base of these enormous atria, whose shafts of light from above would enliven all of this new activity.

These dramatic atria, more refined and thinner than that of the central core of the building, recall the drama and awe-inspiring canyons of gothic cathedrals. If one could access these spaces via a simple spiral metal stair, perhaps integrated with some water feature, plants, and artwork, a vertical pathway to the roof garden could begin from this third level, a personal journey by foot reminiscent of such national treasures as the Washington Memorial.

A Roof Garden for the 21st Century

In addition to Mayor Menino's call for a rooftop restaurant, there have been several suggested uses for this potential one acre space. What could become the tenth floor of the building currently houses two rather large one and two story mechanical penthouses and ineffective roof windows, quite visible from the street and clearly unrelated to the design of the building below. LeCorbusier, one of the great modern architects who certainly inspired Kallmann and McKinnell, saw the roof garden as an instrumental component of this style of architecture he helped create. While the weather in Boston can't be compared to that of some of Corbu's sites in the south of France, strips of garden and potential swing spaces for greenhouses could be successfully located along the edge of this roof. A promenade for strolling and viewing the city might also be directly connected by elevator to the street and the newly restored public spaces below. Being the center point of the city and ten stories up, the views are sensational and surely due to improve when the expressway no longer cuts off the harbor from downtown.

23.7 Five Star Restaurant
A rendered view from the proposed restaurant atop Boston's renewed City Hall.

Providing a crown to the center portion of the building would reclaim 30,000 s.f. of restaurant and conference space at this tenth floor level, with a loft space at the peak of this new structure. This plane could double as a structure to mount the latest in translucent solar electric skylights which turn sunshine directly into electricity while providing properly shaded natural light to the space below. Working with the "one million solar roofs" initiative now being sponsored by the Federal Government, these panels (that help power state of the art ecological buildings in Europe and Japan) could turn Boston City Hall into the largest demonstration project of photovoltaics in the Northeast. This project is in fact currently financeable.

New Shops and Arcade for Congress Street

The approach to City Hall from the east and Faneuil Hall holds what is perhaps the greatest opportunity in this renovation. In addition to the bridge at level three mentioned above, the building on the two lower levels would instantly attract shoppers from one of the nation's busiest shopping areas located just across the street. Behind the 300 foot long brick wall that runs along Congress Street and wraps the corner to the north entry of the building is 20,000 s.f. of parking for 24 City Councilmen as well as mechanical and dead storage, space that could all be efficiently relocated to more appropriate areas in the building. By punching some holes in this brick skin to create a covered arcade, this whole facade could come alive with shops and commercial activity that could open through to the lower atria of the first two public floors and the ticket areas mentioned above.

By extending the existing north entry and making it visible from Congress Street and the plaza, the grand recess it now occupies could be filled with a lobby and more retail space. In this way even more area could be reclaimed on five levels without compromising the original look and feel of the building from the outside. Transforming these two faces of the building on the east and west would effect an enormous improvement on the historic architectural neighbors of City Hall, the Blackstone Block, and the Marketplace. Whatever development is decided on for this end of the Plaza and/or the Federal Building would also now be directly open to and engaged with the revived public entrance and activities of the mound and the grand atria above.

Security would have to be considered with the increased flow of people through the building. However steps could be taken to cordon off certain areas at night or after business hours for the City Offices without sacrificing any of the opportunities mentioned above. The building is currently open to the publics' free movement during regular working hours.

Economic and Energy Efficiency

At Wentworth Institute of Technology, we studied the building from an environmental perspective. The results were simple but profound. Imagine for a moment that the efficiency of buildings can be measured like cars. Instead of miles per gallon we in the building industry call it BTUs (British Thermal Units) per square foot. Every human body is in fact a little heat machine that in a state of rest puts out about 450 BTUs per hour. The fuels that power a building like City Hall are ultimately similar to gasoline, as they burn oxygen and pour more unwanted carbon into the atmosphere. In fact, what is surprising to most people is that buildings produce close to 40% of the carbon being pumped into the atmosphere today, while trucks and autos produce closer to 33%.

Working with a national program called Vital Signs set up in 1995 to analyze a wide range of buildings across the country, we set out to determine how much energy City Hall used on an annual basis and how that compared to the national standard. Working with the Office of Property Management at City Hall who provided us with all of the energy invoices from 1995-1997 for the building, we determined that the energy utilization rate of City Hall was about 277,000 BTUs per square foot. Our building was using 2.5 times (277/110) more energy annually than a standard building built today, and 5 times more than a building built to current high efficiency standards. The combined costs of powering and fueling City Hall come to $1.6 million per year, 2 and 1/2 times more costly to operate than a standard building built today.

Our next step was to develop a three part strategy on how to bring the energy use down and in the process save the city 1 million dollars a year. The simple three prong strategy was to (#1) Upgrade the existing 30 year old mechanical system, (#2) salvage and reactivate the existing computer control center, and

(#3) renovate the interior court and provide a new insulated glass and panel skin to the exposed vertical faces of the structure and the roof openings.

In the process of review and analysis, my colleagues, students, and I realized that we could save this money and the associated pollution as well as retrieve close to 100,000 s.f. of new space in the building. In the process of retrofitting we could in fact address all of the opportunities outlined above regarding the open core and the roof garden from Congress Street and the North Entry. In April of 1997 we shared our enthusiastic results in a full presentation to Property Management and Commissioner Michael Galvin, members of the Trust for City Hall, and the Chief Architect for the City. Mr. Galvin, whose office had initially provided all of the raw data for our calculations was equally moved, and invited us to present to the Mayor and his cabinet on July 8, 1997. The presentation was well received and lasted twice the allotted time.

Center for Ecology and Sustainability

Demonstration / Research Center

To insure the successful implementation of such an ambitious project, we propose the development of an ecological center for New England that might be housed in several thousand square feet of the reclaimed space. Through a collaboration of universities, museums, corporate, private, and public sponsors, this Center could become a regional source of learning for sustainable practice and planning, with the green renovation of City Hall as its built-in demonstration and teaching model.

23.4 Boston
City Hall andf City Hall Plaza is located in the open space in the middle of photograph.

The purpose of the center would be threefold. The first would be to minimize the energy and material inflows and outflows for the renovated City Hall and new facilities currently being planned by the Trust. The plan would integrate issues of sustainable / renewable sources of energy, lighting, indoor air quality, transport and parking, food and nutrient cycling, waste and recycling, indoor and outdoor water use, building material selection, as well as ongoing maintenance of the buildings themselves.

Second, demonstrations of a variety of cutting edge technologies in each of these areas would be made accessible to the public for regular tours and presentations. The Center would actively serve to raise public awareness with events and educational programs related to the history and transformation of the city and its environment (urban, rural, natural, and cultural). By reaching out to educate the public as the Mayor's Environmental Committee and the Sustainable Boston coalition has done, City Hall Plaza would become an inspiration for healthy future development for Bostonians and all who come to visit this center.

The third focus of the center would be to serve as a nerve center for monitoring the state of the metro region and the larger New England ecosystems. Pertinent information related to a sustainable region would be the focus of computer and data services in the Center. This monitoring would include the long term life lines and infrastructure of the city. Partnerships would be forged with universities, museums, and other regional agencies to create the appropriate linkages of data so that the entire puzzle of a healthy region could be analyzed, synthesized, and envisioned for the general public and civic leaders charged with creating legislation that is informed and up to date. By renovating the plaza and City Hall in a sustainable / restorative fashion, Boston will be working from the ground up, truly recognizing itself as an active participant in the process.

This Center would not only act as a living example of responsible development to the entire city, it could also thrive as an economic magnet for the rest of the plaza and the downtown district. It would go hand in hand with developing a renewed sense of place with this historic spot of the first taxi, the beginning of Paul Revere's ride, and the invention of the telephone. The Center would be a proactive and pragmatic agent of positive change from our current paradigm of waste and polluting to the vision of a sustainable future with environmental and economic security for the 21st century.

City Hall as a National Model

Sustainable development will become the dominant paradigm of new construction in the 21st century. The deterioration of the natural environment, the subsequent stresses on our built environment coupled with trends in population growth and increased consumption suggest that we adopt a proactive stance in developing sustainable projects and programs in ecological architecture to support the planet's health and the lives of the next generations.

Greenhouse gases such as carbon dioxide and carbon monoxide, forty percent of which are a result of the construction and operation of buildings, are now being linked by scientists around the world to global climate change. Eighty percent of greenhouse gases come from the developed world (the United States is a major contributor), which hosts only 30% of the world's population. The average American uses twice as much energy as the average European. Changes in temperature patterns are greater now than any seen in the geological record of the past 9000 years. Scientists agree that resultant rises in sea level pose a growing threat to coastal communities like Boston.

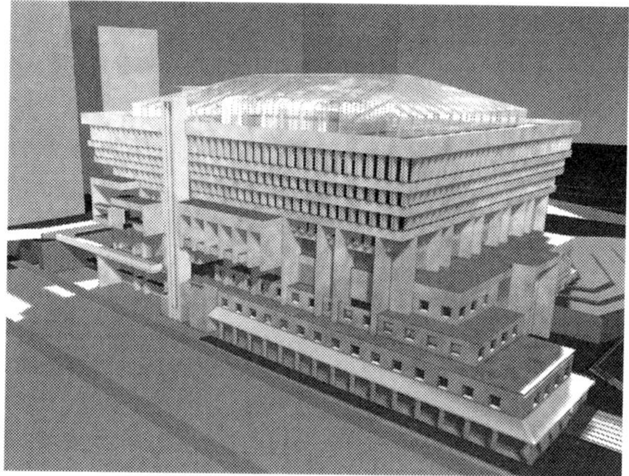

23.8 Proposed Renewed City Hall, Design my Wings Lane Collaborative

Most of the technology and design tools required to implement ecological design are currently available and are being implemented in civic, commercial, and residential projects throughout the world. Case studies from Glasgow, Scotland and Oslow, Norway featured in the1996 International Council for Local Environmental Initiative (ICLEI) report show citywide programs realizing significant savings of natural resources and energy. These buildings are much less costly to operate, and they provide dividends that repay initial costs in a short time.

The ING Bank's 50,000 s.f. International Headquarters in Amsterdam is a good example. Built in 1986, it has a 50,000 BTU/s.f. energy utilization strategy. As a result, the Bank recaptured its $700,000 energy system investment in the first four months of operation. Avoided costs from utilization are joined by savings on health insurance costs as a result of improved employee health and significant cuts in employee absenteeism. The ING Bank reported in 1994 (*In Context*, No. 35) savings in excess of $1.4 million due to reduced absenteeism alone.

Another project closer to home is the Greening of the White House, a comprehensive energy analysis program coordinated by the Rocky Mountain Institute in Snowmass CO. By adopting sustainable or energy efficient heating, cooling, lighting, and insulation strategies, the sustainable rehab of the White House is projected to save American taxpayers close to $250,000 per year.

The 1996 ICLEI report states that because cities have power over land use, transportation, building construction, waste management, and energy supply, they will play a vital role in reducing energy use and greenhouse gases. The report also suggests that cities like Boston join the international organization Cities for Climate Protection which helps local governments address global warming through proper municipal energy policy.

Boston City Hall and Plaza are landmarks of modern architecture at a historic crossroad of revolution, innovation, and dynamic change. It is fitting that they carry the vision of sustainable culture into the 21st century. By using cutting edge sustainable technologies and design to cut waste, save money, create vital community space, and generate economic activity, we can make Boston City Hall and plaza into a demonstration model for the country and the world. The Center for Ecology and Sustainability placed at a key site in the Gaia Matrix of North America, would send the values of a renewed human relationship with the Earth across the continent. The seed energy of Boston would once again be used to promote the evolution of human consciousness.

Since our meeting with the Mayor's cabinet, this proposal has become a major focus of Wings Lane Collaborative, a group of architects, engineers, contractors, planners, and educators dedicated to building ecological as well as economic solutions that are both sensitive and sensible for the 21st century. Our collaborative has been invited to present this proposal at ten different national and international conferences, four of which have published the proposal in their proceedings, including the American Institute of Architects National 1998 conference on the internet. We have also developed an international group of advisors and endorsing agencies working on similar eco-center developments in other cities. Boston is a place where limits have traditionally been surpassed. In support of Mayor Menino's vision for the highest quality of life and the strongest economy of any major city in America, an ecological renovation to Boston City Hall and its plaza can set a new standard that the entire country will ultimately follow in preserving the Earth for our children well into the next millennium.

Reanimating the Landscape

The restoration of our ecology and reintegration of this "Paradise of Culture" with nature is also a restoration of our attitude towards the planet, towards each other, and towards ourselves. As part of this re-animation of the city, we must continue to honor the spirit of the place as well, to re-examine what it is beyond a career or a family that brought to each of us as individual souls to where we are on the planet. In seeking a deeper connection with Gaia we will find an even deeper understanding of our full divine/ human nature.

As we pull our lives back into comprehensive working land use patterns that embrace traditional and restorative values, we will be able to start walking the more sensitive song-lines and ley lines that directly connect us with the grid patterns of Gaia herself. We will be able to reestablish the sacred ways of our ancestors and re-tune our rhythms to hers. The ties and connections we have to our European and Native American ancestors and their connections to each other is another part of the story that is now emerging.

Now it is time to develop relationship with the landscape to see where the sacred stones were placed, where the rituals were held, and praying villages were sited. We need to remember how to get still so as to dowse and feel the landscape with our students and children on a more regular basis. We might also study the geometry our Masonic forefathers understood as they established city plans like Washington DC in the form of a cathedral itself.

One interpretation of this plan came to me after I was told that every soul carries within himself or herself a king or queen, a warrior, a lover, and a magician. It seemed to me that the soul of Washington could be found at the cruciform on the Mall, created by the White House (the king/queen), Congress (the warrior), the Lincoln Memorial (the lover), and the Jefferson Memorial (the magician). The heart stone is just a few feet from the Washington Memorial, the tallest free-standing masonry structure in the world. In this model it is interesting to note that the Jefferson Memorial (the magician) has the White House (the king) within his sights and not the other way around. Just as Merlin knew what was best for Arthur, our forefathers might have inscribed this balance into the soul and form of our nation's capital.

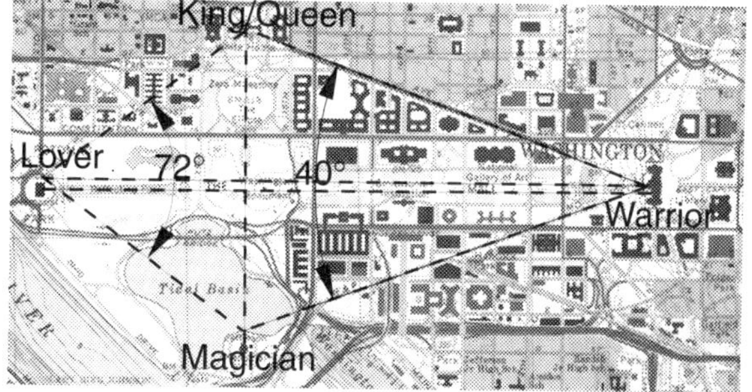

23.9 Warrior, Lover, King, Magician
Washington DC, cricifform geometry and romboid inscribed by roadways and alignment of district center.

With the discoveries of Arkhom and the Gaia Matrix, the heart and essential geometry of Boston is established. A new geometry is brought to light from which a new process of restoration can begin. A sustainable city is wanting to be born to this new millennium, conscious of its impact on the health and mind of the Gaia Matrix. In this process, it is important to remember that...

> [17]...a new image of the city which does justice to all of its dimensions can be no simple overnight job: for it must include the form-shaping contributions of nature, of river, bay, hill, forest, vegetation, climate, as well of those of human history and culture, with the complex interplay of groups, corporations, organizations, institutions, personalities. Let us not then unduly regret our slowness in arriving at an expressive and unified form of the modern city.

In the days ahead as we become more sensitive to these geo-metrys (measures of the earth), we can also work toward a better understanding of the study of geomancy and earth energies. The technology behind the planetary grid system studied and written on by Fuller, Critchlow, Becker, Hagens, Winter, Childress, Michell, Champoux, and other contemporary researchers, provides further leads on the theories of ancient temple builders, Plato, the Templars, and our Masonic forefathers.

Geomantic researcher and writer Steve Nelson notes in his work how the straight line that connects Mexico City (the root), Washington (the solar plexus), New York (the throat) , Boston (the third eye) and London (the crown) can be viewed as one entire chakra system. As one begins to layer the various insights and studies over one another, the patterns and principles that we have inherited, and those that can guide us into the 20th century, will begin to emerge and become more clear.

These straight tracks that circumnavigate the planet are part of these patterns and principles that have never left us. In fact they may have even played a major role in determining where and how we have settled these modern cities in such large numbers. These principles have been sleeping for some time now, and soon will awake to a new millennium, just as our friend Julian West did a century ago, to view his dream ... of this city ... by the bay.

Henry P. MacLean AIA is an Architect and Adjunct Professor of Architecture at Wentworth Institute of Technology. Henry is also a founding member of the Wings Lane Collaborative. He can be reached at Timearch@AOL.com.

17.Lewis Mumford, *The Urban Prospect*, Harcourt, Brace, and World, Inc. NY, 1956, p. 164

List of Illustrations

Power of Seven

7.1 Seven Squared
7.2 Fire / Solar Temple
7.3 The Heptagon
7.4 Council Rock
7.5 Spin Field

Compass Rose

8.1 Winnipesaukee 'Compas Rose'
8.2 Winnipesaukee Lake Panorama
8.3 Ossipee Geology
8.4 Mount Chocorua

Four Directions

9.1 Turtle Island
base Mountain High Maps data
9.2 Four Winds
9.3 Gaian Inter- Course

Chakra System

10.1 The Chakra System
10.2 Willoughby Panorama
10.3 Vermont Artist in Residence
10.4 From the Heart
Susan Franklin Wilson Photographer

Harmonic Expansion

11.1 North American Cycles
11.2 North American Tectonic Plate Yin Yang
base from NGS data
11.3 Antarctica
base Mountain High Maps data
11.4 India, Center of Eurasia
Mountain High Maps data
11.5 Fractals of India
11.6 Sathya Sai Baba
courtesy of Sathya Sai Book Center,
with permission, Robert M. Baskin, Esq.
11.7 Easter Island -
altered base composite

Inner Life

12.1 Inner Geometry Proof
12.2 Stonehenge Geometry
Stonehenge survey by A.Thom
12.3 Flux Field
12.4 Sojourner Truth, c.1797-1883
unidentified Photographer
National Portrait Gallery, Smithsonian Institute
12.5 Shelburne Falls Center Point
Thanks to USGS and *Natural Designer*
12.6 Inner Names
12.7 Arkhom Inner Leys
12.8 Inner Geology
base USGS Massachusetts geology

Universal Ark

13.1 Hazart Inayat Khan's Universel
courtesy of Sufi Order International
13.2 Steiner's Goetheanum
Photo by Thomas Spalinger,
** Rafael-Verlag*
13.3 Universal Symbol
13.4 NewArk
13.5 Shelburne Falls Temple Obelisk

Cycles of Destiny

14.1 The Life of a Nation

Three Democracies

15.1 First Harmonic
15.2 Three Democracies
15.3 Longhouse
15.4 Democracy Spin Fields
15.5 High Point, New Jersey
15.6 Montreal Panorama
15.7 Biosphere
15.8 Montreal Regional Geometry
15.9 The Vesica of the Island of Jesus and the City of Mary

Three Biomes

16.1 Three Biomes
16.2 Maritime Biome
16.3 Great Lakes Biome
16.4 Pilot Mountain
16.5 Southern Biome

Masonic Age

17.1 Three Cities
17.2 The Boston Hub
17.3 City Hall and Sunken Garden
17.4 Boston Inner City
17.5 Boston Hexagon
17.6 New York City Arrow
17.7 Albany Skyline
17.8 Albany Pyramid
17.9 Albany Towers
17.10 Albany's Egg
17.11 Washington DC
17.12 Xochipilli
17.13 John Brown, Geomancer
courtesy of West Virginia Historical Society
17.14 Washington DC Region

Western Wheels

18.1 Grand Teton Wheel
courtesy of Daniel Shaw, Rosetta Publishing. Base map by Raven Maps, Medford, Oregon
18.2 Four Corners
USGS data base
18.3 Western Wheels
18.4 Joseph Smith Obelisk
courtesy of a Mormon Sister
(natural light on granite)
18.5 The Harmonic Expansion of Mormonism
18.6 The Angel Moroni on Hill Cumorah
18.7 Lakota Medicine Wheel
18.8 The Gaia Matrix

Conclusion

19.1 Christ and Compass
altered from base of "The Creator", Bible Moralisee, France, c. 1250, Bodeian Library, Oxford.

The Celestial Basket

by Elizabeth A. Hagens, Ph.D.
All Courtesy of E. A. Hagens

21.1 The Celestial Basket
21.2 Solstice Zodiac
21.3 Plato's Sphere and Virus
21.4 Five Platonic Solids
21.5 Chinese Elements
21.6 Sacred Hoop of the Sioux
21.7 "Map" of Earth
21.8 Celestial Maps

Arkhom- Gift From the Future

by William Stuart Buehler

22.1 Westford Knight
from Frank Glynn, Frederick Pohl,
Dr. Donnell, B. Young.
22.2 Resh "the Chief Headstone"
by Buehler
22.3 Arkhom geometry
by Champoux
22.4 Bakhira Grid
by Buehler
22.5 Metatron's Breastplate
by Buehler
22.6 Eye of Ra
22.7 L-Gate
by Buehler

Restoration of Traditional City: Boston in the 21st Century

by Henry P. MacLean

23.1 Then and Now
copyright BSA/Architecture Boston,1976
23.2 Emerald Necklace
courtesy of B.R.A. Archives
23.3 Figure Eight
by H.P. MacLean
23.4 Boston
from *Architecture Boston*
circa. 1976, photo by Aerial Photos of
New England, Inc.
23.5 The Mound
photo by H.P. MacLean
23.6 Boston City Hall, circa 1999
photo by H.P. MacLean
23.7 Five Star Restaurant
Rendition by Dan Douglas of Wings Lane design
23.8 Proposed Renewed City Hall
3-D graphic rendition by Dan Douglas
of Wings Lane design
23.9 Warrior, Lover, King, Magician
by P.Champoux, concept by H.P.Maclean

Bibliography

Alexander, Christopher, *A Pattern Language*, Oxford University Press, New York, 1977.

Andrews,Ted, *Sacred Sounds*, Llewellyn Publications, St. Paul, MN, 1992

Bradley, Michael, *Holy Grail Across the Atlantic*, Hounslow Press, Willowdale, Ontario, Canada, 1988

Catlin, George, *Letters and Notes on the Manners, Customs, and Conditions of the North American Indians, Written during Eight Year's Travel (1832-1839) amongst the Wildest Tribes of Indians in North America* (In Two Volumes), Dover Publications, Inc., New York, 1973.

Chevalier, Jean and Gheerbrant, Alain, *Dictionary of Symbols*, Penguin Books, Harmondsworth, Middlesex, UK, 1996

Childress, David Hatcher (compiler of collection), *Anti- Gravity & the World Grid*, Adventures Unlimited Press, Stelle, IL, 1987

Feuchtwang, Stephan D.R., *An Anthropological Analysis of Chinese Geomancy*,Vithagna, unknown pub. manu.

Houston, Jean, *Manual for the Peace Maker, An Iroquois Legend to Heal Self & Society*, The Theosophical Publishing House, Wheaton, IL , 1995. [Interactive, experiential group activities included with legend of The PeaceMaker.]

Jennings, Francis, *History and Culture of Iroquis Diplomacy*, Syracuse University Press, 1985

Johnson, Steven F., *Ninuock (The People) The Algonkian People of New England*, Bliss Publishing Company, Marlborough, MA,1995

Krupp, E.C. (ed.), *In Search of Ancient Astronomies*, Doubleday & Company, 1978; McGraw-Hill, 1979.

Lawlor, Robert, *Sacred Geometry:Philosophy and Practice*, The Crossroad Publishing Company, New York, 1982.

Lonegren, Sig, *Spiritual Dowsing*, Gothic Image Publications, Glastonbury, Somerset, UK, 1986.

The Pendulum Kit, Simon & Schuster, New York, 1990.

Lissau, Rudi, *Rudolf Steiner, Life, work, inner path and social initiatives*, Hawthorn Press, Wallbridge, UK, 1987

Mails, Thomas E., *The Hopi Survival Kit*, Penguin Books Ltd, Arkana, 1997.

Mann, A.T., *Sacred Architecture, Great Britain*, Element Books Limited, U.S.: Element Inc., 1993.

Mann, Nicholas R., *Sedona/ Sacred Earth Ancient Lore, Modern Myths - A Guide to the Red Rocks Country, Zivah* Publishers, Prescott, AZ, 1991.

Mavor & Dix, Manitou: *The Sacred Landscape of New England's Native Civilization*, Inner Traditions, Rochester, VT, 1989.

McHarg, Ian L., *Design with Nature*, Doubleday/Natural History Press, Garden City, NY, 1971.

McNeil, William, *The Secret of Ancient America*, Pittsfield, MA, 1986.

Michell, John, *City of Revelation*, London: Garnstone Press Limited, 1972, Ballentine, New York, 1977.

The New View Over Atlantis, Great Britain, Sago Press, 1969, Harper & Row, New York, 1983.

The Dimensions of Paradise, Harper & Row, San Francisco, CA, 1988.

Michell, John and Rhone, Christine, *Twelve Tribe Nations and the Science of Enchanting the Landscape*, Thames and Hudson, Ltd., London, 1991.

Murphet, Howard, *Sai Baba Avatar - A New Journey into Power and Glory*, Birthday Publishing Company, San Diego, CA,1977.

Prevost, Robert, *Montreal A History*, McClelland & Stewart Inc., Toronto, Ontario, Canada, 1993.

Renehan, Jr. Edward J., *The Secret Six, The True Tale of the Men Who Conspired with John Brown*, University of South Carolina Press, Columbia, SC, 1995.

Richer, Jean, *Sacred Geography of the Ancient Greeks*, State University of New York Press, Albany, NY, 1994.

Roadside Geology Series, Mountain Press Publishing Company, Missoula, MT, 1987.

Schwenk, T., *Sensitive Chaos*, Rudolf Steiner Press, London, UK, 1965.

Screeton, Paul, *Quicksilver Heritage The Mystic Leys: Their Legacy of Ancient Wisdom*, Thorsons Publishers Limited, UK, 1974.

Simmons, William S., *Spirit of the New England Tribes, Indian History and Folklore, 1620-1984.*, University Press of New England, Hanover, NH, 1986.

Spence, Lewis, *The Myths of the North American Indians* (originally published in 1914), Dover Publications Inc., New York, 1989.

Swan, James A., *The Power of Place: Sacred Ground in Natural & Human Environments*, Quest Books, Wheaton, IL, 1991.

Wilbur, C. Keith, *The New England Indians*, The Globe Pequot Press, Old Saybrook, CT, 1978

Wood, David *Genisis, The First Book of Revelations*, The Baton Press, Turnbridge, Kent, UK, 1985.

Ordering Information

Please copy this order form:

Ordering additional copies of Gaia Matrix is easy. We accept credit cards, checks, and money orders, we can also send your order COD. Visit our website for information on volume discounts, we cater to small businesses and study groups.

E-mail or Website Orders: www.arkhom.com (our ordering shopping cart for credit card purchases is secure)

Boyd / Franklin Media Publication Center 800-877-2693

Postal Orders: Franklin Media, PO ~~Box 448, Washington, MA 01223-0448~~ 19 James Street Franklin Media Greenfield, MA 01301

Yes! I want additional copies of Gaia Matrix.
Please send me_____ copies at $25 (US) each, plus $5 S&H/book.
Massachusetts residents please add $1.25/book sales tax.

Gaia Matrix - Number of Copies_________x $25 =_________ *

Massachusetts residents: Add $1.25 / book sales tax =_________

Domestic Shipping and Handling: $5 / book = _________

Total = _________

Total payable to Franklin Media

Name______________________________ Business______________________________

Street Address or PO Box______________________________

City, State, Zip______________________________

______Check ______Money Order ______COD
______Credit Card #____________________Exp.________Signature____________________

No credit accounts. All orders must clear first.
Credit Card and Money Orders assure the fastest delivery.
Quantity discounts available -- catering to small business and study groups.

*Please check this box so that $5 of your book goes toward public support of the nonprofit educational organization - Arkhom, Inc.

☐ Voluntary contribution -- CHECK THIS BOX to contribute $5 per book sale to- Arkhom, Inc.

Thank You!

Please copy the following quick form, or fill it out online at www.arkhom.com.

Dear Reader:
We appreciate your taking a few moments to give us some feedback about the book.
We are a small, independent publisher, and your help will allow us to serve you better in the future.
Please comment on the main author as well as the contributors.

Reader Survey: Age___ Sex___ Do you have access to the web? /_/ Yes /_/ No

What interested you most in Gaia Matrix ? (such as topics, chapters, details, specific content)

____

____

What did you dislike most about the book?

____

____

How did Gaia Matrix benefit you?
/_/ greater sense of place /_/ greater spiritual connection /_/ other (please explain)

____

____

What themes would you like to see further developed?

____

____

Do you have or know of information you think should be included in future editions?

____

____

What is your personal experience with the energies or sites described in Gaia Matrix ?

____

____

Can we quote you in promoting Gaia Matrix ? If so, may we identify you by name, initials, specialty, or location?

____

____

Would you recommend Gaia Matrix to others? /_/ Yes /_/ No
Comments: ____

____

Are there organizations or publications that you think would like to hear about Gaia Matrix (name, address, etc.)?

____

____

Staying in touch: Yes, I'd like to be notified of future publications and events in my area.
My intrest is: ______________________

Name ________________________ E-mail ______________
Street Address or PO Box ______________ City, State, Zip ____________

Thank You!

Colophon

Printed with soy ink on acid free archival paper
70-lb., Finch Fine VHF, Bright White
Paper manufactured in Glens Falls, New York
Adobe Jenson MM, text 12 point
Adobe graphic software used throughout book
Book layout done with Adobe FrameMaker
Files completed 25 August 1999
Macintosh Computers
Printed by Boyd Printing, Albany, New York
High-speed web press
Perfect bound, cover lay flat laminate

Some say it took

incredible courage

to do this ---

others who know us say it was

love and heart.